AMERICA'S GREATEST PROBLEM:

THE NEGRO

BY

R. W. SHUFELDT, M. D.,

MAJOR, MEDICAL CORPS, UNITED STATES ARMY.

Membr. Assn. of American Anatomists; Cor. Membr. Academy of Sciences of Chicago; Cor. Membr. Biological Soc. of Colorado; Member and Trustee of the Medico-Legal Soc. of New York; Cor. Membr. Linnæan Soc. N. Y.; Cor. Membr. Academy of Natural Sciences of Philadelphia; Cor. Membr. Soc. Italiana d'Antropologia, Ethniologia e Psicologia Comparata, F orence, Italy; Cor. Membr. Zoölogical Soc. of London; Fellow of the American Ornithologists' Union; Membr. Nat. Geogr. Soc.; Medical Soc. New Orleans; Membr. l'Alliance Scientif. Universelle de France; Hon. Membr. Royal Australasian Ornith. Union (Melbourne); Membr. Cooper's Ornith. Club; Membr. Wilson's Ornith. Club; Art Workers' Club, N. Y.; Hon. Membr. British Soc. Psychical Research (London); Membr. Connecticut Academy of Arts and Sciences, etc. Formerly Membr. Cosmos Club of Washington, D. C.; Philosophical Soc.; Biological Soc.; Anthropological Soc. Washington; Soc. Nat. Eastern U. S.; Amer. Soc. Psych. Research; Hon. Associate in Zoölogy Smithsonian Institution; Membr. Internat. Copyright League; Authors' League of America, etc., etc.

ILLUSTRATED

ISBN: 978-1-63923-776-0

Printed: March 2023

Published and Distributed By:
Lushena Books
607 Country Club Drive, Unit E
Bensenville, IL 60106
www.lushenabks.com

ISBN: 978-1-63923-776-0

A Congo Warrior and his Wife.

TO THE MEMORY

OF MY

LEARNED AND HONORED COLLEAGUE

THE LATE

EDWARD DRINKER COPE

THIS LITTLE VOLUME IS DEDICATED

AS A SLIGHT TRIBUTE TO THE NAME OF ONE OF AMERICA'S PROFOUNDEST PHILOSOPHERS, AND AS AN EXPRESSION OF MY HIGH APPRECIATION OF HIS VOLUMINOUS WORK IN BIOLOGY, AND OF THE SINCERE EFFORT HE ONCE MADE TO MAINTAIN THE PURITY OF THE RACE, OF WHICH HE WAS SO DISTINGUISHED A REPRESENTATIVE.

PREFACE.

To me, there seems to be but little need for a foreword to the present work, inasmuch as nearly all that is usually said along such lines occurs in my Introduction, which here follows next in order. The reader will not have proceeded very far in his or her perusal of the volume ere the fact will be appreciated that, in so far as the work may be considered an historical one, it is squarely up to date in all particulars, even to happenings that occurred but a few weeks prior to the completion of the presswork upon it and the manufacture of the volume.

This is due to the truly marvelous rapidity, associated with expertness and accuracy of the highest order, evinced by my publishers, the F. A. Davis Company, in passing the work through their reading-rooms and press. It is with pleasure that I extend to them my thanks for all this, and for their uniform courtesy throughout while the book was in course of manufacture.

Moreover, I am deeply indebted to many friends who have, from time to time, encouraged me to undertake and complete this task, while to others my acknowledgments are doubly due, for they have not only brought inspiration to my researches, but directly furnished contributions to various chapters in the volume. For such timely and appropriate assistance it affords me especial pleasure to express my gratitude to Dr. William Lee Howard, the eminent alienist and psychologist; to Dr. James Bardin, of the University of Virginia, a distinguished expounder of the negro question in this country and a valuable contributor to various allied subjects; to Mrs. Annie Riley Hale—a widely known lecturer and writer from the South, and an authority on the conditions existing in the Black Belt—for a thoughtful letter which occurs in an appropriate place beyond; to Prof. A. H. Keane, the very eminent British anthropologist, for his active interest throughout in my studies of this national question; to Dr. Edward A. Balloch, of Washington, for the use of his original manuscript on certain points in the myology of negroes; to Dr. Havelock Ellis, of England, the renowned authority on all matters sexual and the author of many most valuable works on the subject; to Col. Walter D. McCaw, Medical Corps United States Army and the late Dr. Robert Fletcher for the loan of valuable works from the library of the Army Medical Museum; to Dr. Robert Wilson, Jr., of Charleston, S. C., for furnishing valuable statistics on public hygiene in the South, as affected by the presence of the negro, and to not a few others who have, either directly or indirectly, assisted me in the present volume, by means of which it is to be hoped that this question of all questions at the present time may be brought before the people in a form by means of which it may be comprehended and fully appreciated.

Finally, I have reserved my most pleasant duty for this last paragraph, written but a few hours prior to the volume passing on to the press: to once more thank my wife, Alfhild, for the indomitable way in which she has lent her aid throughout the entire preparation of this my second formal attempt to preserve the unmixed purity of the blood of the Caucasian people in this country. She has very materially aided me in the reading of proof matter. The entire work, from title-page to Index inclusive, was typewritten by her in the most accurate manner possible; and finally, with but hasty instruction from me, she prepared the Index for the volume in a way that but few experts could equal. This valuable assistance, so persistently and cheerfully rendered, allowed me to complete a large quantity of scientific work I had on hand, which would otherwise have been delayed by being performed at irregular intervals.

R. W. S.

WASHINGTON, D. C.,
March 1, 1915.

CONTENTS.

LIST OF ILLUSTRATIONS.

INTRODUCTION.

In years gone by I have written a number of articles on the negro question in this country, and they have been published in various magazines and medical journals. Appearing in this way, their effect, though good as far as it goes, has but a transitory influence over the public mind, and such efforts are soon forgotten. It is my hope that the present work will be of a more enduring character, and at least demonstrate to the people of this nation that we have a condition on our hands urgently demanding a prompt solution, and not a "problem," as it has been termed by many who appear to be incapable of grasping the nature of the terrible state of affairs, representing this question as a whole, which now constitutes a veritable menace to our much boasted-of civilization.

When the material that makes up the present volume had all been collected together and gone over by me, I submitted it to several of my friends for a final revision, both with respect to facts and to other matters. Among these I may name the distinguished historian, Alexander Del Mar, of New York City, an American author of great renown; Professor A. H. Keane, LL.D., then Vice-President of the Royal Anthropological Institute of England, and others, several being well-informed students of the conditions with respect to this question, and residents of different States in the South.

As already pointed out elsewhere, I had, and have now, but one object in view in publishing a book on the negro in this country: to point out, from scientific premises, the effect that that race has had and will continue to have upon the progress and civilization created and established by the white population of the United States—morally, physically, and otherwise. Personally, I have no prejudice whatever against the negro race on account of its color; the very thought of such a thing would be absurd. I have no prejudice against the natives of India or Arabia, and many of these are as black as negroes.

One might as well charge a naturalist with prejudice against a vulture and with favoring a blackbird. Both are *black;* but what a vulture *stands for* in nature, and what a blackbird stands for, are two entirely different things. The habits of the first-named are repulsive, while the charms of such a gentle and refined songster as the blackbird captivate all who come within his influence.

As I say, I have no color-prejudice against the negro; but what that color *stands for* in him is most repulsive to me.

This book presents a truthful account of what I know about the negro, and what effect his presence among our people involves—the presentation of my observations in all cases being molded by such information as I possess of the sciences of anatomy, physiology, anthropology, ethnology, psychology, medicine, and organic evolution.

Some of my critics have averred that, as a Northern man and a member of the medical corps of the army, I have never enjoyed the proper opportunities to study the negro, and therefore am not competent to pass upon the influence he has as an ethnic factor in the conglomerate population of this country.

In reply to this I may say that I have been a student of the various sciences named in a previous paragraph for over half a century. As long ago as 1862 I became familiar with the lives of the slaves of Cuba and of the free negroes in Hayti. I was for a long time on the first-named island, and I was in Cape Haytien during the revolution. I have seen the "slaver" off the coast of Cuba, when the dead bodies of the captured negroes were being tossed overboard, prior to the entry of the vessel into the harbor of Havana. At different times I have been in every Southern State of the Union, and I have lived two years in New Orleans. I have intimate knowledge of the employment of negroes in the army and navy and many other government departments; of what they have accomplished in business, the trades, and the professions; of the terrible influence their immense hordes are having upon our people in Southern cities, and of their crimes and diseases. I have dissected males, females, and young of both negroes and mulattoes. Further, I have studied the literature of the subject, and these people, as a whole, in the United States, in connection with the influence they are exerting upon our morals, our natures, our politics, and our general welfare for over fifty years.

As previously stated, the bringing of the negro to our shores requires no special comment other than what I have given in its proper place in the body of the work, beyond inviting the attention of the reader to the fact that the taking of Africans out of Africa and settling them in this country by no means makes Americans of them. It would be quite as reasonable to expect zebras to become horses when similarly transported. Nature cares not a straw for human laws and politics, and the passing of a race into any new political area does not make another race of it. Profound and comparatively rapid changes can be effected only through crossing with other races, and this is what is happening in the case of the African in the United States. It is, therefore, only to the hybrids thus produced that the recently much-used appellation "Afro-American" can be truthfully applied. The unmixed African in this country is just as much of a negro today as his ancestors in Africa were before him. He simply stands upon our soil, in every individual case, as a potential ethnic factor, threatening at any and at all times to do his share toward debasing the blood of the white race in America. There is no greater danger assailing American civilization than this; there can be no greater danger than the presence of anything that tends toward the degradation of a race. It is the presence of this danger which has compelled me to write this book. I desire to add my voice to the voices of others who have pointed out this danger—perhaps more potently than I have here—as well as to lend encouragement to those who will raise their voices in a similar manner in the future.

With respect to the matter of lynching it scarcely devolves upon me to say that I am opposed to all forms of lynch law, but the negro is with us; savagery and barbarous acts beget savagery and barbarous acts. Religion has no more to do with it, has no more control over it than the bursting of a soap-bubble has to do with an earthquake. In spite of everything, lynchings will continue to occur in the United States of America just so long as there is a negro left here. He can no more help his instincts than he is responsible for the color of his skin.

So far as transporting any considerable number of the most undesirable class of negroes—a few millions, for example—out of this country is concerned, I have little to add beyond what I have said in Chapter XI of this volume. The National Academy of Sciences might recommend such a step to Congress; but the Academy, as a rule, does not make such use of its knowledge of ethnology, history, or biology.

There is not a negro or mulatto in the United States today that can trace any part of his or her African pedigree *in Africa;* they know absolutely nothing of their transatlantic genealogy; they cannot trace their pedigree to that of the Old World stock, in the case of any individual, as well as we can for many of our blooded dogs and horses. They are absolutely lacking in pride of country, these negroes; and had they been a white race instead of a black one, and been subjected to all that they have up to the present hour, the innate instinct of race alone would have risen within them *as a people,* and, through sentiments of indignation, been the cause of their uprising and the representation of their right to be returned to their own land, the land of their forefathers!

The constant *irritation* they cause in the majority of the whites, in centers where they equal—or nearly equal—the latter in number, has, of itself, a most baneful influence upon the *temper* and upon the formation of our *character* as a nation, standing for all that the human race has attained in the matter of progressive civilization. What is true of the individual is true of the race, and the psychologist well knows what it means to a refined person to be forced to associate and live with a non-moral, diseased, and objectionable one. In time, but one of two things can happen: either complete segregation or else assimilation to the detriment of the person of refinement and the very questionable improvement of the undesirable one.

Here in Washington, as well as in other Eastern cities, we take great pride in safeguarding the morals of our citizens. Every audience that faces a motion-picture reel must first be assured on the screen that the reel has been passed upon by "The National Board of Censorship." This assurance is flashed in the faces of hundreds of thousands of our people every evening of the week; but these same authorities *and the people* utterly ignore the ever-present object-lesson they left on the street, as they entered the building where the aforesaid moral, elevating and permissible picture-reel was to be seen.

Upon the aforesaid street, lighted as it is by the brilliant glare of hundreds of arc-lights, there is to be observed a perambulating crowd of human beings, made up of the representatives of our own civilization, of an equal number of the descendants of an imported black race from the cannibal tribes of Africa, and an army of light-colored hybrids that represent the offspring of hundreds of couples of the two first-named races. What each of these hybrids stands for in all things is now fairly well known to most intelligent people in this country; so it is to the *moral* lesson that we turn.

Almost without exception, every one of these have been born *out of wedlock,* the offspring of a white man and a negress,—a phase of immorality sufficient to damn any nation and degrade it to the level of any group of animals *below* man! These bastards constitute the group representing the *improved* Afro-Americans; they stand for the stock upon which the politicians in power draw, in order to have "the race" represented in places of power and preferment. Their ancestors have been and are the great disseminators of the venereal and other diseases in the United States, as statistics have long ago proven to be the case. It is this mixed, rapidly increasing, bastard stock for whom we have paved the way to represent the white race of the United States for all ensuing generations!

The time is certain to come, however far off it may be,—if stronger and cleaner nations of futurity allow it to arrive,—when the admixture will result in the complete rotting of the old Anglo-Saxon stock in this country, and when no one of our descendants can trace an unsullied pedigree back to the grand old civilizations of the Old World, with all that that means and all that that has accomplished. *This* is what we are passing down to posterity.

It is to help avert such a degradation of our Anglo-Saxon stock in this country that this book has been written.

CHAPTER I.

Man's Place in Nature from a Biological Standpoint.

There never has been but one certain way to decide man's position in the system of nature; it consists in examining man anatomically, physiologically, and psychologically, and comparing the information thus obtained with the corresponding data, secured through similar methods from other living forms now existing upon the earth. Man and his career in the world, up to the present time, may also be examined historically, palæontologically, and anthropologically, as far as the discovered data will permit us to carry the investigation. In fact—in order to establish correctly the place man holds in nature—it becomes necessary to compare and intercompare every possible thing we can find out about him, both in past and present time, with a similar knowledge—as far as we have mastered it—of all other animals in the world, and with especial care in regard to those forms which are universally conceded to—and do—most resemble him; such an investigation should, as far as possible, be exhaustive. Science has done this, and has come to a finding based upon the evidence secured. This evidence has been accumulating since the dawn of history, and in amount and number of established facts is absolutely overwhelming. As a whole, as well as in part, it has passed through the test-crucible of time; at each step in its history, its refinement has been secured through the most intense fire in the furnace of criticism, and we thus have the solution of this long-debated question in our possession and settled forever. The comments of the ignorant upon the findings of science in this matter are no longer regarded by the intelligent; the fire, the protest, and the ridicule that followed this investigation, step by step, throughout its entire course, from its birth to its final solution, have died out.

Man's place in nature is now as thoroughly known and established as is the fact that the earth is enveloped in the sea of its own atmosphere. And it was by no means altogether through the pen, the brains, and the philosophy of Charles Darwin that science was enabled to arrive at the truth of the question,—for the matter of that, his grandfather, Erasmus Darwin, years before him had foreshadowed the finding ("The Temple of Nature," 1804, pp. 67, 68). This finding has been the outcome of the labor and investigation of a great army of workers, and the minds, the scalpels, the microscopes, and the pens of the individual researchers have each and all, directly or indirectly, knowingly or unconsciously, contributed to the result. As an anthropological fact, it has passed out of the realm of mere hypothesis into the full blaze of established fact. In touching upon the question of man's place in nature, a rational writer of the present would no more think of introducing the subject to his readers in an argumentative way than he would were he called upon to write about the atomic theory, the law of gravitation, or the form of the earth, for it is a fact far better established than any of these. Moreover, we can actually handle the material upon which the evidence is based; and the new evidence that is coming to light in ever-increasing masses, as each day rolls by, brings but solid confirmation to science's verdict,—not only as to the place occupied by man and mankind in nature, but exactly as to how he came to be there.

One can enter any public or private library today and pick the works of the time where one will, from school-book to lexicon, from fact to fiction; history will have but one thing to say on this particular point. We find it tersely epitomized for us in the great dictionaries of the time; for example, in the Century Dictionary we find "man" defined as "a featherless, plantigrade, biped mammal of the genus *Homo; Homo sapiens* of the family *Hominidæ* or *Anthropidæ,* order *Primates,* class *Mammalia,* of which there are several geographical races or varieties." (Vol. v, p. 3601.) There is no question what is meant by this definition.

Again, in the same authoritative work, we find *Hominidæ* defined in the following words: "A family of mammals, represented by the single genus *Homo*, man, of the suborder *Anthropoidea* and order *Primates;* mankind. It is characterized by the complete withdrawal of the fore-limbs from the office of locomotion, and consequently the habitually erect attitude except in infancy; the perfection of the hand as a prehensile organ, and the specialization of the foot as a locomotory organ; the regular curvature of the line of the teeth, which are of the same length and in uninterrupted series, without diastemata; the nakedness of most of the body; and the large facial angle. These are the principal zoölogical characters by which the *Hominidæ* are distinguished from the *Simiidæ* or anthropoid apes. Physiologically, mankind is peculiar chiefly in the capacity of civilization, or the ability to create progressive institutions (including the formation and use of speech). Psychologically, man is separated by a very wide interval from the nearest *Simiidæ*. The family is the same as *Anthropidæ*; it is conterminous with its single genus *Homo*, with the order *Bimana*, and with the subclass *Archencephala*." (Century Dictionary, vol. iv, p. 2866.) This is clear enough, and certainly amply good enough for a dictionary definition; however, as a generic diagnosis it offers us some exceptions. In the first place, negroes are to be found that possess the upper and lower canines—especially the former—much lengthened. Again, both men and women have been found, and exist at the present time, in whom the body (including the head sometimes) is completely covered with a thick and heavy growth of hair. In a Burmese family, every member, some eight or ten individuals, was so covered, even including the entire face. It is more frequently seen in the white than in the black-skinned races. Finally, there is a great variance in the openness—or the reverse—of the facial angle.

With these and a few other slight exceptions, there is not a biologist in the world today who will not fully indorse the definition of man and the family *Hominidæ*[1] as quoted above from the Century Dictionary. So far as man's place in nature is concerned, it epitomizes the case as stated by anatomists the world over for the last half-century or more, and it obviates the necessity of pointing out what Sir Richard Owen

[1] It would seem that Carl Linnæus, the great Swedish naturalist, in his classification of the various races of mankind, referred the negroes to one species, namely, to the species *Homo afer* (10th ed., p. 22, 1758). In my opinion, this view is a thoroughly untenable one.

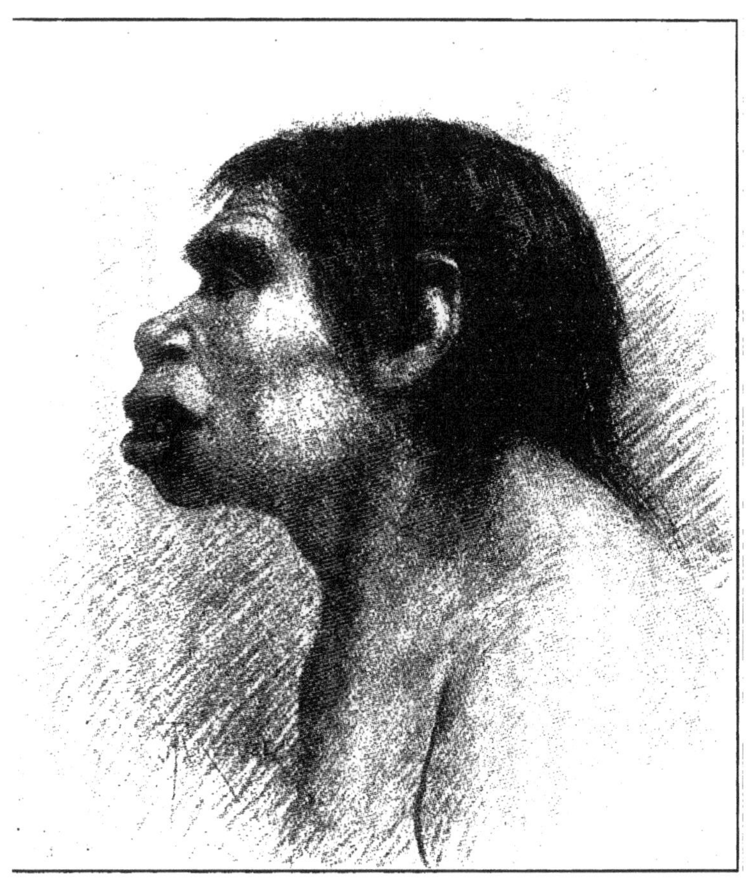

Fig. 1.—The Man of Sussex.

This is from the reconstruction made by Mr. A. Forestier, of the art staff of *The Illustrated London News,* who was assisted by Dr. A. Smith Woodward, of the British Museum.

has said on the subject, or Professor Huxley, or Darwin, or Gegenbaur, or hundreds of other biologists who have personally and exhaustively examined for years the material upon which such an opinion is based. It puts man and mankind squarely in the group *Mammalia* and classifies him accordingly. His speech, his civilization (whatever that may mean), his present progress—if in reality man is progressing mentally, morally, and physically—and all that separates him from any other animal in general, and from the higher apes in particular, are included. Anatomically and structurally he is no better fitted to do what he is doing in the world than is the gorilla in the forests of darkest Africa physically qualified to lead its particular life. Furthermore, man is subject to the same diseases and injuries that the simians are, or even, in some cases, the mammals below them; he will eat and live upon anything that any other animal will eat, be it cooked or uncooked. He is insectivorous, carnivorous, —indeed, omnivorous. He will thrive upon insects, snails, corn, the slain animals—young and old—of other genera than his own, as well as upon those of his own species. His young are born just as the young of many other mammals are, and for many weeks, *in utero,* they cannot be with certainty distinguished from fœtal gorillas. In fact, and taken as a whole, man's reproduction offers nothing different from what we see among many other mammals.

Man experiences pain and pleasure just as other mammals do, and the same may be said for the other emotions and feelings, as anger, fear, grief, spite, hatred, selfishness, greed, cowardice, bravery, and every other qualification of the kind known. The sensations experienced on the part of a frightened man and a frightened monkey are identical in every particular, and in many instances the behavior is the same under the same circumstances. As for grief, spite, and other passions, I have seen monkeys, dogs, and many other animals that possessed just as keen a sense of right and wrong as the average of mankind does; and as for the refinements of cruelty of all kinds toward their fellow-species, man outclasses any other group of animals in the known world. Indeed, man is the most cruel animal in existence, and by no means, as a rule, always the most cleanly. Men steal and murder, —so do other animals; men deceive in no end of ways, —and so do other animals; men slay their own fathers, mothers, mates, children, and friends,—and so do other animals, though, in proportion, not as frequently. Men cohabit with their own relatives,—so do other animals. Auto-erotism in all its forms is practised by both sexes. Homosexuality is common in mankind, and far more so than among other animals; it is met with in both sexes. As a matter of fact, whether induced by disease or indulged in by the normal man or woman, there is no animal—or group of animals—on earth, outside of man, that practises a wider range of sexual perversions, psychopathia sexualis, and the most inconceivable departures from normal coition to a natural end than does the genus *Homo;* he actually out-animals,—yes, out-beasts the bestiality of the very beasts themselves. Along these lines no other animal can compete with him, nor rival him in the contraction of disease as a consequence.

With respect to instinct and reason, they differ but in degree, while typical instinct and the ordinary instincts are the same everywhere and in all organizations. Reason has been brought to a higher plane only in the best of mankind: those enjoying the most exalted intellectual development; while thousands of men and women exist in all parts of the world, in whom the reasoning faculties are no keener than in intelligent foxes, dogs, and elephants; ethnologists have proven this fact over and over again.

Man is the most conceited being in the entire world's menagerie, and on what account, pray? Surely not because of his shape or his anatomy! No, only in consequence of his higher reasoning powers, which, in the course of his psychological evolution and his morphological and physiological adaptation, have advanced him to a stage in which he is fitted to utterly annihilate every other animal on the face of the globe, —an operation he is accomplishing with a rapidity and swiftness truly interesting to contemplate. His civilization consists in replacing much that formerly existed in nature with his machines, his habitations and places of pleasure, his improved passage-ways, and other contrivances that subserve the ends of education and the acquisition of knowledge. He is nevertheless a *Primate,* and ever will be, with all that this word means. His place in nature is as fixed as is the fact that if his head be cut off he will die.

That man has a place in nature there is no manner of doubt, and the truth has been told when we admit that in reality it *is in nature,* and that he has risen to this place in time and along developmental lines in every way similar to the lines followed by all other animals in nature in their evolution, starting, as they have, and as we all have, in common from the simplest animals known to us and which existed in the world with the first manifestations of life of any kind.

In commenting upon this fact in his "Evidences as to Man's Place in Nature," Mr. Huxley said: "Science has fulfilled her function when she has ascertained and enunciated truth; and were these pages addressed to men of science only, I should now close this essay, knowing that my colleagues have learned to respect nothing but evidence, and to believe that their highest duty lies in submitting to it, however it may jar against their inclinations. But desiring, as I do, to reach the wider circle of the intelligent public, it would be unworthy cowardice were I to ignore the repugnance with which the majority of my readers are likely to meet the conclusions to which the most careful and conscientious study I have been able to give to this matter has led me.

"On all sides I shall hear the cry—'We are men and women, and not a mere better sort of apes, a little longer in the leg, more compact in the foot, and bigger in brain than your brutal Chimpanzees and Gorillas. The power of knowledge—the conscience of good and evil—the pitiful tenderness of human affections, raise us out of all real fellowship with the brutes, however closely they may seem to approximate us.'

"To this I can only reply that the exclamation would be most just and would have my own entire sympathy, if it were only relevant. But it is not I who seek to base Man's dignity upon his great toe, or insinuate that we are lost if an Ape has a *hippocampus minor*. On the contrary, I have done my best to sweep away this vanity. I have endeavored to show that no absolute structural line of demarcation, wider

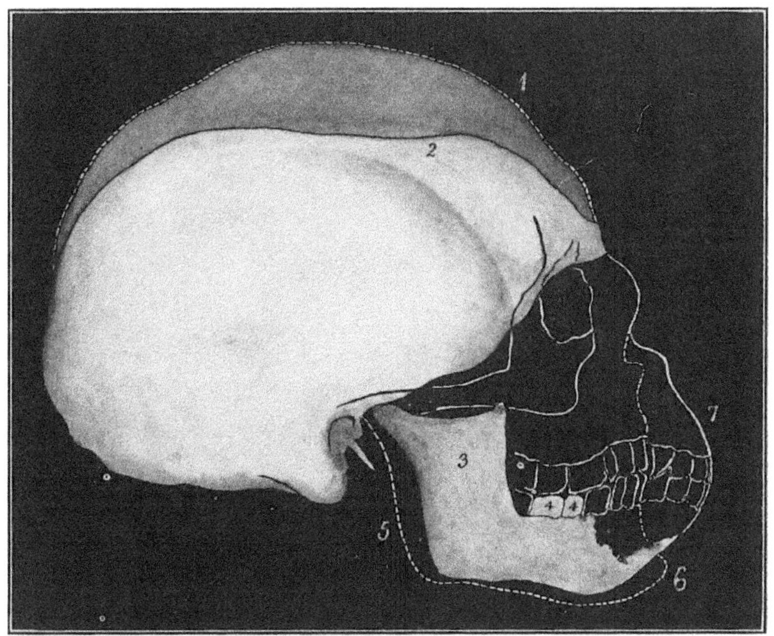

Fig. 2.—Study of the Cranium and Jaw of the Sussex Man.

1 (dotted line), outline of the cranium of highly developed Indo-European—white man; 2, including all the light shaded area, the cranium of the Sussex man (solid line); 3, the lower jaw of the Sussex man, and 4, two of his molar teeth; 5 (dotted line), the lower jaw of the Indo-European skull; 6, the projecting chin of the latter; 7 (solid line), the prognathous or projecting teeth and jaws of the Sussex man, as in apes and many negroes. Drawn by the author.

than that between the animals which immediately succeed us in the scale, can be drawn between the animal world and ourselves; and I may add the expression of my belief that the attempt to draw a physical distinction is equally futile, and that even the highest faculties of feeling and of intellect begin to germinate in lower forms of life. At the same time no one is more strongly convinced than I am of the vastness of the gulf between civilized man and the brutes; or is more certain that whether *from* them or not, he is assuredly not *of* them. No one is less disposed to think lightly of the present dignity, or despairingly of the future hopes, of the only consciously intelligent denizens of this world.

"We are indeed told, by those who assume authority in these matters, that the two sets of opinions are incompatible, and that the belief in the unity of origin of man and brutes involves the brutalization and degradation of the former. But is this really so? Could not a sensible child confute, by obvious arguments, the shallow rhetoricians who would force this conclusion upon us? Is it, indeed, true, that the Poet, or the Philosopher, or the Artist whose genius is the glory of his age, is degraded from his high estate by the undoubted historical probability, not to say certainty, that he is the direct descendant of some naked and bestial savage, whose intelligence was just sufficient to make him a little more cunning than the Fox, and by so much more dangerous than the Tiger? Or is he bound to howl and grovel on all fours because of the wholly unquestionable fact that he was once an egg, which no ordinary power of discrimination could distinguish from that of a Dog? Or is the philanthropist or the saint to give up his endeavors to lead a noble life, because the simplest study of man's nature reveals, at its foundations, all the selfish passions and fierce appetites of the merest quadruped? Is mother-love vile because a hen shows it, or fidelity base because dogs possess it?" (Pp. 128-131.)

In the work from which these rather long quotations have been taken, Professor Huxley answers these questions himself, and in a manner which leaves not the slightest doubt in the mind of any reasonable person as to their correctness. There are still, however, unnumbered thousands of people in the world who can afford to read his words with advantage; they are as true and as logical as any of the demonstrations in Euclid's geometry.

No thoughtful, reading, and intelligent man or woman today believes that the beginning of mankind was in a miraculously created pair, in no way differing from representatives of the human race of the present day, or that the man was the result of a separate act of creation, and the woman the outcome of a miracle. That fable has had its day, and those who still profess to believe it are either simply hypocrites or ignorant as a native Hottentot. It is not at all necessary to enter further upon this question.

As we shall see in a later chapter, there is no doubt as to the existence of vast differences that in many ways distinguish the various races of men now peopling the earth; yet this truth is no better established than is the fact that the entire family of mankind has, in common with all other existing mammals, descended from a common progenitor, and that at the present time the genus *Homo,* and the various genera of the higher simians, are all members of the same group.

In line with the facts set forth above, now comes the important discovery of the "Man of Sussex" (England),—an ape-like being, with characteristics which place him squarely in the homo-simian pedigree; more man than ape, to be sure, but nearer, very much nearer, the latter than any form heretofore known to us. The discovery of his remains, which consist of the vault of his cranium and the imperfect lower jaw, took place in December, 1911, and science at once recognized the important light it shed upon the history of the human race. Mr. W. P. Pycraft, of the British Museum, has this to say, in *The Illustrated London News,* with reference to these remains (Dec. 28):—

"The evidence for the interpretation which has been placed on them is incontrovertible. In the first place, the lower jaw is unmistakably ape-like, while presenting other features indubitably human. It is ape-like in its massiveness, in the absence of a chin, and in the absence of a peculiar ridge along the inner surface which in the typical human jaw is extremely well marked, and serves for the attachment of muscles concerned with the act of swallowing. Another simian feature is the shortness and great breadth of the upper branch whereby the jaw is hinged to the skull. As to the teeth of this ancient Briton, it will suffice to remark that they resemble those of the celebrated Heidelberg jaw, and in so far are of the human type; but they are ape-like in the greater length of their grinding surfaces. But there is reason to suspect that the canine or 'eye' teeth projected, at any rate slightly, above the level of the rest,—an ape-like character met with in savage races today, tho' never to the same extent as in apes.

"Another ape-like character is afforded by the trend of the grinders, which shows that the teeth in the complete jaw must have run in a straight, parallel series,—not in a horseshoe curve, as in modern men. . . .

"Happily, enough of the skull has been found to allow of the restoration of the whole of the cranial portion, which encloses the brain. And this shows us that the beetling brows so excessively developed in the celebrated fossil man of Java, discovered some years ago, were in the Sussex man far less developed; while the brain capacity of this ancient man had just under two pints, which is nearly twice as much as that of the highest apes, tho' considerably less than that of the average European, which is, roughly, about two pints and a half."

This man was in existence some hundred thousand years ago—possibly a million—and it is quite probable that either he or his immediate forbears lived during the latter part of the Pliocene age.

"As to his personal appearance one would not like to dogmatize," says Mr. Pycraft, "but, with the help of Mr. Forestier, I have been enabled to make what is probably a near approximation to the truth. He was a man of low stature, very muscular, and had not yet attained that graceful poise of the body which is so characteristic of the human race today. But he was by no means lacking in intelligence. Living in a genial climate amid a luxurious vegetation, and surrounded by an abundance of game, he may be said to have led a life of comparative ease. Of clothing he had no need;

FIG. 3.—A MALE GORILLA.

This photograph of the largest gorilla known was taken immediately after death by Herr Paschen, of Yaunde, and gives an excellent idea of the size of these animals as compared with negroes. The animal weighed 400 pounds.

nor was there any reason to bother much about housing accommodation; tho', for safety's sake, he may have been forced to devise some kind of shelter by night. Elephants and rhinoceroses, of species long since extinct, roamed in herds all around him. These and the hippopotamus no doubt he killed for food, and, besides, he must have hunted a species of horse long since extinct, while the lion, bear, and saber-toothed tiger afforded him plenty of opportunities for hair-breadth escapes. He had probably inherited the use of fire from his forbears, and this useful ally served to harden the ends of his wooden spears, and perhaps to cook his food. His only other tools were furnished by flint stones chipped to the rough semblance of an ax, but used in the hand, not wielded by a shaft. From the peculiar character in which it was flaked from the rough nodule selected, this implement is known as the 'Chellean' type, and tho' one of the more primitive types of Paleolithic weapons, it showed better workmanship than is displayed by the still earlier 'Strepyea' and 'Mesvinian' types, and a great advance on the much-discust 'eoliths.' These earlier weapons, it may be remarked, are the only evidence we have of the existence of men older than the makers of the 'Chellean' implements, but they speak as surely as did the footprints found by Robinson Crusoe.

"Finally, these fragments of man from the Sussex gravel tell us that already at this early period the human race had begun to split up into different peoples, which had spread far over the earth's surface, as is witnessed by the remains found in Java and at Heidelberg. And these three, we must point out, belong, roughly, to the same period of time in the world's history; these three, more than any others, bear witness to man's kinship with the apes."

In the London *Sphere* (Dec. 28), we read the following account of the discovery of the remains of this man. It is given by Mr. Charles Dawson, who, with Dr. Smith Woodward, described them at a meeting of the Geological Society (Dec. 18), Mr. Dawson being the spokesman. In the course of his remarks he said: "Water filled the gravel-pit until the end of May, but excavation was begun early in June, and by the end of September had resulted in the finding of sufficient fragments of the skull to restore the whole and also in the recovery of half the lower jaw. At the same time the diggings revealed fragments of two primitive elephants, a hippopotamus, the common red deer and horse, and a beaver. Numerous flint implements of a very primitive type were also found. While the diggings were in progress he examined thoroughly the geology of the whole neighborhood, and came to the conclusion that the position of the gravel and its nature proved great antiquity. Since the gravel was deposited, the Ouse itself has cut down its channel to a depth of eighty feet."

CHAPTER II.

THE ETHNOLOGICAL STATUS OF THE NEGRO.

INDISCRIMINATING people speak of the inhabitants of the great continent of Africa in the loosest possible manner, designating them collectively as negroes; this is, however, as every well-informed person knows, by no means the case. In the first place, all the northern tier of countries bordering upon the Mediterranean are inhabited by races of an entirely different description and possessing important histories. So it is with the most of the east side of the continent and southward for some considerable distance. In the extreme southwest, too, we have the Bosjesmen and the Hottentots, neither of which belong to the negro or negroid races; their stock is quite different. Apart from the inhabitants of Africa just indicated, and those who have made Africa their home, coming from divers countries of Europe and other continents, there still remains to be taken into consideration some hundred and thirty-odd millions of others; then there are the negro or negroid races, composed either of pure and original stock, or those produced by hybridization or interbreeding with the foreigners or with other African nations.

This enormous mass of people occupy four great regions on the continent of Africa, namely, the region of West Soudan and Guinea; of Central Soudan and the Chad Basin; of East Soudan and Upper Nile; and of South Africa, where the Bantu family resides. These four regions contain from four to eight great groups of black or dark-colored people, often representing very widely different races, speaking dissimilar languages, entirely different in their appearances and customs, and having altogether separate histories. Some of these races we know a good deal about; some of them we know but very little about, and of the great mass of them—many millions in number—we know almost nothing. We do know, however, that some twenty-five millions of negroes and their descendants are living in other parts of the world besides Africa. Their descendants are either true negroes or else hybrids resulting from the former's crossing with the whites, with Indians, or with other nationalities. Many of these negroes and half-castes are to be found in North and South America and the West Indies, having been forcibly introduced there through the slave-hunters of by-gone years. It is reckoned that there are some ten millions of negroes and half-breed descendants in the United States alone, and in some sections these are increasing with great rapidity, especially in the Southern States, where the climate, food, and other conditions are favorable to their propagation.

As this book is chiefly devoted to a consideration of the negroes and their descendants in this country, I shall not attempt to pay attention to the major part of the great hordes of those peoples to be found in Africa, but only incidentally refer to those on the west coast—the Gold or Slave coast of the African continent—and to the other tribes or races as occasion requires, for the purpose of drawing upon them for additional illustrations in the matter of their histories, their mental, moral, and physical characters, or any-

Fig. 4.—Negro Boy and Apes.

On the left side of the figure there is a young Chimpanzee, and on the right a young Orang-utan. This is a wonderfully interesting comparison.

thing that may shed light upon the special subject with which I am dealing.

In Chapter I, the position of the genus *Homo*—man and mankind—in the animal world was briefly set forth. Man is an animal and belongs directly in the mammalian series. To this law there has never been found an exception or a single departure since the earth became a planet. It applies just as rigidly to the men and women of the present day as it did to the earliest forms of men that were evolved from the pristine simian stock thousands of years ago. It applies with just as much truth to one individual as to another, and to the world's anthropofauna as a whole, both past and present. It is as true of the highest as of the lowest, in every and all particulars, of men everywhere; and, finally, it is as true of the population of Africa, severally and individually, as it is of the population of the United States, severally and individually. But then, when we come to the mental, moral, intellectual, and psychological attributes of man—of men, mankind—the existing differences in these respects among various representatives of the genus *Homo,* in all parts of the world, as applied to the individual or to the race or group, are simply, in many instances, immeasurable.

Throughout the entire history of the world, both men and women have exhibited vast differences in regard to culture, refinement, knowledge, and mental capacity. They have also exhibited similar differences with respect to their philosophical caliber, and the ability to employ the reasoning faculty in its varied fields, as applied to logical ends, and to the solutions of practical and theoretical questions. Linnæus, von

Humboldt, Huxley, Darwin, and other great men were just as much of the animal world as the lowest Yorubas, Bushmen, or Australian natives; but the gulf that separated them is marked by an enormous period of evolution.

We are now in position to consider the mental, moral, and physical characters of the negroes and negroids, especially the tribes found in the West Soudan, the Congo Basin, the Slave and Gold coasts of Africa,—in fact the stock from which was derived the negroes that were brought to the United States as slaves. These are the negroes, and the descendants of them are of the race or races that interest us here in this country. It is these we have upon our hands, and it is these we have to deal with in the condition of affairs widely known as the "negro problem."

The word *negro* seems to be of Spanish origin, and is derived originally from the Latin *niger,* meaning black. Anthropologically, it distinctly characterizes the race of negroes to be described in the present volume. All others are of negroid or even sub-negroid blood, and it has been advanced that the original stock came from the land of Lemuria, that hypothetical region now submerged beneath the waters of the Indian Ocean. These were the lands that constituted the cradle of the negro stock which is now found in a pure state only in the Benua and Shari basins; in the Gaboon; on the coast of Guinea, and along the lower Zambesi River. Here are located the villages of the unnumbered hordes of blacks that occupy the lowest position in the scale of evolution of the genus *Homo.* Among them are the relatives of many of the negroes in the United States, and, indeed, large numbers of the latter are no further removed from the most degraded standard of savagery than the former are. Typical representatives of these true negroes anywhere are markedly uniform with respect to their moral and physical characters,—more so, in fact, than any other people of whatever nationality they may be. For this reason they offer us material for comparison—morally, socially, and morphologically—with not only the higher forms of existing apes and their allies, but with human races standing above them in the evolutionary scale.

Taking up first some of their external characters, it will be seen that the hair is short, black, and frizzly, —in fact, distinctly *woolly*. On section, a single hair is elliptical or quite flat. As compared with the simians, the negroes differ in this particular, the former having coats of true hair and not wool as on the heads and other parts of the latter. Keane states that P. U. Brown, in his *Classification of Mankind by the Hair,* "shows conclusively that, unlike true hair, but like true wool, the negro hair is flat, issues from the epidermis at a right angle, is spirally twisted or crisped, has no central duct, the coloring matter being disseminated through the cortex and intermediate fibers, while the cortex itself is covered with numerous rough, pointed filaments adhering loosely to the shaft; lastly, the negro pile will felt, like wool, whereas true hair cannot be felted. Observing that the negro domain is also the habitat of the most anthropoid apes —gorilla and chimpanzee—and that these bimanous and quadrumanous species are both of a pronounced dolichocephalic type (index nos. 72-75), some anthropologists have suggested the direct descent of the former from the latter. But against this view may be urged the different texture of the pile, which, although black in both, is woolly in the negro, but true hair in the ape."

The negro has a large black eye, with the sclerotic coat tinged with yellow,—a distinctive character frequently noticed in the typical west-coast negroes. The jaws exhibit decided prognathism, or projection forward, the facial angle being seventy degrees against the eighty-two of the average white man. Another marked feature is the nose, which is broad and flat, with dilated nostrils, and with the ridge concaved, often showing the red inner surface of the mucous membrane. The lips are very large, protruding and heavy. Sometimes they are everted, displaying the red mucous membrane of the mouth. The malar bones and zygomatic arches being prominent, the cheeks are made equally so. These full-blooded negroes have black skins, or a deep brownish tint. Climate has nothing whatever to do with this, nor has any special pigment. It is due to a superabundance of coloring matter between the true and the scarf skins. Soft and velvety to the touch, the negro epidermis is, for the most part, quite free from hair, and would be interesting were it not for the outrageous odor it emits, especially under heat and excitement. This is sometimes so strong that I have known persons of our own race brought almost to the stage of emesis when compelled to inhale it for any length of time.

Usually the negro is of but average height, and by no means always erect, presenting curves due to the prominence of the back of the head, the shape of the spine and pelvis, and the general morphology of his frame. The anterior pair of limbs are long as in the apes, and frequently slender; while the pelvic extremities may be weak, deficient in calves, and with a low instep to the feet, which are broad and flat. The heel projects backward, and the hallux or big toe is slightly independent and tends to become prehensile. As an example of this it has been noted that negro and mixed breeds ride with the great toe in the stirrup-iron. Again, the hand of the typical negro often has much about it to remind us of the manus in the gorilla. In two instances I met with very black negroes in the South, both men, in whom the ears were conspicuously pointed at their upper margins as in many *Quadrumana.* The projecting point on the helix, as described by Darwin, I have noticed far more frequently in negroes than in the white races. It is undoubtedly a vestigial character, indicating that man arose from a pointed-eared animal. The ear in the fœtal orang is likewise pointed. Certain external organs are enormously developed in the negro, and the hair is coarse and kinky as it is on the head. I dissected an old negro man at the National Medical College in Washington, D. C. As a subject, he was particularly simian in his organization, and one thing noticed about him more than anything else was the structure of his toe-nails. These were, on all toes—but especially on the great toes—marvelously thickened and curved, reminding one of the claws on certain animals. Those peculiar structures were over twenty times as thick as the ordinary toe-nail, and evidently had not been trimmed for years.

The same winter I dissected a rather light-colored negress who had double breasts,—one above the other. All four were fully developed and functional in life.

The development of a tail—that is, a free, movable caudal appendage, with rudimentary vertebræ in it—is very rare. In the skull of the negro the cranial capacity and the brain itself are much under size. On the average, the former will measure thirty-five ounces as against forty-five for the Caucasian skull. In the negro the cranial bones are dense and unusually thick, converting his head into a veritable battering-ram; moreover, *the cranial sutures unite very early in life.* This checks the development of the brain long before the same takes place in other races, and this fact accounts to some extent for the more or less sudden stunting of the negro intellect shortly after arriving at puberty. Filippo Manetta has pointed out that "the negro children [on the plantations in the South] were sharp, intelligent, and full of vivacity, but on approaching the adult period a gradual change sets in. The intellect seems to become clouded, animation giving place to a sort of lethargy, briskness yielding to indolence. We must necessarily suppose that the development of the Negro and White proceeds on different lines; while with the latter the volume of the brain grows with the expansion of the brain-pan, in the former the growth of the brain is, on the contrary, arrested by the premature closing of the cranial sutures and lateral pressure of the frontal bone." (*La Razza Negra nel suo stato selvaggio,* etc., Turin, 1864, p. 20.)

In his internal anatomy the negro exhibits a much closer approach to the anthropoid apes than does any other race of the genus *Homo.* Perhaps it would be nearer the truth to say that he has not been so completely differentiated from the simian stock as have the other races of mankind.

Many vestigial or rudimentary organs and structures that are constant in the case of the animals below man appear far more frequently in the negro than in the white race. It will not be necessary to enumerate all of these when a few will answer our purpose, especially when taken in connection with the external characters already given above. I believe that it will be found that the supracondyloid foramen of the humerus (feline carnivora, gorilla) is more frequently present in the negro, and I am quite sure the *psoas parvus* muscle is. Dr. Edward A. Ballock was interested in this subject a number of years ago (September, 1891), and read a paper upon it before the Washington Medical Society (D. C.), he being a resident of that city. He has sent me the original MS. of this paper, and as it is short and to the point, I find it useful to include in the present chapter. It is entitled "On the Relative Frequency of the *Psoas parvus* Muscle in the Colored Race," and I may say that what its author found to be the case is confirmed by my own experience, on the dissecting table as well as in my reading. Dr. Ballock says:—

"For a long time I have been impressed with the fact that American anatomists were neglecting a field fertile in promise, rich in opportunity, and certain to yield fruitful results to careful cultivation. I refer to the investigation of the anatomical peculiarities of the negro, including in that term both those of pure and mixed blood. This field is peculiarly our own, and, from the necessity of the case, must long continue to be so. We owe it to ourselves no less than to our science to investigate it thoroughly. We should not let slip this opportunity to make and record careful observations.

"A recent search through the literature bearing on this point, made in another connection, enables me to say that, by the European anatomist, an opportunity to study a negro subject is an especial privilege. Each organ and structure is carefully examined and all anomalies noted. Thus Turner in England and Chudzinski in France have put on record detailed accounts of dissections of this character, and evidently they are regarded as of high scientific value. With us the very abundance of such material leads to its neglect. Were negro subjects so much of a rarity with us as they are abroad, we may easily imagine with what care each one would be dissected.

"It seems to me that we have here a remarkable chance to make solid additions to our science, particularly in the line of comparative anatomy, which, to my mind, is the only scientific anatomy.

"In isolated instances this has been done, and the literature of medicine and anthropology contains not a few allusions to this matter. Among others, Parker has noted important differences between negro and Caucasian brains, and Baker has recorded many myological differences; but, so far as I am aware, the matter has never received the careful and systematic investigation it deserves.

"I have thought it opportune to bring it to the notice of the Society at this time, in the hope of stimulating interest in it and leading to its further development. The isolated fact of today may become

Fig. 5.—A Spider Monkey in Erect Attitude.
(Courtesy of Mr. F. Ashman Carpenter, of San Diego, California.)

the generalization of tomorrow, and if each will contribute his mite we shall soon have a body of facts sufficient to warrant us in deducing the laws of agreement and difference, if such there be.

"During a somewhat extended service as demonstrator of anatomy in one of our local medical schools, using negro subjects entirely, one myological peculiarity of the race was forcibly impressed upon my attention. I refer to the almost invariable presence of the *psoas parvus* muscle, on both sides and well developed. I regret that I kept no exact record, but I feel warranted in saying that the presence of this muscle is the rule, and its absence a noteworthy exception. It was equally present in the two sexes.

"This muscle occurs constantly in the lower animals and serves an important purpose; but as we ascend in the scale it grows smaller and more rudimentary until in man it is generally stated to be absent or a mere fasciculus.

"Meckel is the only authority who regards this as a constantly present muscle. He states that it is sometimes absent, but that this is rare. Every other anatomist is against him. Theile's language is especially emphatic; he says: 'I consider the *absence* of the small *psoas* as the normal condition in man. In over twenty bodies, where I have searched especially for it, I have only found it a single time.'

"Holden gives its frequency of occurrence as one in eight or ten subjects; while Wilson, Quain, Cruveilhier, and others state in general terms that it is more frequently absent than present. Allen regards it as an accessory bundle to the great *psoas*. This may be true in the white, but I hardly think it will hold true of the negro. The muscle is invariably fairly developed, with entirely separate and well-defined points of attachment and having its own aponeurosis.

"I am inclined to regard the presence of this muscle in the colored race as a reversion toward the lower type of mammals, especially when taken in connection with other equally striking myological peculiarities, and I trust that I may be able, by this note, to cause someone, whose opportunities will permit, to study carefully the comparative myology of the two races. From my own limited experience, I am positive that a mine of information lies awaiting the explorer who shall uncover it, and I hope that its treasures may soon be added to the literature of our science."

Darwin has said that "we have seen that the mental powers of the higher animals do not differ in kind, though greatly in degree, from the corresponding powers of man, especially of the lower and barbarous races; and it would appear that even their taste for the beautiful is not widely different from that of the *Quadrumana.* As the negro of Africa raises the flesh on his face into parallel ridges 'or cicatrices, high above the natural' surface, which unsightly deformities are considered great personal attractions;[1] . . . as negroes and savages in many parts of the world paint their faces with red, blue, white, or black bars, so the male mandrill of Africa appears to have acquired his deeply furrowed and gaudily

[1] Sir Samuel Baker: "The Nile Tributaries of Abyssinia," 1867.

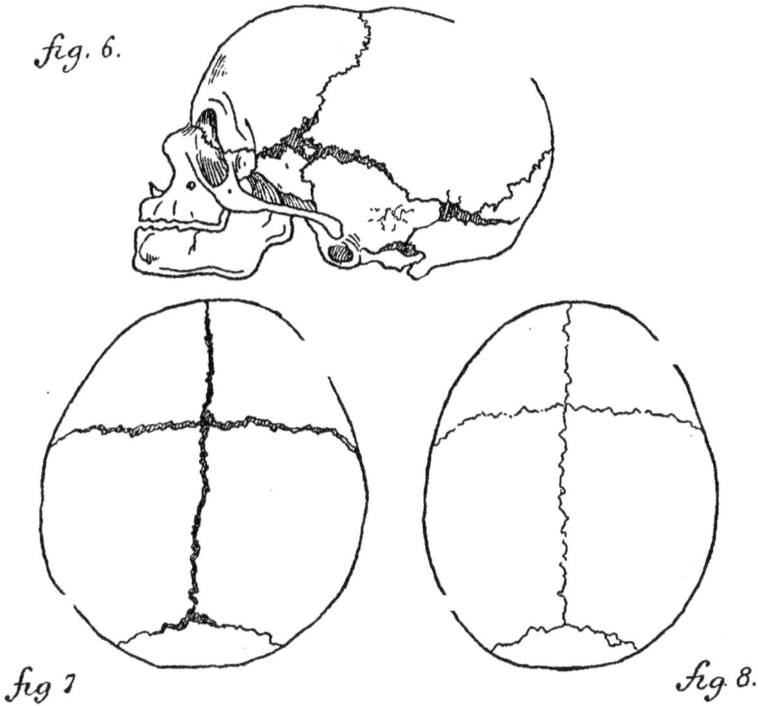

FIGS. 6, 7, AND 8.—SKULLS OF CAUCASIAN AND NEGRO CHILDREN.

Fig. 6 represents the skull of an average white child at the time of birth, left lateral view. Here the lateral fontanelles and cranial sutures are plainly seen; being far from closed up, they admit of the general expansion of the brain-mass for a long time during the growth of the individual.

Figs. 7 and 8 are partly diagrammatic representations of vertical aspects of the skulls of two children at about the time of puberty. It will be observed that in the white child (Fig. 7) the cranial sutures in this region still remain unclosed, thus allowing brain-growth and development; while in the negro (Fig. 8) they have coössified, thus preventing any further brain expansion and the results that naturally follow. (Drawn by the author.)

colored face from having been thus rendered attractive to the female."[2]

And again: "In regard to Colour, the new-born negro-child is reddish nut-brown, which soon becomes slaty-grey; the black colour being fully developed within a year in the Soudan, but not until three years in Egypt. The eyes of the negro are at first blue, and the hair chestnut-brown rather than black, being curly only at the ends."[3]

In short, as has long been known, whether living in Africa or living in America, the typical west-coast negro is, in his physical organization, as near the anthropoid apes as are any of the savage races of mankind,—perhaps the nearest. He is untold ages nearer than is the typical representative of the best in the white race.

We may say the same thing of his mental and moral qualifications. Further along in the present work I shall touch more fully upon these points. Professor Keane states that the mental and moral differences between the negro and the white races are quite as well marked as the physical ones, "and as both are the gradual outcome of external conditions, fixed by heredity, it follows that the attempt to suddenly transform the negro mind by foreign culture must be, as it has proved to be, as futile as the attempt would be to suddenly transform his physical type,"

---

[2] Darwin, Charles: "The Descent of Man," pp. 540, 541. The comparison made here is an especially good one, and will be appreciated by anyone who has had the opportunity to see, as I have, the native Africans paint up their faces, wrinkling them up in the manner above described, and also to study the face of the African mandrill, a most remarkable simian.

[3] *Loc. cit.*, p. 557.

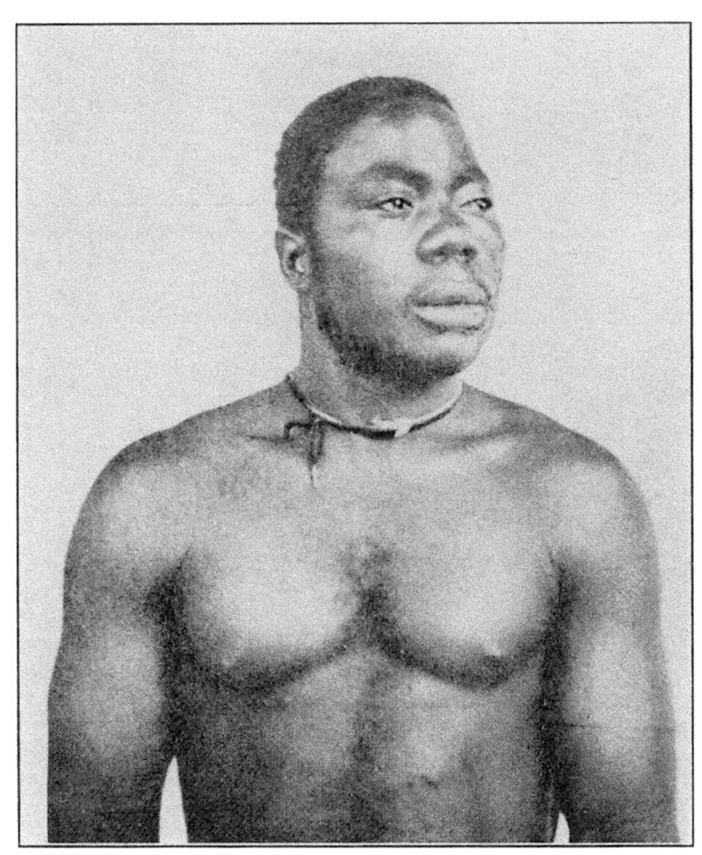

FIG. 9—A KRUMAN: WEST AFRICAN NEGRO.

(Photo by Sir Harry Johnston.)

—a point that the untutored masses in the United States fail to see. The negro has, in fact, no morals, and it is therefore out of the question for him to be immoral; in other words, he is non-moral rather than immoral.

In speaking of the condition of the blacks in the Southern States in 1883, the Rev. Dr. Tucker is quoted as having said, at the American Church Congress for that year, that he knew of whole neighborhoods "where there is not one single negro couple, whether legally married or not, who are faithful to each other beyond a few weeks. In the midst of a prayer-meeting I have known negroes to steal [money] from each other, and on the way home they will rob any henroost that lies conveniently at hand. The most pious negro that I know is confined in a penitentiary for an atrocious murder, and he persists in saying he can see no offence against God in his crime, though he acknowledges an offence against man."

Mention was further made of negro missionaries guilty of the grossest immorality, living in concubinage, addicted to thieving, lying, and every imaginary crime, yet all "earnest and successful preachers, and wholly unconscious of hypocricy. Their sins, universally known, did not diminish their influence with their race. It was impossible to doubt their absolute sincerity."

"A much darker picture," says Keane, in his work on the negro, "is presented by the independent negro commonwealth of Hayti, for eighty years the scene of almost uninterrupted fratricidal strife."

Throughout the entire historic period of man's career upon the earth, the chapter on the negro is practically a record of the lowest savagery, soon lapsing back into the mere tradition of wild and untutored tribes, whose social institutions are at the lowest possible level, with fetichism for religion, coupled with torture, cruelty, slavery, cannibalism, and a common belief in sorcery. Where not checked by the presence of the European, the native shambles in the middle Congo Basin are still hung with choice cuts of human bodies, and these continue to be sold in the open marketplace. In Africa they even barter their dead relatives, and those securing the corpses in this way eat them. (Stanley, "Heart of Africa," vol. ii, pp. 18, 19.) They will even disinter them for the same purpose and eat them after decomposition has set in. The negroes who still practise this in Africa are several millions in number, and close blood relations of the race in the United States.

To quote Professor Keane once more on the state of the African negro, he says: "When visited in 1879 by Dr. Buchver, this potentate [the Muata Yanvo of Ulunda], to impress his guest with his power, caused one of his subjects to assume the part of a chief just arrived from a remote province of the empire. The sham cortège of soldiers and women advanced to the throne thickly plastered with mud from head to foot, and the 'chief,' approaching on all fours, deliberately rolled himself in the sand at his majesty's feet as a proof of his respect.

"The administration of justice is regulated not by any sense of right or wrong, but by the caprice of the king, who is himself often in the power of the navumbala, or witch-detector. Beyond what has been acquired from without, of letters there is absolutely no knowledge, unless an exception be made in favour of the invention or adaptation of a rude syllabic system some years ago by a native of the Vei tribe. Hence literature is purely oral and limited to a few tribal legends, some folk-lore, proverbs, and songs of the simplest kind. The arts also are exclusively of an industrial character, restricted mainly to coarse weaving, pottery, and the smelting and working of copper and iron. Architecture has no existence, nor are there any monumental ruins or stone structures of any sort in Negroland proper.

"No full-blooded negro has ever," says Keane, "been distinguished as a man of science, a poet, or an artist, and the fundamental equality claimed for him by ignorant philanthropists is belied by the whole history of the race throughout the historic period." Professor Keane says "no full-blooded negro" has ever thus distinguished himself,—a fact that cannot be denied. From an ethnological standpoint, the place occupied by the West Soudan negro and his relatives in the United States is now clearly defined; he has been carefully studied by many minds fully capable of undertaking the task, and his status, not difficult of comprehension, is fairly set forth in the foregoing brief chapter.

CHAPTER III.

FURTHER COMPARATIVE ETHNOLOGICAL DATA.

MANY writers of the present and of the past have invited attention to the mental, moral, and physical characters of the negro, a few of which have been briefly described in the last chapter.[1] Heusinger, for example, long ago recognized the fact that the black races of mankind came nearer the anthropoid apes than any of the white races did, and in his work he cites many authorities who have touched upon this question.[2] Shortly before his memoir appeared, Tiedeman had published one which contained a far greater amount of information on this point, illustrated by excellent plates, comparing the brains of negroes with those of the simians.[3] He clearly pointed out, as many other writers had done before him, that the negroes of Africa were more nearly related to the higher apes than were the white races of Europe. Indeed, as their writings testify, such dis-

1 All the citations made here are from works personally examined by me, and in this connection my thanks are due to Colonel Walter D. McCaw, U. S. A., in charge of the Army Medical Museum at Washington, and to the late Dr. Robert Fletcher, of the library of that institution, for the loan of several valuable volumes from the Library of the Surgeon General's Office, which were forwarded to New York for my examination.

2 Heusinger, Dr. C. F.: "Vier Abbildungen des Schädels der Simia Satyrus von verschiedenem Alter, zur Aufklärung der Fabel vom Oran utan." Marburg, 1838. Large quarto, 44 pp. Plates of skulls of Orang-utan.

3 Tiedeman, Dr. Friedrich: "Das Hirn des Negers mit dem des Europäers und Orang-outangs vergleichen." Mit sechs Tafeln. Heidelberg, 1837. The tables in this memoir are very valuable.

FIG. 10.—YOUNG MENDE GIRL, OF EASTERN SIERRA LEONE.

(Photo by Mr. Cecil H. Firmin.)

tinguished anatomists as Cuvier, Camper, and Sömmering entertained the same opinion.

White, who in 1799 published a memoir entitled "An Account of the Regular Gradation in Man, and in Different Animals and Vegetables," says: "Taking the European man as a standard of comparison, on the one hand, and the tribe of simiæ on the other; and comparing the classes of mankind with the standards, and with each other, they may be so arranged as to form a pretty regular gradation, in respect to the differences in the bodily structure and œconomy, the European standing at the head, as being farthest removed from the brute creation" (p. 83). He further says that "the African, more especially in those particulars in which he differs from the European, approaches the ape."

Lawrence states in his "Lectures on Physiology, Zoölogy and the Natural History of Man": "In all the particulars just enumerated, the negro structure approximates unequivocally to that of the monkey. It not only differs from the Caucasian model, but is distinguished from it in two respects: the intellectual characters are reduced, the animal features enlarged and exaggerated. This inferiority of organization is attended with corresponding inferiority of faculties, which may be proved, not so much by the unfortunate beings who are degraded by slavery, as by every fact in the past history and the present condition of Africa." (London, 1819, p. 363.)

Hume was of the opinion that all negroes were inferior to the whites, that "There scarcely ever was a civilized nation of that complexion [black], nor ever any individual eminent either in action or speculation.

No ingenious manufactures amongst them, no arts, no sciences. On the other hand, the most rude and barbarous of the whites, such as the ancient Germans and the present Tartars, have still something eminent about them, in their valour, form of government, or some other particular."[4]

"The colour of the skin of genuine negroes," says Haeckel, "is always more or less of a pure black. Their skin is velvety to the touch, and characterized by a peculiar, offensive exhalation. Although negroes agree with Kaffres in the formation of the woolly hair of the head, yet they differ essentially in the formation of their face. Their forehead is flatter and lower, their nose broad and thick, not prominent, their lips large and protruding, and their chin very short. Genuine negroes are moreover distinguished by very thin calves and very long arms. This species of men must have branched into many separate tribes at a very early period, for their numerous and entirely distinct languages can in no way be traced to one primæval language." Of these same negro tribes he further says: "They have barely risen above the lowest stage of transition from man-like apes to apelike men, a stage which the progenitors of the higher human species had already passed through thousands of years ago."[5]

The attitude of the genuine African negro toward women has already been touched upon on a previous page of the present work. Every day the daily newspapers of this country take it upon themselves to re-

---

[4] Essays and Treatises on Several Subjects, vol. i, note M.

[5] Haeckel, Ernst: "The History of Creation," vol. ii, pp. 313, 364, 1880.

cord the cases that have occurred within the day passed exemplifying this attitude. Thousands of such cases are never recorded, and the perpetrators seem to become more brutal and dangerous as time goes on. Letourneau has said: "We have previously seen how lamentable the fate of woman is among the negro Africans, and how excessive are the 'rights of the father of the family,' since he can traffic in his children without rebuke. This virile despotism may easily coexist with the adoption of uterine filiation. In one Kaffir tribe, the men used their own children to bait their traps for catching lions, and yet maternal filiation prevails in Kaffraria; only it does not govern inheritance."[6]

Such customs are by no means uncommon today in Hayti and in the interior of Jamaica, barring the trap-baiting one, as there are no lions there. The non-morality of thousands of negroes in this country has already been described, and is not to be wondered at when we come to look into the history of their African ancestors.

"As for all the negroes of Africa," says Letourneau, "whatever the degree of their civilization or savagery, they have not even a suspicion of the monogamic *régime.* But, in Africa also, sensuality is only one of the secondary causes of the plurality of wives so strongly desired by the blacks. Their polygamy is chiefly founded on economic motives.

"Naturally the last sentiments we may expect to find in African households are those of delicacy or

---

[6] Letourneau, Ch.: "The Evolution of Marriage, and of the Family." London, 1900, p. 305. See also Layland in Journal of Ethnological Society, 1869.

moral nobility. Humble to servility in the presence of the master, the women give rein to their shameless excesses as soon as they can do it without danger.

"In Bornou a wife never approaches her husband without kneeling. When a Poul orders one of his wives to prepare his supper, which implies that the master desires her company for the night, this signal favour is received with transports of joy. The chosen wife hastens to obey, and when the repast is ready she proudly goes to seek the master, thus humiliating her female colleagues, who retreat in confusion to their cabins to await their turn. But all this abject behaviour is merely by compulsion, and the women recoup themselves well for it whenever they have the chance. . . . In all negro Africa the husbands are generally strangers to the jealousy of honour which exists among the intelligent husbands of civilized countries. They do not care for moral fidelity, based on affection and free choice." (*Evolution of Marriage,* pp. 127, 128.)

Monteiro, the African traveler, says: "The negro knows neither love, affection, nor jealousy. During the many years that I have spent in Africa I have never seen a negro manifest the least tenderness for a woman—put his arms around her, give or receive a caress, denoting some degree of affection or love on one side or the other. . . . They have no word in their language to signify love or affection." This statement is quoted both by Herbert Spencer in his *Sociology* (vol. ii, pp. 284-293) and by other authoritative writers on morals and marriage among negroes. Such characteristics as these can only pertain to a people who delight in torture, and torture of

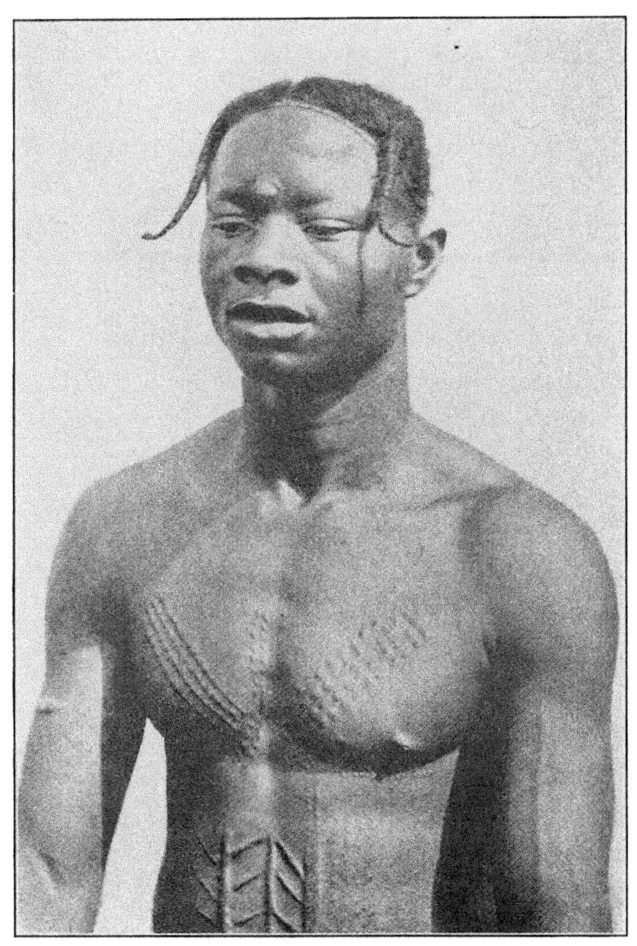

Fig. 11.—Type of Congo Native.

every conceivable kind. We must cease to wonder, then, when Monteiro further informs us that the negro "has not the slightest idea of mercy, pity, or compassion for suffering. A fellow-creature, or animal, writhing in pain or torture, is to him a sight highly provocative of merriment and enjoyment. I have seen a number of blacks at Loanda, men, women, and children, stand around, roaring with laughter, at seeing a poor mongrel dog that had been run over by a cart, twist and roll about in agony on the ground till a white man put it out of its misery."[7] To prove that the unmixed negro in this country is still indifferent to feeling when confronted with fearful suffering in others, it is but necessary to remind the reader of the numerous instances where they have raped and murdered little white girls, for years past, in all parts of the United States. Cruelty is an instinct that militates against everything that is good and noble in a progressive civilization; and can anyone believe for an instant that these Africans among us have lost this instinct, or that we, as a nation, are strong enough or numerous enough to 'civilize it out' of the millions of them that are now mixed up with us, and where, through that mixture, hybrids are, by the hundreds, being daily produced? Never!

"Immorality," says Fritsch, "is too deeply rooted in the African blood to make it difficult to find an occasion for indulging in it; wherefore the custom of celebrating puberty is made the occasion for lascivious practices; the unmarried girls choose companions with whom they cohabit as long as the festival lasts. . . . usually three or four days."[8]

[7] Monteiro, J. J.: "Angola and the River Congo," p. 134.
[8] Fritsch, G.: "Die Eingeborenen Süd-Afrikas," p. 112.

Finck, too, has gathered together for us not a little literature shedding light upon the non-morality, the utter depravity, the bestiality, and the cannibalism of the native negroes in Africa; and, as has been said before, there are a sufficient number of examples in the world that go to prove that negroes, however long they may have enjoyed the influences of the highest civilization, when by themselves will always lapse into the very lowest stages of barbarism. Finck says: "In 1891 the Swedish explorer Westermarck published a book describing his adventures among the cannibal tribes of the Upper Congo. I have not seen the book, but the Rev. James Johnston, in summing up its contents says: 'A man can sell his wife and children according to his own depraved pleasure. Women are the slave drudges, the men spending their hours in eating, drinking, and sleeping. Cannibalism in its worst features prevails. Young women are prized as special delicacies, particularly girls' ears prepared in palm oil, and, in order to make the flesh more palatable, the luckless victims are kept in water up to their necks for three or four days before they are slaughtered and served as food.' "[9]

But it is not necessary to go further into this side of the genuine negro's character, for it is all too well known to the intelligent reader. The higher sentimental qualities of love are totally lacking in true negroes of both sexes in this country today; this fact is easily discovered by anyone who will take the pains

[9] Finck, Henry T.: "Primitive Love and Love Stories." New York, 1899, p. 394. Johnston, J.: "Missionary Landscapes in the Dark Continent," p. 193. This work I have not personally examined, and so rely entirely upon Finck for the correctness of the passages here quoted.—R. W. S.

to study their natures with a keen psychological insight. In thousands of instances they undertake to mimic us in this quality as in much else that has for ages pertained to the higher race; as a matter of fact, from first to last, it is the gratification of the sexual appetite that comes up in their minds when typical negroes are brought together, the matter of pure love being constitutionally unknown to them. All this is a question of inheritance with the race in this country. How very, very rare it is that we see two negroes kiss each other, or exhibit any true sentiment in their love-making! The animal instincts arise at once, and the rest of the story is known to us. Many animals below man manifest a far greater amount of real affection in their love-making than do the negroes, and hundreds of cases might be cited even among the various groups of birds.

In support of all this we may note what Zöller says:: "A negro woman does not fall in love in the same sense as a European, not even as the least civilized peasant girl. Love, in our sense of the word, is a product of our culture, belonging to a higher stage in the development of latent faculties than the negro race has reached. Not only is the negro a stranger to the diverse intellectual and sentimental qualities which we denote by the name of love; nay, even in a purely bodily sense it may be asserted that his nervous system is not only less sensitive, but less well developed. The negro loves as he eats and drinks. . . . And just as little as a black epicure have I ever been able to discover a negro who could rise to the imaginative phases of amorous dalliance."[10]

[10] Zöller, Hugo: "Forschungsreisen in die deutsche Colonie Kamerum," iii, 68-70.

When my former work on *The Negro* appeared, it received a very large number of reviews, but a no more scientific one than at the hands of the distinguished ethnologist, Dr. A. H. Keane, of London. Doctor Keane's remarks first appeared in *The Savannah Morning News* (Georgia) of June 7, 1908, p. 7, and were extensively reproduced by a number of magazines and periodicals throughout the country. Notwithstanding the fact that his contribution contains one or two quotations that have already appeared in a previous chapter of the present work, they are allowed to remain in order to not interfere with the line of his argument, and his criticisms are here reproduced *in extenso*:—

"EDITOR MORNING NEWS: May I, as an outsider, but not 'an alien,' crave a little of your valuable space for a few remarks on this work, to which my attention has recently been called, as again raising the whole question of the black 'eye-sore' in an acute form. Equipped as he is with all the armature acquired from his ethnological and anatomical studies, and from long and close contact with the negro, the author speaks at first hand with a commanding voice that few others could pretend to. Hence, when he tells us that when writing the book he was 'actuated by no other motive than that of telling the truth most plainly and fully,' his conclusions on the many complex factors of the problem will at least be taken into serious consideration, though they may not succeed in securing universal assent. The issues raised are too numerous and involved to hope for an immediate solution, and, for the present, all that can be reason-

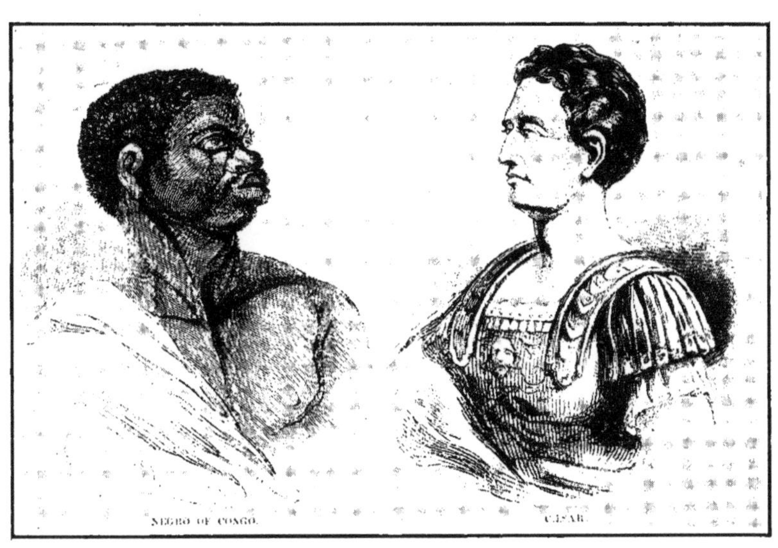

FIG. 12.—COMPARISON OF THE PHYSIOGNOMY OF A CONGO NEGRO AND CÆSAR.

ably expected is some such full and frank statement of the case as is here presented to the reader.

"In support of Dr. Shufeldt's general argument, I should like here to dwell more particularly on two points, to wit: The negro's intellectual stagnation, and the effects of miscegenation—on both of which I may claim to speak with some confidence, if not altogether convincingly.

"*First.* I believe I was amongst the first anthropologists to enter a strong protest against the assumptions of those philanthropists and sham sentimentalists who, on political, social, and religious grounds, rashly proclaimed the fundamental equality of all races, and preached the doctrine that the Zulu-Kaffirs and the Africans stood on the same mental level as the Aryan-speaking white peoples. As far back as the year 1884 I pointed out, in the Encyclopædia Britannica (9th edition), that such equality was belied by the history of human culture, and disproved by the physical structure of the black man's brain-cap. The cranial sutures close much earlier in the negro than in other races. To this premature ossification of the skull, preventing all further development of the brain, many pathologists have attributed the inherent mental inferiority of the blacks, an inferiority which is even more marked than their physical differences. No one has more carefully studied this point than Filippo Manetta, who, during a long residence on the plantations of the Southern States of America, noted that the negro children were sharp, intelligent, and full of vivacity, but in the adult state the intellect seemed to become clouded—animation giving place to a sort of lethargy; briskness yielding to indolence. With the white, the volume of the brain grows with the expansion of the skull; with the negro, the growth of the brain is, on the contrary, arrested by the early closing of the cranial sutures. ('La Razza Negra,' Turin, 1864, p. 20.) Later the same phenomenon causing stagnation of both the mental and moral faculties was noted by other observers, such as Col. A. B. Ellis and Capt. Binger, the latter declaring that to this intellectual stagnation should be ascribed in these regions (the Soudan) the closing of the cranial box; the development of the skull ceases and prevents the brain from further expansion.

"That the moral no less than the pure intellectual qualities remain at the animal stage, is evident from the unbiased testimony of such observers as Capt. Ruffin, of Richmond, Va., and especially the Rev. Dr. Tucker, who stated at the American Church Congress of 1883, that he 'knew of whole neighborhoods where there is not one single negro couple, whether legally married or not, who are faithful to each other beyond a few weeks. The most pious negro that I know is confined in a penitentiary for an atrocious murder; and he persists in saying that he can see no offence against God in his crime, though he acknowledges an offence against man.' He had not yet grasped the distinction between sin and crime. His moral faculty was still infantile, and it is this very infantile condition of the negro temperament, combined with an ineradicable strain of animal ferocity, that makes the negro element such 'A Menace to American Civilization.' I may incidentally remark that the cranial capacity, on which the mentality depends, stands in Soudan at about 1300 c.c., as compared with Dubois'

Pithecanthropus erectus (900 or, perhaps, 1000), and the average American (1600). The average negro is thus intellectually about midway between the human precursor (early Pliocene man) and the present most advanced civilized people; in other words, he lags, in terms of time, at least one million years behind. Such is the inference to be drawn from the data supplied by physical anthropology.

"*Second.* Racial temperaments resemble physical temperaments in that the union of two of either results in equilibrium. Hence the union or the intermingling of two races, at different cultural levels, means the relative upheaval of the lower at the expense of the higher. Consequently the Afro-American, now much spoken of, is necessarily a debarred creature, compared with the typical Anglo-American aborigine of more or less pure Anglo-Saxon or British descent. It follows that, if this Afro-American element is on the increase, the Anglo-American element has entered on a process of decay, which must end in all-round debasement unless arrested. Can such a dismal prospect be looked upon with equanimity even by that 'Little American' section of the community, which, like our (I fear) still more numerous 'Little Englanders,' have always the first word for the alien, the second only for themselves? For it is to be noticed that the degradation would not be confined to the Southern States, but would inevitably spread like a pestiferous contagion over the whole Union. Indeed, it already threatens to spread, and a silent Northward movement appears to have recently set in; the Southern blacks even now pouring into the city of New York, as I am informed, not by alarmists, but by cool-headed observers there. On this aspect of the question I read almost with terror the warning note raised by Dr. Shufeldt, who tells us that 'there are plenty of people in this country of ours who would far rather see the entire white race here rotted by heroic injections into their veins of all the savagery and criminality there is in the negro, than have any number of the latter in any way inconvenienced by their being returned to the country from which their ancestors came.'

"Such fanatical regard for the susceptibilities of a race which, after all, is entitled to scant respect, becomes a crime against humanity, and, if persisted in, would end in national suicide. Surely they cannot shut their eyes to the deadly results of miscegenation in Latin America, although there the crosses have mainly been between whites and American aborigines, the latter being in most respects a far superior race to the blacks, so that the resultant Hispano and Lusitano-American Mestizoes must be assumed to be of better type than the Afro-Americans. Dealing with the various degrees of intermixture, Sir H. Johnston aptly remarks that the white and black stocks 'are too widely separated in type to produce a satisfactory hybrid.' This observer, who has had more to do with the African aborigines than any other man living, also holds that the pure and unadulterated negro cannot advance with any certainty of stability above his present level of culture without the admixture of a somewhat higher race, such as the Indian Coolie. Then, the blend of these two races 'would give the Indian the physical development, which he lacks, and he, in his turn, would transmit to his half-negro offspring the industry, ambition, and

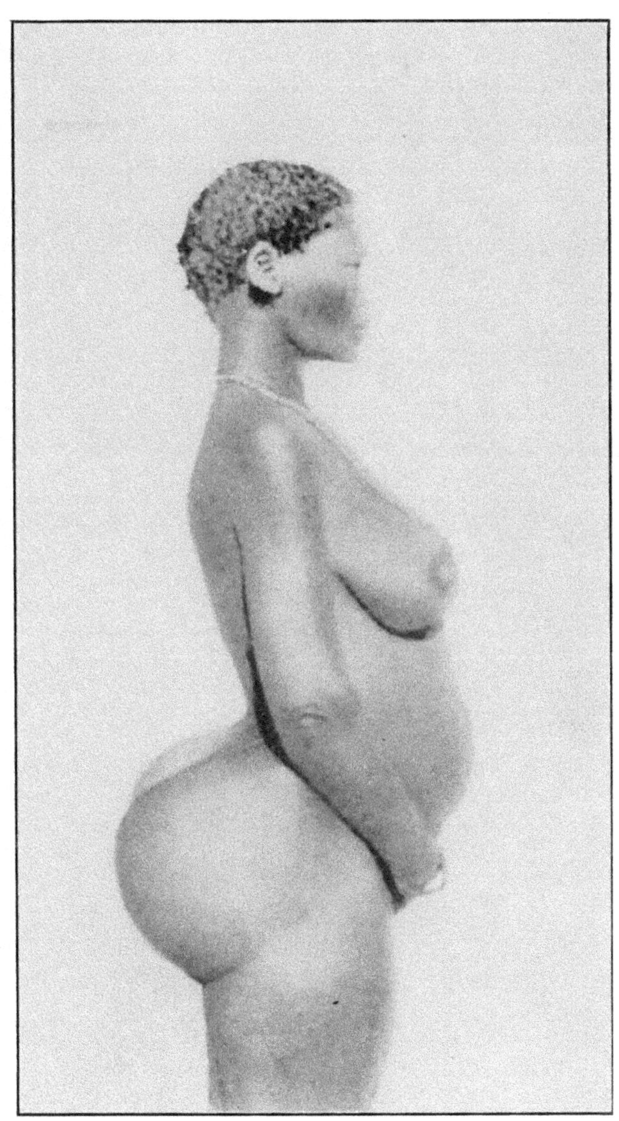

Fig. 13—A Steatopygous Hottentot Woman.

(By the author, after Stratz.)

aspiration toward his civilized life which the negro so markedly lacks.' (Quoted in my "Man, Past and Present," p. 265.) The infusion of such a Hindu strain has even been suggested as a possible means of improving or elevating the North American negro. But I do not consider such a project as at all practicable, and I hold, with Dr. Shufeldt, that the only ultimate remedy for the growing evil must be in separation, or, in plain words, removal or excision from the body politic. But a consideration of the various schemes by which it is proposed to effect this, and thereby disperse the 'black cloud,' does not fall within the scope of the present communication. I am, Sir, yours faithfully, A. H. KEANE, LL.D.,

"Late Vice-President of the Anthropological Institute,

"London.

"Aram-Gah,

"79 Broadhurst Gardens,

"South *H*ampstead,

"London, N. W.,

"May 7th, 1908."

Passing from this phase of the ethnological status of the negro, we may touch upon a few more points, in a comparative way, regarding his anatomical structure as observed by various writers.

"In some skulls," says Huxley, "the brain-case may be said to be *'round,'* the extreme length not exceeding the extreme breadth by a greater proportion than 100 to 80, while the difference may be much less.[11]

[11] "In no normal human skull does the breadth of the brain-case exceed its length."

"Men possessing such skulls were termed by Retzius 'brachycephalic,' and the skull of a Calmuck,[12] of which a front and side view are depicted by von Baer in his excellent 'Crania selecta,' affords a very admirable example of that kind of a skull. Other skulls, such as that of a negro. . . . from Mr. Busk's 'Crania typica,' have a very different, greatly elongated form, and may be termed 'oblong.'[13]

"In this skull the extreme length is to the extreme breadth as 100 to not more than 67, and the transverse diameter of the human skull may fall below even this proportion. People having such skulls were called by Retzius *'dolichocephalic.'*

"The most cursory glance at the side views of these two skulls will suffice to prove that they differ, to a very striking extent, in another respect. The profile of the face of the Calmuck [or the skulls of the Europeans and ancient Roman, cited above] is almost vertical, the facial bones being thrown downwards and under the fore part of the skull. The profile of the face of the negro, on the other hand, is singularly inclined, the front part of the jaws projecting far forward beyond the level of the fore part of the skull. In the former case the skull is said to be *'orthognathous,'* or straight-jawed; in the latter it is called

[12] The same features are to be observed in the skull of the intellectual European, shown in Fig. 20 of this work, or in the skull of the ancient Roman shown in Figs. 21, 22.—R. W. S.

[13] The skull here referred to is reproduced in Figs. 16 and 17, and the same characters are admirably shown in the negro skull I have photographically copied from Quatrefages, shown in two views in Figs. 14 and 15. There is no mistaking the prognathous skull of the genuine negro, nor the fact that it is more simian-like in character than the skulls possessed by the intelligent Anglo-Saxon. —R. W. S.

'prognathous,' a term which has been rendered, with more force than elegance, 'snouty.'

"Various methods have been devised in order to express with some accuracy the degree of prognathism or orthognathism of any given skull; most of these methods being essentially modifications of that devised by Peter Camper, in order to attain what he called the 'facial angle.' "[14]

Professor Huxley then proceeds to show that "any 'facial angle' that has been devised can be competent to express the structural modifications involved in prognathism and orthognathism, only in a rough and general sort of a way." He then offers a far more accurate method of computing this angle in all skulls of the Mammalia, though it places the negro skull in the scale where it truly belongs, among the very lowest of existing races.[15]

As every student of comparative vertebrate morphology is aware, "in the lower vertebrates, the surface of the cerebral hemispheres is smooth; in the higher, it becomes complicated by ridges and furrows, the *gyri* and *sulci,* which follow particular patterns. . . . The general nature of the modifications observable in the brain as we pass from the lower to the higher *mammalia* is very well shown by the figures of the brain of a Rabbit, a Pig, and a Chimpanzee."[16] (Figs. 28, 29, and 30.)

---

[14] See Figs. 23, 24 and 25 of the present work. In the matter of the *facial angle,* the typical negro stands between the gorilla and the intelligent white man, and this will hold true for a typical series of skulls.—R. W. S.

[15] Huxley, T. H.: "Evidence as to Man's Place in Nature," 1863, pp. 169-171.

[16] Huxley, T. H.: "The Anatomy of Vertebrated Animals." New York, 1872, p. 60.

By comparing these figures with those shown in Figs. 31, 32, 33, and 34, it will be observed that "the brain of man differs far less from that of the chimpanzee than that of the latter does from the Pig's brain." Huxley says, further: "As to the convolutions, the brains of the apes exhibit every stage of progress, from the almost smooth brain of the Marmoset, to the Orang and the Chimpanzee, which fall but little below man. And it is most remarkable that as soon as all the principal sulci appear, the pattern according to which they are arranged is identical with that of the corresponding sulci of man. The surface of the brain of a monkey exhibits a sort of a skeleton map of man's, and in the man-like apes the details become more and more filled in, until it is only in minor characters, such as the greater excavation of the anterior lobes, the constant presence of fissures usually absent in man, and the different disposition and proportions of some convolutions, that the Chimpanzee's or the Orang's brain can be structurally distinguished from Man's."[17]

In other words, when we come to study and compare the skulls of all monkeys, anthropoid apes, and the lower and higher races of man, their several cranial capacities, the facial angles, and other characters *in a sufficiently large series,* and setting aside all rare exceptions in these particulars, it will be appreciated that the great mass of typical, unmixed negroes in America and elsewhere must be classed as probably the lowest race of people now in existence on this planet. To properly understand the most important

[17] Huxley, T. H.: "Evidences as to Man's Place in Nature," 119, 120.

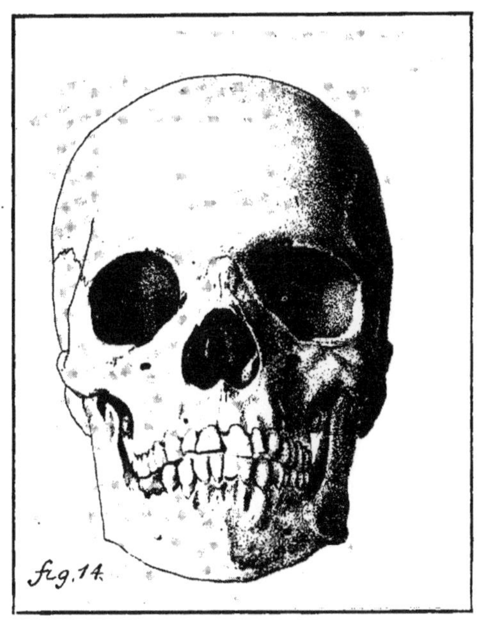

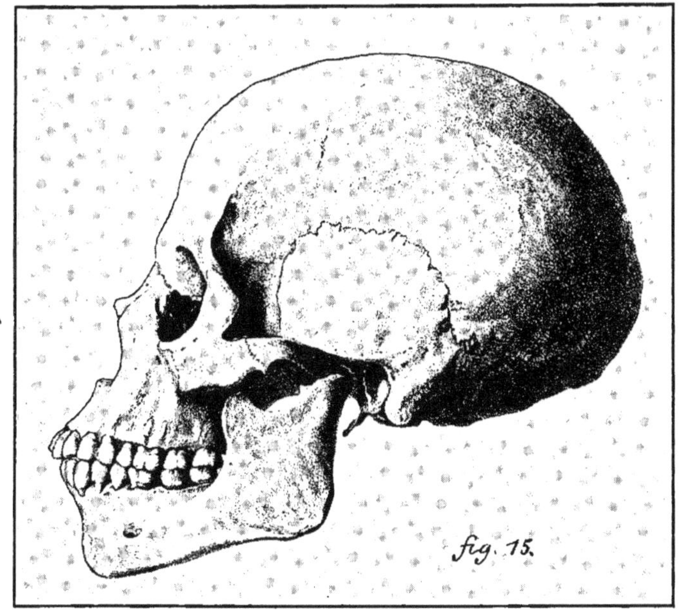

FIGS. 14 AND 15—ANTERIOR (FIG 14) AND LATERAL (FIG 15) VIEWS OF THE SKULL OF A NEGRO FROM THE CONGO.

(Photo by the author, after Quatrefages et Hamy: "Crania Ethnica les Cranes des Races Humaines," Pl XXXVI, Figs I and II) The prognathous jaws of the negro race are well seen in this skull They exhibit the simian affinities and the very low intellectual plane occupied by these people

of these differences, one has but to study and compare the various figures of skulls, brains, and facial angles offered in the several examples of the present work. I have many times examined the actual material and compared such as is here described, and anatomists are practically of one opinion in regard to the facts as I have presented them, or quoted them from the writings of other authors. This I have intentionally done and will continue to do to the end of this chapter, in order that I may, as far as possible, escape the charge of confining myself to my own studies and observations for proof of what is here brought forward.

Dr. Chamberlain, in quoting Dr. Shute, says: "As 'anatomical peculiarities, which, taken together, stamp a race as high or low,' Dr. Shute mentions the following, which are more or less simioid: —

"1. Cranial sutures simple and uniting early.
"2. Nasal aperture wide, with nasal bones ankylosed.
"3. Jaws unduly projecting and chin receding.
"4. Wisdom teeth well developed, appearing early and permanent.
"5. Humerus unduly long and perforated.
"6. Calcaneum (heel-bone) elongated.
"7. Tibia flattened.
"8. Pelvis narrow.

"According to Dr. Shute,[18] 'measured by these criteria, the Caucasian stands at the head of the racial scale and the negro at the bottom.' "[19]

---

[18] Shute, D. K.: "Racial Anatomical Peculiarities," Amer. Anthro., vol. ix (1896), pp. 123-132.

[19] Chamberlain, Alex. F.: "The Child, A Study in the Evolution of Man." London, 1900, p. 432. This excellent work contains a mass of information tending to prove the low plane occupied by the negro in America.

Few people understand the negro better than does Sir Harry H. Johnston, and in one of his works he says that if left to himself he is a *fine animal,* incapable of any progress, while "in his wild state he exhibits a stunted mind and a dull content with his surroundings, which induces mental stagnation, cessation of all upward progress, and even retrogression towards the brute. In some respects I think the tendency of the negro for several centuries past has been an actual retrograde one. As we come to read the unwritten history of Africa by researches into language, manners, customs and traditions, we seem to see a backward rather than a forward movement going on for some thousand years past—a return towards the savage and even the brute. I can believe it possible that, had Africa been more isolated from contact with the rest of the world, and cut off from the immigration of the Arab and the European, the purely negro races, so far from advancing towards a higher type of humanity, might have actually reverted by degrees to a type no longer human."[20]

Huxley refers, in his "Anatomy of Vertebrated Animals," to some few other anatomical characters in comparing Apes, Negroes, and Whites, which may be

[20] This quotation is from Dr. A. H. Keane's "The World's Peoples," etc. (London, 1908), p. 73), a work full of valuable information in regard to the negro races and the low plane they occupy in humanity's scale of development. In it, on pp. 72, 73, Dr. Keane says: "Even when some progress has been made under the stimulus of higher influences, the removal of those influences is inevitably followed by a relapse into the former state, as in Hayti. Here the reversion to Voodu and other pagan rites, to snake-worship, cannibalism, and similar horrors, is attested to by Sir Spencer St. John, who had official knowledge of these matters, and, after twenty years' residence in the 'Black Republic,' tells us that, the better influences removed, the negro gradually retrogrades to the African tribal customs."

referred to with advantage; he says: "It appears in some of the lower races, *e.g.*, Negroes and Australians, the forearm and hand and the foot and leg are often longer in proportion than in Europeans. From not wearing shoes, the hallux is much more movable in these races, and the foot is commonly employed for prehension.

"There is no proof of what is so commonly asserted, that the heel is longer in proportion to the foot in negroes."[21]

There are not a few characters in the skeleton of the trunk and limbs wherein the genuine negro more often agrees with the simians than with the whites. In Fig. 26 a comparison is made between the skeleton of a European and a Gorilla, introduced for the purpose of showing how very closely the skeletons of these two mammals resemble each other.

For a similar purpose I have likewise introduced two of Sir Richard Owen's figures (Figs. 35 and 36), comparing the plantar surface of the foot of a Gorilla and in Man, both dissected out to show the arrangement of the muscles. Reference has been made in a previous chapter to the great prehensibility of the foot in certain Africans, and in this particular they more closely approach the anthropoids than do the Europeans or their American descendants. It must be remembered, however, that in this respect it never in any way approaches the truly hand-like member as found among the Apes and Monkeys.

[21] Dr. A. H. Keane, in his "The World's Peoples," differs on this point, and in giving the "physical characters" of the negroes he says: "*Foot* flat and broad with low instep and larkspur heel" (p. 16). It is a common assertion, at least throughout the United States, that "a nigger's heel will make a hole in de groun'."

The foot of the Gorilla is well shown in Fig. 3, a picture wherein some other useful comparisons can be made, as for example the physiognomy of the great ape with that of any of the three negroes who stand behind it. Even a more interesting comparison of this nature is to be found in Fig. 4, where the expression of the young negro's face so much resembles that of the young chimpanzee on the left, especially about the eyes and the nose. The pure animal type of the unmixed negro, however, is well exemplified in Fig. 39. Here, indeed, we have a good example of many of the negroes that are now interbreeding with the whites in this country, and a glance at this man's features should be ample to convince any intelligent person of the great undesirability of such a mixture.

Of all the African colored races, Dr. Keane claims that the Vaalpens, or Kattea, are the most degraded, being the most perfect "embodiment of the pure savage still anywhere surviving." They are a negroid people.

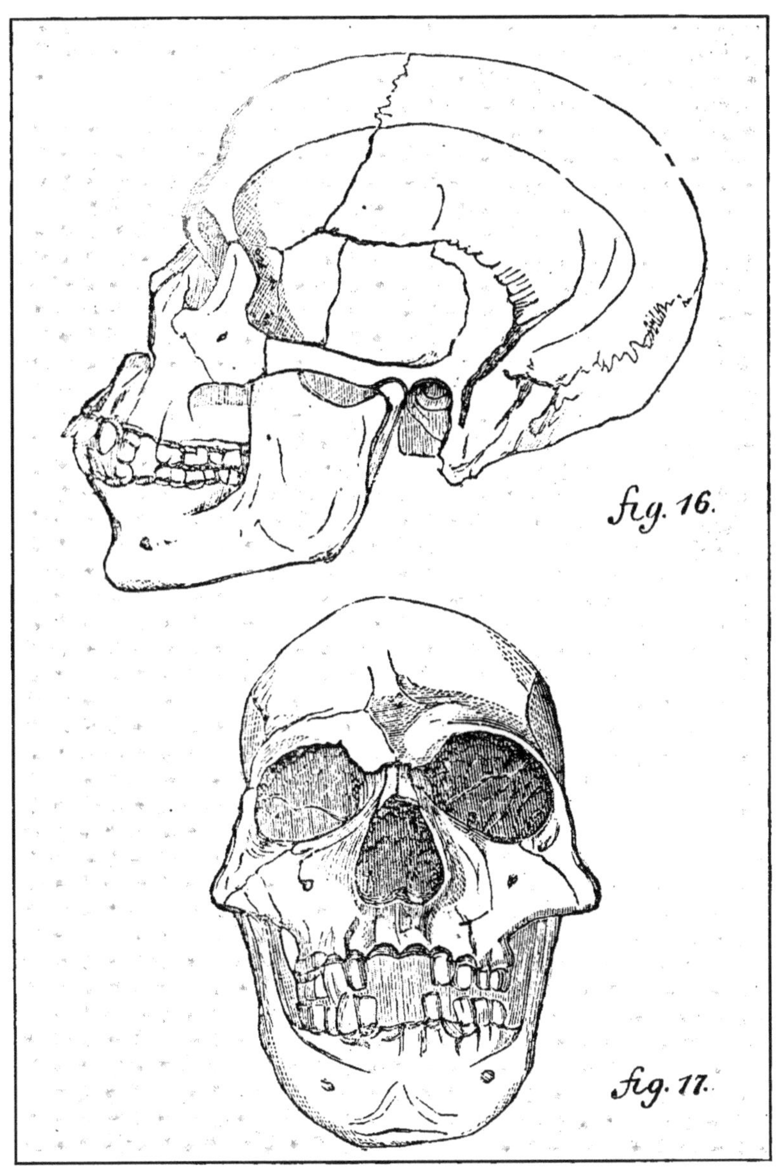

FIGS. 16 AND 17.

Fig. 16, lateral view, and Fig. 17, anterior view, of the oblong and prognathous skull of a negro. After Huxley, by the author. ("Evidence as to Man's Place in Nature," Fig. 28.)

CHAPTER IV.

The Introduction of the Negro into the United States. The African Slave Trade.

Early in the 60's my father was the American Consul General in the city of Havana, Cuba, and while there I not only saw and visited the African and coolie slavers in the harbor, but for two years I had the opportunity of studying the treatment of the slaves on the island by their masters. The barracoons were a familiar sight to my eyes, and I have seen many a slave punished either by the owner or by the government overseer. At Cape Haytien in Hayti, a year or so later, I had the opportunity of studying negro life in a negro city,—a city of Spanish and French building, but at that time—in a dilapidated condition—in the hands of the blacks, who had gained it through an insurrection against their masters. During the American Civil War I was in the South in the service of the Federal Government. For forty years I have studied the African negro in America, in every situation ever occupied by the race, whether its representative was of pure African stock, a half or other fractional caste, a slave or a freedman.

The existence of human slavery, in one form or another, dates back to the very dawn of American history. An account of the millions of beings who have thus been enslaved, their histories, their lives, their deaths, and their fates afterward, would be a tale of the rankest injustice, most dastardly murders, tortures unspeakable, fiendish cruelties, slaughter, de-ception, unbridled lust, tyranny,—indeed, every crime, both petty and capital, that the mind can conceive of, or the hand of man has ever committed. Millions of our own species have been dealt with in this manner, and make up a tremendous death roll; no part of human history can in any way compare with it.

England, Holland, Spain, Portugal, Brazil, and many other countries were deeply engaged in it, but none of these more so than was America, whose record in the slave trade is quite as foul, shameless and abominable as that of any other nation on earth during the time it lasted. In the present volume I shall have nothing to say on the subject of slavery in the far East, where it still exists in many places, as it does in many parts of Africa among the negroes; neither shall I refer, except ever so lightly, to the slave trade of Great Britain and other European countries. My main object in introducing it at all is to picture to the reader the character of the negroes that were brought over to America as slaves; their mental, moral, and physical natures; their numbers, the treatment they received in the way of fitting—or unfitting—them for colonization; how the slave trade was conducted, and how it was brought to an end. Of all these questions the most important by far is: What kind of people, what kind of *stock* were these negroes? This point has been avoided by the so-called twentieth century leaders among the negroes in the United States; and naturally so. This avoidance is seen in their published works as well as in their addresses and teachings. A few exceptions to this rule occur, however, exceptions met with in the writings of those having very little negro blood in them.

So far as we can ascertain from history, the first African slaves landed in the Northern States were brought there by the Dutch in August, 1619. John Rolfe, the husband of Pocahontas, was in Jamestown at the time, and a part of his account of the affair has been preserved. In his diary we read that "a dutch man of warre that sold us twenty Negars touched at Jamestown this year." Little more is known about it, and it is not even ascertained from what part of Africa these negroes came, or how they were captured. The history of the North American slave trade dates from this event. The Dutchman came here because on the high seas, when he had his slaves on board, he met with a Virginia ship, the *Treasurer,* and those aboard of the latter told him that they wanted slaves in Jamestown. Afterward the *Treasurer* herself brought negro slaves to Virginia, and indeed she was the first ship especially fitted out for the slave trade in this country. Subsequently she had quite a history which has been very well told in the *Magazine of American History* (November, 1891) by a writer of authority. In the year 1636 we see, in the ship *Desire,* the very first craft *built* in the United States for the very purpose of this nefarious traffic. Still other vessels landed them along the coast at various points, yet in 1649 not over fifty negro slaves had been imported into Virginia. The negro president of the colored institute at Tuskegee, Alabama, in his book entitled "The Future of the American Negro," ignores the introduction of the tens of thousands of slaves that were landed in this country during the subsequent slave-trade period, and makes the attempt to hoodwink his readers by asking them to believe that all the negroes in the United States at the present time are descended from those constituting the first cargo brought to Virginia. He makes the statement thus: "The first slaves were brought into this country by the Dutch in 1619, and were landed at Jamestown, Virginia. The first cargo consisted of fourteen. The census taken in 1890 shows that these fourteen slaves had increased to 7,638,360."

That he meant this exactly as it is said is proved by what he restates on pages 22 and 23 of the same book in the following words: "I know that, whether the Negroes are increasing or decreasing, whether they are growing better or worse, whether they are valuable or valueless, a few years ago some fourteen of them were brought into this country, and that now those fourteen are nearly ten millions." These statements are false. In the first place, *twenty* of these African cannibals were brought here upwards of two and a half centuries ago, instead of "a few years;" many thousands were added to them from 1619 to 1862, and of the ten millions of negroes he speaks of as now being in the United States, more than half are hybrids.

Mr. William Hannibal Thomas, in his work on "The American Negro," had reason to say of him: "He lies with avidious readiness, and in all moods and degrees of enormity, without undergoing the slightest remorse, and often without any apparent sense of prevarication. He lies to please, to evade, to conceal, to excuse, to command. He lies to be heard, and will not be silent, though he has no truth to utter." And again: "There is a cunning astuteness about the nature of a negro which renders him an adept in de-

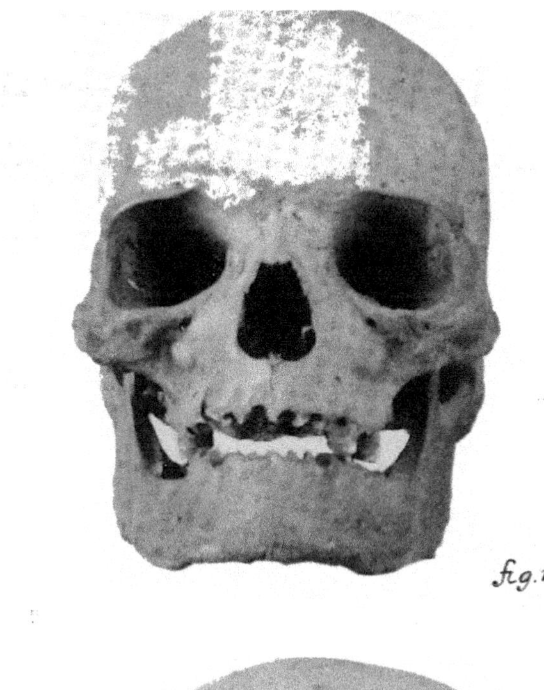

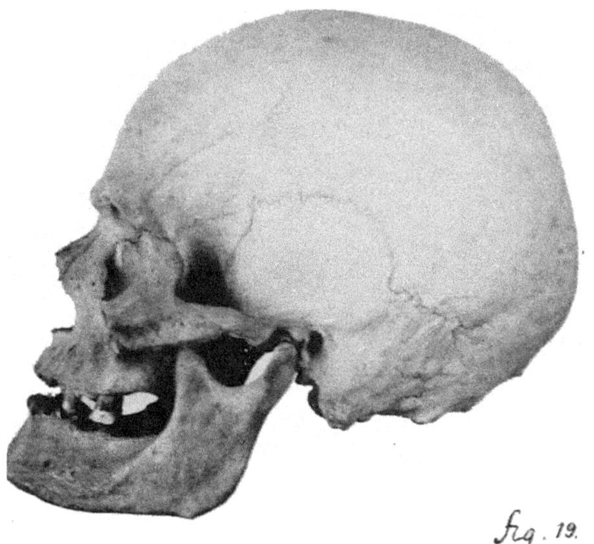

FIGS. 18 AND 19.

Fig. 18, anterior, and Fig. 19, lateral views of the skull of a hybrid. (Negro and Indo-European.) The subject murdered a cashier of a bank in Baltimore many years ago. The author purchased the head for dissection after the execution, when the body was secured by the Medical College. The skull is still in his private collection. It is of especially brutal aspect. (Photo by the author.)

ception, and consequently enables him to hide many of the shams of his life."

It has been contended that the colonists, in first introducing the negroes into this country, were to some extent inspired by *religious* motives, and that the "soul-saving" proposition was at the bottom of it; but in course of time the cloak became woefully threadbare, to be finally converted into a shroud in no way concealing the cadaver that might fitly stand for the emblem of this disgusting traffic. Slavery at first prospered in the colonies, and, seeing this, not a few attempts were made to enslave the indigenous redmen; but it was an utter failure.

At an early date the British entered the field as slave traders, and they succeeded in this undertaking from the very start. Royal Companies were formed, treaties were drawn and ratified, and British slave trade soon became a powerful institution (1713). "In those days," says an authority at hand, "the ship-chandlers of Liverpool made special displays in their windows of such things as hand-cuffs, leg-shackles, iron collars, short and long chains, and furnaces and copper kettles designed for slavers' use. The newspapers were full of advertisements of slaves and slaver goods. The young bloods of the town deemed it fine amusement to circulate hand-bills in which negro girls were offered for sale. An artist of wide repute—Stothard—painted 'The Voyage of the *Sable Venus* from Angola to the West Indies.' No doubt much of the same sort went on in the colonies, for New England soon took the lead in the slave trade, as it was a field full of adventure, cruelty, independence, chance for wealth, and unlimited opportunity to gratify the sexual passions with a new and an enslaved race." The colonial Yankees plunged into it with avidity. Moore, in his "History of Slavery in Massachusetts," says: "At the very birth of foreign commerce from New England the African slave trade became a regular business;" and Hopkins, in his "Reminiscences," stated that in 1770 there were no less than 150 vessels belonging to Rhode Island alone in the African slave trade, and that that State was responsible for enslaving more of them than any other one in all New England. Newport, in fact, was started and built up almost entirely on the African slave trade.

The famous Captain John Paul Jones, of the American Colonial Navy, gained his experience and his early reputation along the same lines. He served in the forecastle of the slaver *King George*. But this vile traffic, this fatal, murderous and beastly trade, bred, not only adventurous sailors, but pirates, buccaneers, and every species of rascal and coward.

An average slave-ship was in those days one of about 500 tons burden; she had a length between 60 and 70 feet, and was built with especial regard for speed. Her storage capacity consisted in a capacious hold, in which rum, trinkets, powder, provisions, and slave truck were stowed away. There was an upper deck, with a *space* between it and the hold, known as "'twixt decks." This space is where the slaves were quartered during the voyage. It was less than *four* feet high, and in some slavers even not so much. In here, in this horrid death-pit, this unventilated hole and rotten dungeon, they packed away the poor negroes by the hundreds. The men were usually forward, shackled together two and two; the women and children were aft, and, though confined, were not chained. All of them were pushed along until they touched each other. In some instances they were *rammed in,* and compelled to lie spoon-fashion during the entire trip of many weeks. In a little while the dead and the living were in there together, linked together in the dark. Sometimes death claimed three-fourths of them; hunger, burning thirst, and unmitigated misery assailed them all the time. They wallowed in their own filth, breathing an air pestilential in the extreme. The women were raped and ravaged by the entire crew.

Hundreds of such craft were afloat at one time, swarming the slave-coast of Africa, taking all manner of chances, and conveying their human cargoes to the West Indies, to Europe, to the American Colonies, and to Brazil. Some fine ships were in the trade, though whalers were pressed into the service; also fast sloops, brigs, and brigantines. It was the money-making scheme of the day. Men would clear thousands of dollars on one trip. Slaves were landed all along the American coast. The *Providencia* put 4500 into Brazil in four voyages. She was a steamer. Plenty of small craft were in it, hardly bigger than small oyster-sloops. Some were notorious for their great speed, and in tight places they could down masts and use sweeps.

So far as the great slave markets of America were concerned, during the entire time the slave trade was considered legal, the chief and almost only source of supply was found, says a writer at hand, "along the Atlantic coast of Africa, between Cape Verde at the north, and Benguela, or Cape St. Martha, at the south. The sea here makes a great scoop into the land, as if the Brazilian part of the South American continent had been broken out of the hollow in the African coast. Two great rivers and a host of smaller streams come down to the sea within its limits, and its contour, as a whole, is that of a mighty gulf; but there is neither bay nor inlet throughout its whole extent that forms a good harbor for shipping. And the off-shore islands, too, are few in number and small in extent. The land at the beach is almost everywhere low, though hills and mountains may be seen, flooded with a dreamy haze, in the distance. The rivers wind about through uncounted channels in low delta lands covered with masses of mangrove and palm trees, and haunted by poisonous and vicious reptiles. The yellowish sand of the sea, and the black sand-washings of the uplands, mingle to form low, tawny beaches and dunes, where the river currents are beaten back by the ever-present and ever-treacherous surf. Goree and Gambia, Sierra Leone and Liberia, the Bight of Benin and the Bight of Biafra, Bonny and Calabar, Anamabae and Ambriz, the Congo and St. Paul de Loango, are all familiar names to the student of slave-coast literature."

This was the field of operations on the African side,—a hot, torrid sea; a practically unindented coast-line, washed by a most dangerous surf; an atmosphere reeking with disease; a dense, miry jungle and forest on landing, the very air of which was like breathing death itself; dangers from ferocious beasts and reptiles, from hostile natives,—in fact, everything that places the life of man under such conditions and cir-

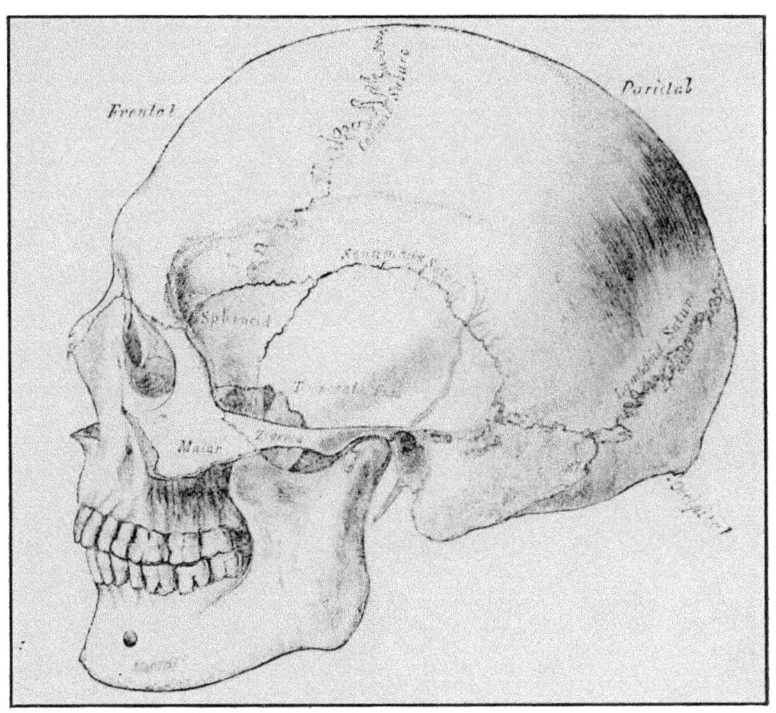

FIG 20.

Left lateral view of the skull of an intelligent white European, showing the relations of the principal bones and cranial sutures. (Photographically copied by the author from Dr. Carter's drawing in Gray's Anatomy.)

cumstances in jeopardy, while inward, beyond it all, lay the land of the vast unknown.

More or less near in this latter lived the various races and tribes of black people that furnished the slaves, the relatives and descendants of which are the close blood-relations of the stock now commonly designated as American negroes. They were, and are still, a savage, superstitious and cannibalistic people. In their religion of fetishism they see their world peopled with evil and malevolent spirits at war with nature and themselves. Lightning, thunder, rain, reptiles, witches, beasts and birds of prey, the cowards and the cunning among their own or other races, were one and all under the control of malignant and antagonistic spirits. Hundreds of negroes in the Southern States of North America still believe in such things, and it is perfectly natural that they should, for it is not so many years ago that they left their human flesh-eating relatives in Africa.

These people are not only superstitious and degraded to the last degree, but ignorant, non-progressive, and without conception of the barest elementals of civilization. Recorded history they have none.

This was the country and these were the people to whom the slave traders flocked, and who furnished them their human freight to carry on their infamous traffic. Rum had much to do with it. Both the slavers and the natives loved it. The whites drank it; employed it as their medium of exchange, the stuff that got the slaves for them, and out of which their great fortunes were made.

Slaves were few and hard to get at first, the slavers having to purchase them from such tribes as had them for sale on the coast. Everyone considered the *trade* perfectly legitimate and honorable. One coast tribe of blacks being more powerful than a neighboring one, it would, upon defeating in battle the weaker one, capture a number of slaves, and these latter were disposed of to the slavers when they came for them. Not a few tribes were thus pitted against each other; as time passed, and the victorious parties found they had a growing market for slaves, they began making their raids for no other purpose.

Slaves were owned principally by the chief men of the tribe where they were to be found; when it was otherwise, they had become enslaved for various offences to individuals. Not a few negroes were made slaves for debt; for seducing wives of their neighbors; for handling a neighbor's fetish, and for other causes. Until they became numerous, these slaves were well treated by their owners,—almost as members of the family. It was only after the white man came upon the coast that they began to increase in number, to be kidnapped and treated with cruelty, and slain by the score when the danger of discovery was imminent, or when they mutinied against their captors or owners.

The negroes of the period often killed and ate their captured enemies and slaves; sometimes they were butchered, burned, disemboweled, and otherwise used as "sacrifices" on gala days, jubilees, fêtes, on the dedication of a juju-house and on similar festivals. If anyone cares to read of the horrors of the customs and ceremonies of these demons in their native land, customs which are still in vogue, I can suggest no better book than "The Ethiopian," by J. Cameron Grant. This is a work that ought to interest anyone and everyone who may be studying the negro problem in this country; who desires to know from what kind of stock our negroes are derived, and the length, breadth, and thickness of the terrible *black stain* with which we have soiled our racial record,—a stain that unfortunately possesses properties for spreading.

In 1645 slaves were becoming more difficult to obtain; the demand for them in the colonies was great and ever-growing; fortunes lay in the trade,—something must be done. So, in the year when the Boston ship *Rainbowe* was on the coast of Africa, she fell in with some London slavers there who had become somewhat tired of waiting for a cargo. To enliven things the Londoners and the Yankees combined, and on some pretence of a row with the blacks on shore, landed a howitzer—in those days called "a murderer"—and one Sunday morning raided a village, killing scores of the inhabitants, and capturing some of them alive. Captain Smith, of the Boston boat, got *two* of these. He was an *American*,—proud of the feat and of his brilliant slaughter of men, women, and children, and also of the fact that he had been the first to teach the world how to obtain slaves in Africa without waiting for them so long on the coast. Upon his return home this captain was tried in Boston; but, of course, the courts had no jurisdiction over any acts he may have committed on the coast of Africa. So the charges against him of sabbath-breaking, kidnapping, and murder were dismissed, and both slaves were sent back to Africa.

This case cleared the African coast for all Americans who cared to go and do likewise. From a peaceful and orderly traffic—disgusting and cruel though it was—the slave trade was soon enlarged by this added feature of slave capture. Shore stations were established soon thereafter,—veritable hells of iniquity; so these shore attacks began to be far more frequent and on an ever-increasing scale. Not only this, but the slavers instigated the coast tribes to make attacks themselves for the profit there was in it; thus wars were enkindled between the tribes of the coast and the tribes of the interior. Notwithstanding all this, and the hundreds of slaves captured, the supply by no means yet met the demand.

Captain Canot describes one of these raids in the following words: "In my wanderings in Africa I have often seen the tiger pounce upon its prey, and with instinctive thirst satiate its appetite for blood and abandon the drained corpse, but these African negresses [who were of the raiding party] were neither as decent nor as merciful as the beast of the wilderness. Their malignant pleasure seemed to consist in the invention of tortures that would agonize but not slay. A slow, lingering, tormenting mutilation was practised on the living, . . . and in every instance the brutality of the women exceeded that of the men. I cannot picture their hellish joy, . . . while the queen of the harpies crept amid the butchery, gathering the brains from each severed skull as a *bonne bouche* for the approaching feast."

Those that were captured alive were sold on the coast, and the stories of these raids undoubtedly interested the American colonists when they were recited to them upon the return home of the slavers. History goes to show that the colonies were, at this time, quite familiar with all of these outrages.

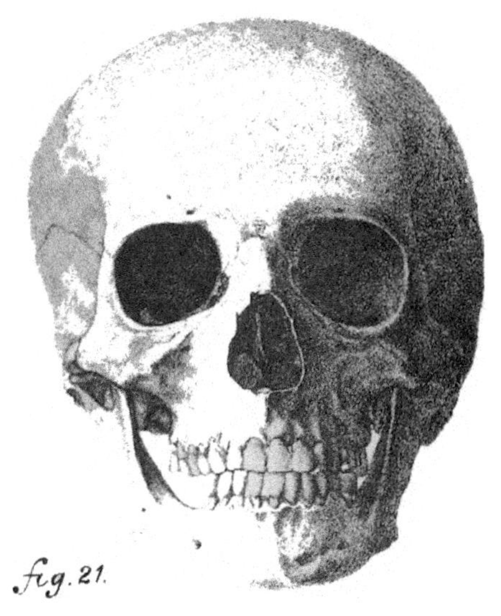

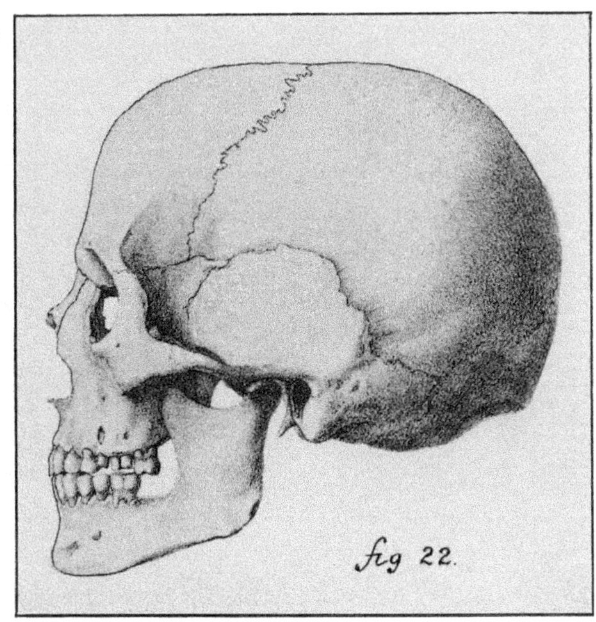

FIGS. 21 AND 22.—ANTERIOR (FIG 21) AND LATERAL (FIG. 22) OF THE SKULL OF AN ANCIENT ROMAN.

The proportions are here particularly good, and the delicacy of the entire structure especially marked (Photo by the author from Quatrefages et Hamy. "Crania Ethnica les Cranes des Races Humaines," Pl. LXXXIV, Figs. I and II.)

English slavers were quite as bad in such matters, as is evidenced by the chapter of treachery and murder done in 1767 on the slave-ships *Indian Queen, Duke of York, Nancy,* and the *Concord,* when they were up one of the rivers on the slave-coast. Scores of negroes were induced to come aboard these four vessels for a pow-wow. After they were made nearly crazy with rum, the crews armed themselves simultaneously for slaughter and capture. The scenes that followed almost defy description, and I am rather glad that my space will not admit of my telling the story.

Both Portuguese and English women engaged in the fascinating slave trade upon their own account, some of them even going to the coast of Africa. Here they lived in the stations on shore or up the rivers,—in those barbaric palaces of wealth, culture, ribaldry, sensuality, and blood-money. The home of Dom Pedro was an example of these, and his sister lived with him. He left the coast in 1839 with a cool million of money. Captain Philip Drake, in his "Revelations of a Slave Smuggler," describes another of these voluptuous fiends (January 5, 1840); the following are his words: "Da Souza, or Cha-Chu, as everybody calls him, is apparently a reckless voluptuary, but the shrewdest slave-trader on the African coast. Whydah was built by his enterprise, and he lived the life of a prince. His mansion here is like a palace, and he has a harem filled with women from all parts of the world. He keeps up a continual round of dissipation, gambling, feasting, and indulging in every sensual pleasure with his women and visitors. . . . His house is the very abode of luxury. He must squander thousands. But what is money to a man who has a slave-mine in Dahomey, bringing hoards of wealth yearly by a hundred vessels! Da Souza enjoys almost a monopoly of the coast trade. Blanco has been his only rival of late years. . . . This morning Cha-Chu met me and proposed to supply me with a wife. 'You shall have French, Spanish, Greek, Circassian, English, Dutch, Italian, Asiatic, African, or American,' he said, laughing."

In 1850 there were 244,985 slaves in the State of Louisiana alone. Virginia was a breeding-place for them. Hundreds of them died because of the severity of slave-life; hundreds upon hundreds of them still continued to die on board the vessels that transported them to our shores; and untold numbers of others were murdered, or destroyed as incidental to attempts at capture.

The raids in Africa were carried a score of leagues inland, and untold and unspeakable atrocities were perpetrated upon the natives. No end of cruelty, no end of bloodshed, no end of diabolical torture was the order of the day. Although growing side by side with America's maiden efforts in a humane civilization, and the introduction of all manner of merciful methods, the treatment of the African slave has nevertheless been, from start to finish, a long drawn-out picture of hellish brutality, unbridled sensuality, and demoniacal practices. No other kind of cattle have ever been thus dealt with in the world's history. It is a panorama of beastly infamy.

Sometimes the cargo of negroes aboard the slaver mutinied; a case occurred in 1844 aboard the American slaver *Kentucky,* which left the coast with 530 slaves aboard. They were in the hold and packed together as usual, chained two and two. The mutiny was quickly suppressed; but the captain decided to make an example of the ring-leaders, so he shot and hanged 46 of the men and 1 negress. The deponent, one of the crew, further says that "after this was over they brought up and flogged about 20 men and 6 women."

The profits of the slave trade were simply enormous, *single trips* clearing as much as from $20,000

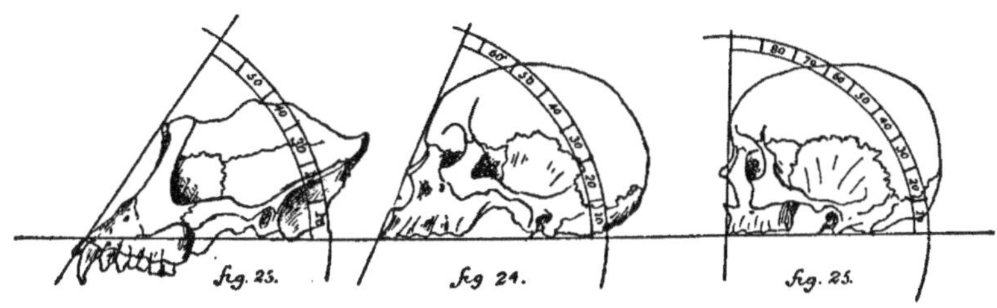

FIGS. 23, 24 AND 25.

The *facial angle* in the gorilla (Fig. 23), in the negro Fig. 24), and in the intellectual representative of the white race (Fig. 25). It will be seen that in the skull of the gorilla this angle is less than 60 degrees; in the negro less than 70 degrees, while in the skull of the white man it almost reaches 90 degrees. (Drawn by the author, from typical specimens.)

to over $40,000. These are *net* profits. In one case the net profit made in six months by a small vessel amounted to $41,438.54.

In 1835 a Baltimore clipper, the *Napoleon,* made on one cargo a net profit of over one hundred thousand dollars; but such facts have little to do with the present work. They simply show the incentive that kept up the filthy enterprise, making men blind to the trouble they were heaping up in this country for following generations to get out of as best they could.

That many of the colonists long foresaw the evils that would some day come from the interbreeding of the blacks and whites in the United States, there can be no manner of doubt. Even as early as 1705 Massachusetts imposed a tax of four pounds on each slave that came within her jurisdiction, and this was distinctly "for the Better Preventing of a spurious or mixt Issue."

Those that sought such sable Venuses were so numerous that the *café-au-lait* progeny, which began to appear in the population, excited the alarm of the legislators of the State. It is a wonder that some of the Southern States did not likewise see this pending danger, especially at a later date, when it must have been still more evident; for be it known, South Carolina, for example, had in 1734 no fewer than 22,000 slaves against a short 8000 white within her limits. Possibly altogether as many as hundreds of thousands of negro slaves were, during the history of the slave trade, brought to the United States from Africa. There may be 4,000,000 of unmixed African negroes in this country at the present writing (1914), but the remainder of the 10,000,000 that writers on the subjcct talk about are half-castes,—hybrids produced by incessant crossing with the whites.

From the time the slaves were first brought into the country, up to and to include the time when they were set free as a result of the Civil War, they were the cause of the framing and enforcing of no end of laws; of starting all sorts of legislation; of the formation of parties for and against the trade; of exciting the Church to action; of strife of many kinds and outbreaks of passion and speech. It is not the intention of the present work to pass into the history of this part of the subject. It is the darkest and dirtiest page in American history, and I must leave it to those who care to follow it along other lines. Indeed, enough would have been said in this chapter had I merely stated the fact that the North American slave trade practically began when the Dutch brought twenty of them to Virginia in 1619, and that upwards of four hundred thousand more of these benighted, ignorant, semi-simian, superstitious and treacherous cannibals were, up to 1862, landed upon our shores. The entire traffic was horrid in the extreme, and the injury it has done and is still powerfully doing those of Anglo-Saxon descent in these United States of America is immeasurable.

CHAPTER V.

Biological Principles of Interbreeding.

Man's place in nature and the ethnological status of the negro have been completely demonstrated and settled for all time, as have the facts that between the years 1619 and 1862 many hundreds of thousands of negroes were imported into this country from the west coast of Africa; that some of these are probably still living at the present writing, and that three or four millions of their actual descendants, together with several millions more of half-castes—produced chiefly by interbreeding with the white race in the United States—now demand consideration. These negroes inhabit principally what is known as the "black belt," an area extending through the Southern States westward, in which latter direction their numbers gradually decrease. Their ancestors, the negro races of the West Soudan, are cannibals,—ignorant, superstitious, cruel, unreliable, and non-progressive in every way; savages of the lowest type, without a recorded history, and almost totally lacking in anything we refer to modern civilization; yet it was from this stock that the negroes of the United States were derived within a comparatively brief space of time,—so brief that it is highly probable that many of the near relatives of the negroes here in the United States are still living as cannibals in their own country in Africa. For example, male negroes, brought to this country in 1860, when they were twenty-five years old, might easily have left living children behind them in

Africa. This would make the fathers here some seventy-odd years old, while their children in Africa would be in the prime of life or less than fifty years of age. So far as I am aware, no single negro in this country has ever made any attempt to hunt up his or her relatives left behind in Africa. No such neglect could ever have happened in the case of a white race. Even had it been ever possible to enslave the latter, they would certainly have made a unanimous attempt to regain their relatives upon being restored to liberty, and in all probability they would have returned to their own country. That the negroes in the United States have never made any attempt of this nature is one of the best proofs of the extremely low position they occupy, in any sort of classification, in the genus *Homo.*

However this may be, it next devolves upon us to examine the biological laws of interbreeding in man and in other animals; it is evident that this is the next question that presents itself for our consideration.

Within the last half-century or more so much light has been thrown upon all things relating to the origin of living forms upon this planet, their reproduction and multiplication, their development, growth, decadence and extinction; variation, the production of races, subspecies and species, natural selection, the survival of the fittest, and, indeed, upon a score or more other questions of the kind, that, with the abundant literature in the field upon such subjects, it would be superfluous to enter, in an argumentative way, upon the discussion of such matters. Much of it has now far outgrown the stage of hypothesis and has been relegated to the realm of the law. The

Asiatic myth of special and miraculous creation has long ago passed into the scientific waste-basket, and the story of the original pair now figures, in the minds of all informed people, simply as a dogmatic pun. There is much that is transcendentally beautiful in nature, and we see it throughout the animal and vegetable kingdoms as well as in the inorganic world; yet, notwithstanding all this, and the surpassing beauty of the garden in which we live and die, there is much in nature, indeed nearly all, which is ordered upon the scheme of the most implacable cruelty. "I have, also, often personified the word nature," says Darwin, "for I have found it difficult to avoid this ambiguity; but I mean by nature only the aggregate action and product of many natural laws,—and by laws only the ascertained sequence of events."[1]

Some of the laws to which Darwin refers are now as thoroughly appreciated as are the facts in physics and astronomy. We no longer believe that the earth is flat, and the sky a perforated crystal to allow the rain to come through; we know much better, and we know, too, that we have no power to alter any of the natural laws or the absolute conditions existing in life. We often hear it said that it is foolish for man to "tamper with nature" and thus cause variability in forms or change in conditions that may militate against his interest or do harm in other ways. To this extent alone can man tamper or interfere with nature; but this by no means implies that he can cause variability in animal or plant forms, or check or prevent it in its operation in nature. The struggle for

[1] Darwin, C.: "Animals and Plants under Domestication," vol. i, p. 17.

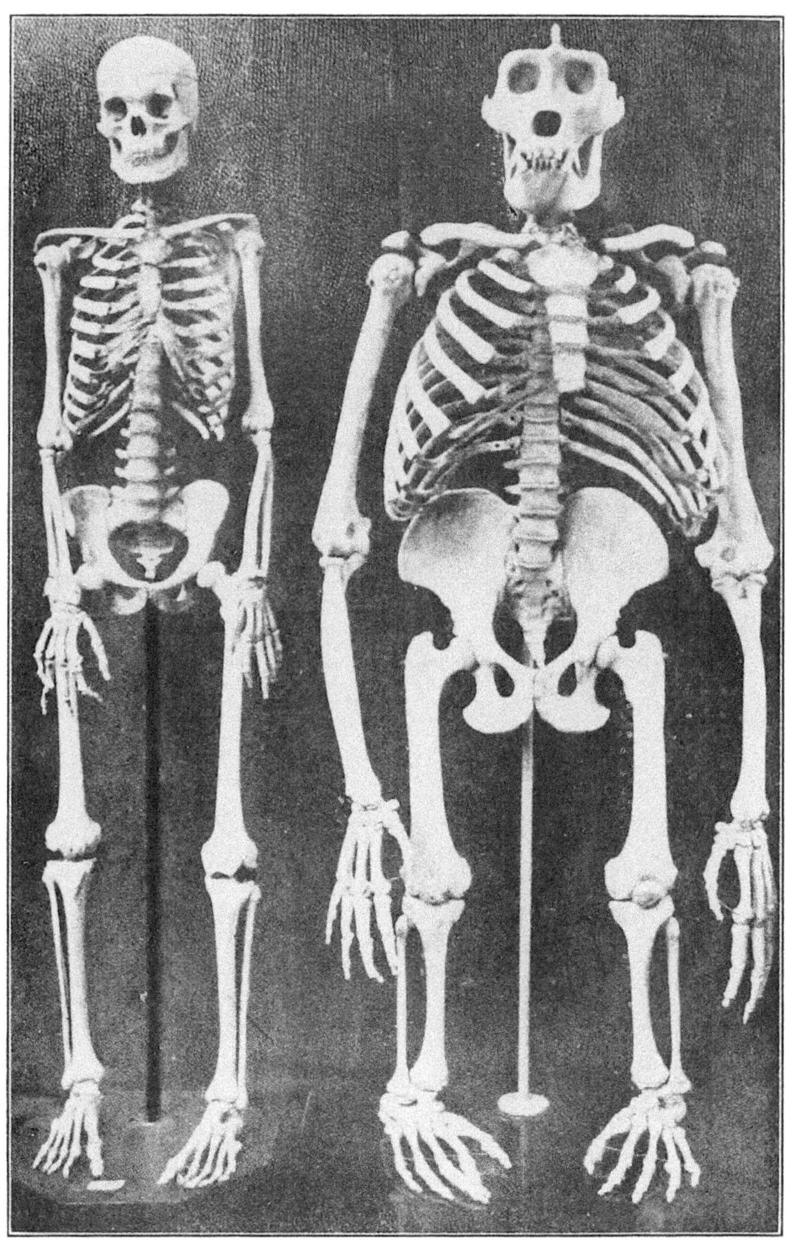

FIG. 26.—SKELETONS OF MAN AND GORILLA

From "The Living Animals of the World" Courtesy of Hutchinson and Company (London) "This photograph shows the remarkable similarity in the structure of the human frame (left) and that of a gorilla (right). This gorilla happened to be a particularly large specimen, the man was of ordinary height." It will also be observed that in the man the hands reach down only to the upper thirds of the femora or thigh-bones, while in the gorilla they come opposite the knee-joints. In negroes the hands frequently reach down to the middle thirds of the thighs or to points between those just

existence commenced with the first spark of life on earth, and it has never ceased, nor will it cease in its operation until every evidence of life in the world is extinct. So, too, with all the natural laws: heredity, variability, natural selection, and others. They all came into force as life and form first appeared in the world, and they will never cease to act so long as living forms of any kind, either animal or vegetable, are in existence through which they may be exemplified. All that man can accomplish is to artificially produce variability in form by a change of environment and by crossing. But in doing this he cannot alter in the slightest degree any of the primal conditions, as climate, or any of the laws controlling variability. Man may expose living forms of animals and plants to these existing conditions and laws, but beyond that his power ceases. Within certain limits, he may cause various forms of animals and plants to cross, and reproduce other forms that differ, in certain particulars, from the parent ones, and so on through successive generations. But his limitations here are equally exacting; for, in the first place, all animal forms are either not fertile *inter se,* or interbreeding is impossible, as would be the case in a giraffe and a bat. Even when possible, the two species cannot be induced to breed, as would in all probability be the case with a wolf and a peccary.

Let us consider a few other examples to make my meaning still clearer. In the group of domestic pigeons we may select and cross certain varieties, with the view of producing particular changes either in plumage or form or both, and this selection and crossing may be persisted in until we have accomplished our object and produced the kind of birds we desired to manufacture. But we should have been absolutely powerless in our efforts here had it not been for the ceaseless operation of the natural laws of variability and heredity to insure the gradual changes. We are told of a variety of domestic pigeon which had been produced by artificial selection, extending through a number of generations, with the view, among other characters, of having the birds have as short bills as possible. The breeder was so successful that he obtained pigeons with bills so short that they could not feed themselves, and the old ones actually had to be fed by hand, otherwise they would soon have starved. Again, we have in this country certain aquatic batrachians called amblystomas; they are related to the tritons, salamanders, and newts; some people call them water-lizards, as they possess the general shape of a lizard, and, at least in the case of the amblystomas, they spend a certain part of their existence in the water. In New Mexico they have the *Amblystoma tigrinum,* and when they are found in shallow water or pools with light-colored, clayey bottoms, the amblystomas themselves are of pale tints; this may also, to some extent, be due to their food. When I was living in New Mexico, a number of years ago, I captured a great many of these amblystomas, several hundred for the Smithsonian Institution, and others for a German lady who was experimenting with them in Berlin. I also experimented with them, as the amblystomas possess what may be termed very plastic organizations. I found that, by keeping them in perfectly clear water in deep glass jars, and feeding them heartily for months on raw beef and nothing else, they changed very markedly in appearance; besides, they became of a deep *black* color, and in the course of time they came to look totally unlike their kin in nature. This was a case where surroundings and food produced the variation; but the variation was due to laws over which I had no control, and which, in fact, I could not fully explain; yet I soon came to know that, if I took from its natural environment a pale-brown amblystoma which was more or less slender and agile, and desired to produce a stouter and more sluggish one of nearly or quite dull black color, all I had to do was to expose him to the above conditions, feeding him as just described, and I was certain to get the result. But the result responding to the treatment was always the same, and the variety produced was uniform; that is, under the same conditions and treatment the amblystomas never became more slender in form, or yellow or pink in color. The same thing can be accomplished with flowers and plants of all kinds. In these instances we do quickly what nature takes a long time to do, and breeders all over the world have been doing this sort of thing for many, many generations. A great variety of flowers have been thus treated, with the view of producing odd and extravagant forms with brilliant and attractive colors. Fruits have been crossed, grafted, and bred to improve their size and flavor and other desirable qualities. In the domestic animals all sorts of crossings and selections have been resorted to in order to accomplish a great variety of ends. Horses have been thus dealt with to improve their speed and form; cows, in order to breed for milk; sheep, for their mutton and wool; dogs, for hunting, running, and guarding; pigs, for pork, and so on with many other animals. Darwin says: "Man, therefore, may be said to have been trying an experiment on a gigantic scale; and it is an experiment which nature during the long lapse of time has incessantly tried. Hence it follows that the principles of domestication are important for us. The main result is that organic beings thus treated have varied largely, and the variations have been inherited. This has apparently been one chief cause of the belief long held by some few naturalists that species in a state of nature undergo change." It is quite a number of years ago since Darwin penned these words, and they are as true today as they were when they were written. All intelligent naturalists of the present time not only believe that species in a state of nature undergo change, but they know it to be a fact. I desire the reader to ponder well upon the real significance of these facts, for a little farther along, when I come to consider the question of their application in the case of man and the higher mammals, I shall return to them.

When different breeds of animals are crossed, the laws of inheritance are ever in operation, and the results are seen in the morphology as well as in the traits, characters, and idiosyncrasies in the descendants of the succeeding generations. If too close interbreeding is practised, sterility is often the result, and this condition also follows sometimes when the breeding animals have been removed from their normal habitats and food, and placed in widely different environments and climate. Having a sufficient number of animals to *select* from, and a knowledge of variability, so far as we now comprehend it, with an understanding of the laws of inheritance, man can, if he chooses, produce great results. Nearly everything in such experiments, however, depends upon careful and scientific selection. Acting in this manner we can, with greater or less certainty, produce, within limits, the forms we desire. If you want black cats with winning and docile natures, you surely would not breed from white cats with cross and ill-tempered natures; and if you wanted black cats with an area of white on the chest, you would certainly select parents so marked—a dozen or more individuals—and by careful selection and a not too close interbreeding, the desired marking will be produced in an ever-increasing proportion of cases. The same thing would happen in nature were such cats left to themselves to breed, and the white area proved to be a strong sexual and attractive character; but in such cases it would take ever so much longer, the balance of the environment being the same, and food and climate favorable. After studying thousands of such cases, Darwin was again led to say that "Man may select and preserve each successive variation, with the distinct intention of improving and altering a breed, in accordance with a preconceived idea; and by thus adding up variations, often so slight as to be imperceptible to an uneducated eye, he has effected wonderful changes and improvements. It can also be clearly shown that man, without any intention or thought of improving the breed, by preserving in each successive generation the individuals which he prizes most, and by destroying the worthless individuals, slowly, though surely, induces great changes. As the will of man thus comes into play, we can understand how it is that domesticated breeds show adaptation to his wants and pleasures. We can further understand how it is that domestic races of animals and cultivated races of plants often exhibit an abnormal character, as compared with natural species; for they have been modified, not for their own benefit, but for that of man."

Having now reviewed some of the better known principles or laws of interbreeding in animals in general, we are in a position to apply these to the case of man. In the first place, it is well to note that every known biological or natural law, having anything to do with organic evolution in its very widest sense, is just as applicable to man as it is to any other animal. This not only applies to normal growth, change, and development, but to similar abnormal conditions and to disease. It has been—and is now—the overlooking of this fact which has been the cause of much misery, crime, disease, and the production of highly undesirable individuals in the human race the world over. Men and women can be varied with just as much certainty as are pigeons, chickens, dogs, or horses, by scientific and judicious selection and crossing. Given the proper material in the way of men and women, the absolute control of it, the time and the conditions, and the other necessary means to carry out the ends in view, and the result will be any desired kind of man or any kind of a woman, within the laws of variability, heredity, and development. No single person could do this, for the reason that the time might be a thousand or even several thousand years; but nature cares nothing for time. The same is true of artificial selection or race-breeding with the view of attaining a certain result. There may be simply hundreds upon hundreds of different kinds of the latter. We may breed men and women for giants or for dwarfs; for any color of hair, eyes or skin; for long noses and flat feet; for immense gluteal proportions, as the steatopygous Hottentot women; for flat heads; for a tail or the development of the caudal appendage beyond the general superfices of the body; for immense strength; for a complete covering of hair; for polydactylism; for curiously shaped ears, and for the elimination of the teeth. In other words, make pointed-cared, edentate, wonderfully hairy, short-tailed, long-nosed, bimanous vertebrates of them, presenting many other curious characters.

Mankind may be dealt with to produce diseased individuals, and this may be carried so far—in the case of some diseases—that the virulence of the latter will wipe out the stock, thus bringing the experiments to a close. All it requires is scientific stirpiculture, close attention, and ample time. If we except the Spartans and the experiments at Moscow a few years ago, no attempt—so far as I am aware—has ever been made to improve, either mentally or physically, a sex or a race in the manner indicated. In the lower races, nature is having some play in the matter, with results by no means always for the best. In the white races it is even worse, and little or no heed is paid to careful mating with the view of race improvement, or even with regard to elimination of diseases and deformities. Here the process is exceedingly slow, and in the vast majority of instances Dame Nature blushes to look her growing progeny in the face. Brainless numskulls cross with opium victims; misshapen dwarfs marry measly maids; in fact, it is all a purely haphazard performance, and done without any regard to giving fine physique, well-trained intellectual powers, and evenly balanced, well-tempered characters any chance at all in the world.

Upon the whole, the ancient Greeks were made of better stuff than the modern Americans, and the latter have been the most disregardful of proper race-breeding. In fact, since the Civil War we have actually imported all sorts of stuff from all parts of the planet, and taken blood of all shades into our veins by converting the United States into a kind of procreation-pen, in which experimentation is going on, apparently with the view of observing how many different kinds of crazy creatures we can turn out! The criminal records in the courts of our large cities show the results; the grave-yards point to others; the hospitals, penitentiaries, insane-asylums, and no end of "charitable" institutions point to scores of still others. Nevertheless, it is not all bad; improvements in sanitation; the rapidly growing interest taken in individual improvement in physique, in health culture, in the spreading of knowledge, and many similar features, are all combining to do something. But all combined are as nothing when compared with what might be accomplished in such directions in a few generations, were the methods more systematic and scientific.

I have now another subject, more or less akin to the one we have just had under consideration, to bring forward; it is this: if, through any cause or causes, large numbers of one race are introduced into a region already occupied by large numbers of a totally different race, and the environment, climatic conditions, and food are favorable to the support and increase of

FIG. 27.—TYPE OF YOUNG MALE NEGRO BOY. (New York City.)

Photographed by the author. The subject has tuberculosis of the lungs, so common to the race in America.

both peoples, such races are certain to fraternize, to react upon each other in various ways, and finally to interbreed. It matters not a whit whether one of these races is highly developed in every way, and the other is savage, superstitious and ignorant,—they will inevitably cross and produce hybrids. In most instances it will be the *males* of the dominant race who will couple with the females of the lower race, while it will prove a marked exception that the reverse of this will be the case. The males of the lower race may occasionally entrap a female of the higher race, or they may succeed, in rare instances, by violence, but all such cases will not amount even to a few in several thousands; whereas the males of the advanced race will easily succeed with the females of the lower or savage stock. The reason for this is not far to seek. The females of the higher types are more refined, more sensitive, and far less passionate. The mere suggestions of a barbarian would be repugnant. No such sentiments control the males of the dominant or advanced and cultured race with respect to seeking the females of the savage people. The pressure or demand to satisfy the sexual appetite in the male—even if he be an individual endowed with refinement—often completely blinds him, rendering him practically irresponsible in many cases, and, the desire for variety coming into play, carries him over almost anything. Black, brown, red, or yellow skin makes no difference whatever, and there will be plenty of representatives in the one race to cross with an equal number of representatives in the other. There will be large numbers of exceptions to this, of course; the females of the advanced race will not interbreed with the males of the lower race, and in the case of the males of the former many will be found who will likewise shun such intercourse, controlled either by sentiment, disgust, self-respect, or by other reasons. Still, the interbreeding will go on with marked increase during certain periods, and falling off at other times. These fluctuations will be due to various causes, but it will nevertheless always be progressing in some degree or other and a hybrid race be continually produced. War, social and political privileges and restrictions, the gradual degeneration of the *morale* of the higher stock, and the increasing push and effrontery of the lower, will, with several other reasons, exert an influence; but, one way or another, nothing will entirely check it. It very soon becomes impossible to separate the two races. A system of fines, however large the amount in any case, would have but a slight deterrent effect. The whipping-post might be more efficient; but I do not believe that even the death sentence as a penalty would be wholly effectual in preventing it. In fact, sometimes the very danger to be met lends a zest to the attempts to gratify the demands of the sexual appetite, and men will seek it and attain it even with their lives in their hands. It is the nature of the animal, and it obtains throughout nature. A thorough comprehension of the entire subject in its widest sense might lead to some effectual remedy; but a *far separation* is, as a matter of fact, the only preventive of interbreeding, when two races come to occupy the same area of country under the conditions I have pointed out above.

From what has been said in the foregoing paragraphs of the present chapter, it is clear that we have, in the case of the negroes in this country, a typical example, on a very large scale, of the introduction of a large number of representatives of one race into an area occupied by a large population representing another and primarily distinct race. History furnishes nowhere a better example of the kind than this; and in so far as the two races are concerned, they were initially as distinct as they could possibly be. One race—the imported one—was as black as black could be; they were as low, sensual, and superstitious a race of cannibals as the world has ever known. On the other hand, the advanced race—the preoccupiers of the soil upon which these two races subsequently fraternized—represented, at least in part, some of the best stock that had developed in the Old World. They were in reality the seeds of a great nation, a nation destined to take its place later on as one of the most powerful, most advanced, and most highly civilized on the face of the globe. Hundreds, nay thousands, of the former, the blacks from the West Soudan of Africa, were interspersed among these in the manner already described in a former chapter. The crossing of the two races commenced at the very outstart of the vile slavery trade that fetched them hither; indeed, in those days many a negress was landed upon our shores already pregnant by some one of the demoniac company that made up the crew of the slaver that brought her over. It is quite likely, too, that many of these negresses were pregnant by blacks in Africa at the time of their capture; some of them died in this state aboard the slavers, and others gave birth to children on the passage across the Atlantic. Some were carrying unborn children upon being disposed of at the end of the journey, and I dare say were considered to be the more valuable on that account. However this may be, there is no question that, from the earliest time the negro slaves came into the United States—during all their years of slavery, and during all their subsequent years of freedom, up to the present writing—the negresses of that race have borne myriads of children to representatives of the white race in this country.

By far the vast majority of these births have occurred in the "black belt" of the Southern States; although in slave days, and even now, in such cities as Washington, Baltimore, Philadelphia, and a score of others to the northward, the males of the white race have not been behindhand in increasing the vital statistics along these lines. Many of the mulattoes thus produced had good, white blood in their veins. In many instances the negro mothers adopted the name of the family that owned or employed them, or that of the male members by whom they had borne children. Cases are even on record where negresses, in bearing twins, would have one white and one black child; for an instance of the kind and its explanation, see Flint's Textbook of Human Physiology, p. 895.

As the years rolled by the effects of all this became painfully visible. Nature never has and never will concern herself about man's interests, however vital man himself may consider these interests to be, and she did not in this matter of race interbreeding; consequently, every child that was born was born with every cell in its body occupying its position according to the immutable laws of heredity and variation. Hence the features and entire organization of each and all of those children responded to the aforesaid laws, just as they do in the case of any other animal, and each came to be the very kind of being, in all particulars, that the operation of those laws would produce, no other organization, in any particular instance, being possible. The same may be said for the innate mental and moral potentiality of any particular child. Of course, during the development and growth of any being, from the moment of birth to the close of its career, it may, to some extent and from a variety of causes, be subject to being molded and changed,—mentally, morally, and physically. In other words, when a child is born to a pure negro mother by a white man, that child is, according to certain fixed laws, prenatally stamped with certain morphological, mental, and moral characters, no particle of which could possibly have been different under the particular parental combination, however that child may come to be molded afterward, either for good or for bad. The knowledge we have of inherited prenatal impressions of all kinds is extremely meager and amazingly hazy in its character. No one can as yet tell why a child resembles one parent more than the other, or, perhaps, a grandparent more than either; nor how it *grows* to be more or less like some member of the family or perhaps one of its ancestors. Yet all such things are evidently controlled by laws, causes, and effects, and by circumstances and conditions, the origin of which we hardly know anything about, though we have many reasons to believe that the produced organism, in the form of the particular child, could not have been, even to the last atom in its composition, other than it was, or turned out to be, from the various forces in operation to produce it. In the life and career of any adult, at any particular instant, there is always a reason why he or she has such and such features, such and such an organization, such and such traits of mind and character, and so on to the ultimate composition of the entire being. There is no element of chance in all this; we are all resultants, at any instant of our lives, of certain laws, causes, and effects, and we could not be otherwise than we are if we tried ever so hard. In the next chapter I shall touch more fully on this question, as it bears upon hybridization, and point out a little more clearly why it is that, in so many white people in our Southern States, one can so frequently recognize a faint, subtle strain of the negro in their faces and forms.

In a number of places in the present chapter I have referred to the remarkable character of the sexual side of the negro's organization. This is a subject of which the laity knows absolutely nothing or little about, and but very few physicians have paid the slightest attention to it, much less given it any serious thought or study. Lawyers and judges, as is only too often the case, ignore it entirely in those trials wherein the accused is a negro man, charged with rape or assault. This is unfair to the negro, and unpardonable ignorance on the part of those who sit in judgment on him.

And finally—as for the mob that makes up a gang of lynchers to hang and torture the negro who has assaulted and perhaps raped a white woman—they, to a man, know no more of the uncontrollable sex frenzy in a male member of that race than the average negro knows of vertebrate palæontology.

Doubtless many of the readers of this volume will question what I have said on this subject, and what I will pass upon again in other places in this book; so I thought it best to have some one of my profession—an authority of the very highest order on the entire subject of the psychology of the negro, and especially his sex psychology—stand as sponsor for my statements with respect to this side of his organization. With this in view, I requested my friend, Doctor William Lee Howard, to prepare me a contribution on this point, as I knew of no writer on the psychology of sex and matters sexual generally, as applied to man, better than he in the United States. Doctor Howard has not only had abundant opportunity to observe and make record of the sensuality of the negro, but he has never neglected the advantage he has thus enjoyed, while his several books and many articles on the subject have rendered him an international authority in that particular field. He is an extremely candid writer, and does not hesitate to refer, in unmistakable terms, to any organ or organs and their several functions, if he finds it necessary to do so, and the complete presentation of his picture and argument calls for it. In doing this, he but plays the part of the true and fearless physician who knows full well that, in order to make clear what he desires to impart to his readers, the Prince of Denmark must appear in the scene.

It is worse than useless to undertake to teach the laity anything of this subject, now so vital to our own race, if we are to omit the very factors that demand the fullest consideration. That Doctor Howard has ever been guilty of this, no one will charge him with who has read his lucid and important articles in *The Ladies' Home Journal* and elsewhere, and his various books on sex. When a dentist discusses any subject pertaining to his profession, it is no more than natural that he mentions the teeth; or when a physician undertakes to make clear to an audience the nature of indigestion, we expect him to mention the stomach in his discourse; then, why should one be surprised when an authority on the nature and pathology of sex mentions the anatomical organs and the functions responsible for the manifestations of sexuality and sensuality? The time for prudery in such matters has passed.

I find I am not altogether in harmony with Doctor Howard in regard to the treatment of the negro, or what to do with him in this country. We cannot cure an ulcer by tickling it with a straw—we must be more radical in our treatment. What he advises with respect to the "loafing negro," may answer for those so addicted,—that is, temporarily; but as a remedy for the problem as a whole, it would be worse than temporizing with the most serious question that this nation now has before it for consideration. This is a matter that I fully treat of in the last chapter of the present volume. What follows below is Doctor Howard's contribution in its entirety:—

"THE BASIC CAUSES FOR THE NEGRO'S SENSUALITY.

"BY WILLIAM LEE *H*OWARD, M.D.

"What has impressed me most as being a stumbling block to a solution of the negro problem in the United States, is the general ignorance of anthro-

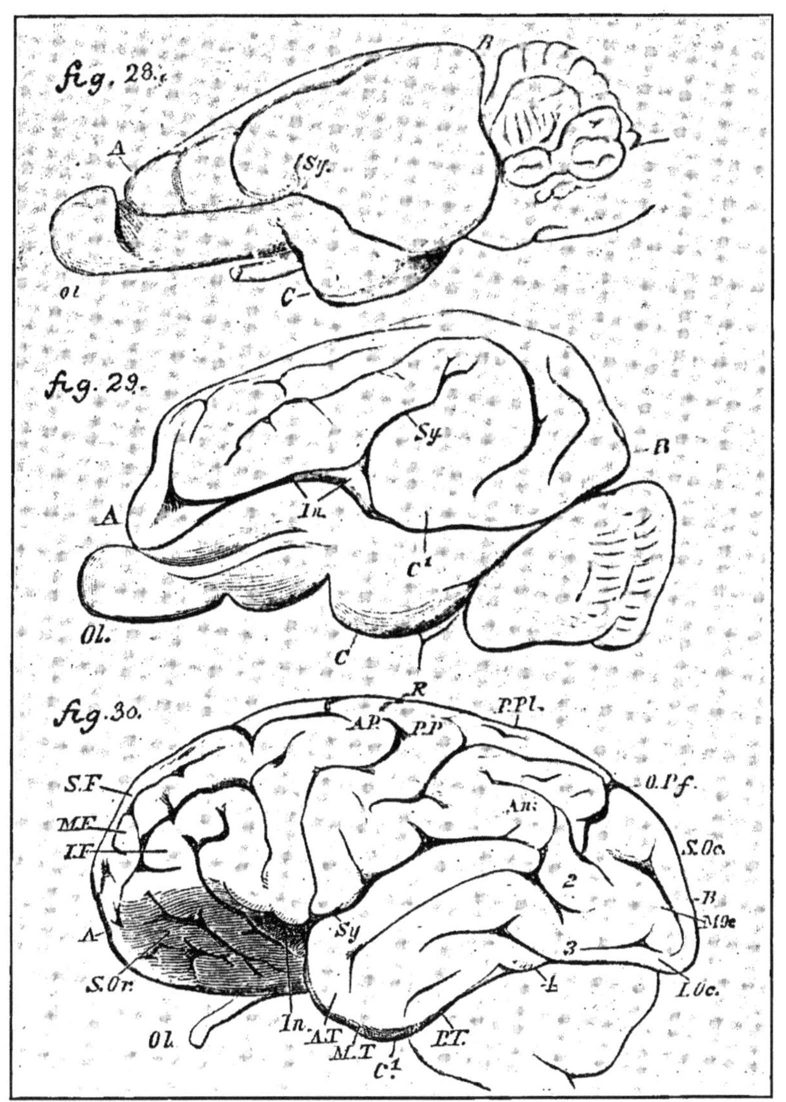

FIGS 28, 29 AND 30.—LATERAL VIEWS OF THE BRAINS OF A RABBIT (FIG. 28), A PIG (FIG 29), AND A CHIMPANZEE (FIG. 30).

(Drawn of nearly the same absolute size) The rabbit's brain is at the top; the pig's in the middle, and the chimpanzee lowest. *O L*, the olfactory lobe, *A*, the frontal lobe, *B*, the occipital lobe; *C*, the temporal lobe; *Sy*, the Sylvian fissure, *In*, the insula; *S or*, supraorbital; *S F*, *M F.*, *I F*, superior, middle, and inferior frontal gyri, *A P.*, antero-parietal, *P P*, postero-parietal gyri, *R*, sulcus of Rolando, *P Pl*, postero-parietal lobule, *O Pt.*, external perpendicular or occipito-temporal sulcus, *An*, angular gyrus; 2, 3, 4, annectent gyri, *A T.*, *M T.*, *P T*, the three temporal, and *S.Oc.*, *M Oc.*, *I Oc.*, the three occipital gyri (By the author, after Huxley.)

pologic facts, ethnic sexual traits, with an unwillingness to study or learn of the fundamental causes for the ineffaceable differentiation between the African and the Caucasian.

"This studied refusal, this denial of the necessity for knowing the real reason for the African's unfitness for any social relations with the white man, is found among the masses and that very large class of supposedly educated men and women of the North, East, and West of our country. Yet it is not strange that this ignorance of the negro's ethnic traits should prevail, because these people have never, through travel or observation, been brought face to face with the negro and his innate habits and instincts.

"More, these people and philanthropists, these well-meaning teachers with their ancestral training in prudery, this mass of the superficially informed, have only lately been forced to listen to plain facts of the sex structure of their own race.

"The havoc venereal diseases are making with our race, the great rôle uncontrolled sexuality plays in our increase of insanity, idiocy, crime, and pauperism, has been a revelation to the general public. But this important fact must be kept ever in mind: that sensuality with us is recognized as antisocial, immoral, a menace to civilization, and the effects of total disregard of instruction and watchfulness, while giving license to the young to do about as pleases their undeveloped impulses.

"Also, the increase of immorality among the white people is mostly seen in those we recognize as unfit, mentally unstable, and not of the pure racial stock. Furthermore, with this recognition is an effort, through laws and social organizations, to control and remedy the conditions. We, as a race, do not accept sexual immorality as a right social condition; the negro, on the other hand, can see no immorality or social wrong in practising sexual rites with their religious and social affairs.

"The fundamental difference between our sexual instincts and those of the African may not be so great; but, while with the negro sensuality is the Alpha and Omega of his whole life, from childhood to old age in both sexes, with us it is controllable, and lechery meets with its proper condemnation.

"It is not controllable in the negro, nor is lechery a state he condemns. In the negro, sensuality is a natural, innate condition, having a biologic origin and physiologic impulse, ineffaceable through education, moral teachings, or environment.

"It was necessary that first the public be awakened to sexual facts and psychology before we could expect it to understand the problem of the negro as it confronts us today. It was the only way for people to understand why the negro must remain a negro, never permitted to reach the height of his ambition—sexual relations with the white girl; prevented from longer believing that his ultimate destiny was social equality among the Caucasians of the United States, and that biologically his sexual traits, instinct, and passions can never be changed by man's methods.

"Five years ago it would have been impossible to have gotten the truth about the African into the mind of the average man or woman living in the United States. Preachers were ignorant of sex psychology, lawyers were indifferent and lacked scientific knowledge, the business man did not dare mention to his family the few facts he knew, and the school-teachers ——Well?

"The African is biologically unfit—get the point? —to associate with a race whose basic sex instincts are as different as the color of its skin. Now I hear from all sides: 'Oh, but the color of the skin does not make any difference: a man with a black skin is just as good as a man with a white skin!'

"True, if black skin and white skin had the same biologic origin; and if the man with the black skin had been reproduced by germ cells containing the same elements as the white man. But the fact that they contained elements which made him black, is suggestive evidence that they also contained elements which made him vastly different in other traits. And this suggestion is proven to be one which leads to facts, as we shall see.

"Now, you will ask, What has this to do with the negro's unfitness to associate with the Caucasian?

"Nothing by itself; only to show that Nature has endowed him with several ethnic characteristics, which must be recognized as ineffaceable by man.

"The germinal sexual elements transmitted to him he transmits unchanged to his children, no matter whether he is a college professor or a laborer, just as he does the color and odor of his skin, his kinky hair and anatomical features, especially the large but flexible sex organ, which adapts itself to the peculiar sex organs of the female negro and their demands.

"These ethnic traits call for a large sexual area in the cortex of the African's brain, which soon after puberty works night and day. When we can outdo

Nature and reduce this area by education, we can also reduce the inherent sensuality of the negro, and replace it by an area where intellectuality and culture, combined with our views of morality, will operate.

"As interesting as it would be to go into the subject of inherited and acquired traits, and to express in technical terms the reasons why *inherited* primal instincts *cannot* be changed by education, I believe much of it would not be thoroughly grasped by the general public. Hence I give the facts about the African's inherited sexual traits devoid of scientific terms and euphemisms.

"Unless you get it clearly in your mind as a scientific fact that *primal* instincts cannot be eradicated by education or social contact, you will be unable to comprehend why the negro must be socially segregated.

"Pugnacity, the instinct to war, is a primal instinct. Has culture or the highest form of education effaced it? Has Christianity, prayers, laws, peace treaties, decreased the fighting instincts of man? Certainly not! and because it is a *primal instinct.*

"The chief, the controlling *primal* instinct in the African is the sexual. Education, laws, Christianity, cannot change one iota this biologic force in the pure race. Of course, artificial procedures—operations, drugs—will kill the cell origin of the instinct. Cohabitation with the Caucasian will reduce the sensual impulses in resulting generations, as well as reduce the positive traits of the respective races. The offsprings of miscegenation are negative beings, having the evil qualities and traits of their parents and none of the good, besides being constitutionally weakened in resistance to all the mental and physical affections of man.

"Operations have no Christian or educational reason for application, while mixture of the races is socially and ethnically destructive.

"The Caucasian as a race is moral; the African as a distinct race is not moral. He is *un*-moral, and no amount of education or training is going to change a non-existing element—a biologic negative.

"This fact should never be lost sight of; it is one of the causes which produces the great sexual differences between the negro and white race. 'These differences may be exaggerated or lessened, but to obliterate them it would be necessary to have all the evolution over again on a new basis. What was decided among the prehistoric Protozoa, cannot be changed by an act of Congress' (Geddes and Thompson).

"The negro problem can be solved only by dealing in concrete facts, not abstract principles. The latter method has been too long accepted and has resulted in a miserable failure. As an example: the belief that the African was capable of living as hygienically and morally as the Caucasian was the great mistake made by those who deal in abstract principles. Physicians and social workers know that this false idea sets in action three of the most powerful and destructive foes of mankind: insanity, tuberculosis, and syphilis, —diseases which have been conscientiously studied by the best minds during the last ten years, and whose causes and remedies we are just commencing to understand.

"No extent of education has produced in the present-day negro any ethical understanding of the necessity of fidelity in married life. He has no code of marital ethics or of morals to control seduction or adultery. What is carefully guarded among all races of the world, is among the African race accepted as natural and treated with moral indifference. This undeniable fact is due to their innate *un*-morality.

"The African has the instinct of sex jealousy well developed, but it is not the jealousy of permanent possession: it is the ferocious instinct of the animal when mating, the lycanthropy of immediate desire. He will attempt to kill or mutilate with razor or axe—any weapon that approximates those of his ancestors—the man who would rob him of a temporary sex mate. But this innate jealousy of possession will give way to be transferred to another woman, as suits his sensual impulses and tastes.

"The anatomic variations of the African show conclusively his ineradicable traits. The phylogeny of the negro will exert itself under all conditions. We can keep him down for a time through fear and restraint; but there comes a time when the libidinous substances flowing in the blood stimulates him to sexual fury. Under these circumstances nothing short of a bullet will stop him.

"Besides the secretions of the testicles which stimulate sexual impulses, there is this libidinous substance which also stimulates the whole genesic system, nerves in the body, sex organs, and sex centers in the brain. In the negro, this latter substance is unquestionably of great force and quantity, and accounts for much of his sensual ideation. You can see this physiologic stimulation working a bull elk to madness when the females are in rut. I have seen the same effect upon a bull elk when menstruating girls paused before his wire enclosure.

"One might as well attempt to reduce by education this overpowering mass of physiologic element in the African's system, as to attempt to reduce the secretions of his odoriferous glands. I have never heard good women and teachers claiming that this could be done, but I have heard them say that kindness, Latin, and some knowledge of ethics would reduce his sexual impulses.

"The whole trouble in getting the facts before the general public is that it does not know the least thing about sex psychology or physiology; that sex forces are fundamentally the greatest forces in all life, and that the Negro, for reasons Nature knew were necessary, was given sexual activities fortunately denied the Caucasian. To me, these reasons are fairly clear; but as an explanation would have to go deeply into social psychology, we shall avoid it.

"Education, as it is understood by the white man, will never, in the full-blooded African, affect centers above those governing the procreative instincts. It is a fact observed by those in positions to study the negro that, with the advent of puberty, all intellectual development ceases; even the 'sound memory,' which is the cause of much apparent precociousness, seems to be submerged by the growth of active sensuality.

"With the oncoming of puberty, the negro shows his genesic instincts to be the controlling factor in his life. In little negro girls, lust is demonstrated to an extent scarcely possible of belief by those who have not been brought into contact with them in hospitals or otherwise. I have never seen a negro virgin over ten years of age, and never heard of one from my colleagues. Such conditions do not call for any ostracism or condemnation. Remember, I am referring distinctly to the negro of African descent.

"Sensuality takes hold of the negro's religiosity, controls his thoughts, governs his actions. It is purely a physiologic state, and one for which he is not responsible, but one we must recognize and see to it that it is confined to his own race,—that is, the operative effects.

"The periodic attacks of sexual madness in the negro are due, as I have said, to overstimulation—from our point of view—of sex centers in the brain from the great amount of glandular secretions. These stimulating secretions may be sublimated or turned into useful channels by one way only: *physical labor*. The outpouring of these substances circulate in the blood and then reach the brain centers. When this occurs, the African *will not work,* for he is under the control of sexual forces which produce a state of physical lethargy and physiologic activity. He never had to work when at home among the forests and streams, and existed under a life of constant sexual stimulation.

"In his native country, this was exhibited and relieved by tribal orgies, lustful dances and ceremonies, initiation into sexual rites and excesses. During the period of slavery in the United States he carried on similar methods of relief and sublimation, and had his women always with him. Yet even here there was considerable lessening of sex fury where

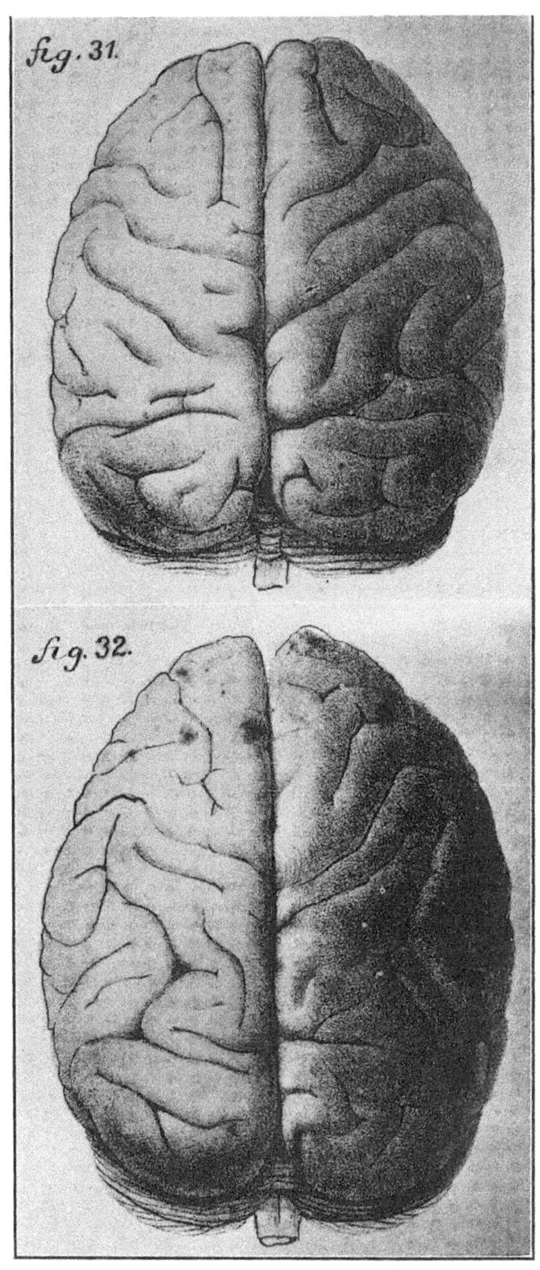

FIGS. 31 AND 32.—BRAINS OF ORANG-UTAN (*Simia satyrus*) (FIG. 32) AND CHIMPANZEE (*Troglodytes niger*) (FIG. 31).

(Superior views, considerably reduced.) The convolutions of the cerebrum in either of these brains should be compared with those given in other illustrations of brains in this work. (Photographically copied by the author from *Das Hirn des Negers mit dem des Europaers und Orang-outangs vergleichen*, by Dr. Friedrich Tiedemann, Heidelberg, 1837. Tafel VI.)

he was *made* to utilize the force through hard physical work.

"But once scattered, free among white people and non-segregated, his one overpowering desire was white women. Now, to his inherent periodic attacks of sexual fury add this incessant determination to enjoy *all* the rights of white men, and you see the real reason for the horrible raping of white girls and women. The almost certainty of being tortured; the knowledge of immediate death in some frightful form—facts which would keep the man with a normal Caucasian brain from risking such ends—is completely submerged by a sex madness, and then we see the explosion of a long train of antecedent preparation.

"During these periods of sexual madness, the negro has all the active symptoms of animalism. There is loss of controlling power over what little higher centers of the brain he possesses. The power of inhibition given the white man, he does not possess—cannot as a negro ever possess. This fact accounts for his skatalogic rites which last for days, his superstitions and lust ceremonies, his education from boyhood to death in matters purely sensual.

"In this country, the negro is supposed to have been ridden of his superstitions. Not a bit of it! The physician sees quite frequently one form of its ineffaceable heredity. No sadder sight can be seen than the little negress who is brought to the hospital suffering from an active venereal disease, due to the belief that a man suffering from such a disease can be cured of it by sexual intercourse with a virgin *child.* You can present a high-school diploma to a negro youth who will attempt a cure of himself by this ancestral belief,—it won't be driven out by algebra or Latin, nor by Sunday-school lessons.

"Let the negro understand in emphatic terms that he cannot aspire to social equality with the white man. Force every loafing negro to work. Put him on Government roads—we need them. Instruct him in the use of tools and farming implements. Take him away from all cultural education. Make it a penal offence to sell or give him alcohol or drugs. Make him the nation's ward, as are the self-respecting Indians.

"Only by some such methods can we put to valuable uses those physiologic by-products which stimulate him to sensual acts and murderous deeds.

"Unconstitutional? Unconstitutional to make such laws and regulations as will be the best for humanity and civilization? Tommy rot! The constitution already looks like a porous plaster."

CHAPTER VI.

Hybridization, Atavism, and Heredity.

In the present chapter it is my intention to deal with the question of hybridization and race hybrids in nature, and to discuss, to some extent, the little we know about them. Most of my remarks will be confined to hybridization, as bearing particularly upon the special subject with which the present volume is concerned, of the Africans and the whites in the United States of America. Very considerable attention has been paid to one phase of hybridization in times past, and is receiving a large share of attention at the present time,—that is, the whole matter of breeding in the domestic animals, and in fruit, flowers, and vegetables used by man.

But little or no attention is being paid to the successful breeding of men and women. We know a good deal of the laws governing the production of hybrids, of artificial selection and evolution, of development and the rest; but we take no effectual steps to utilize them in our own case. In other words, race improvement is with us, at the present time, purely a matter of chance, and in some great movements, in which it has been profoundly involved, we have been quite blind as to the results, and quite deaf to the teachings of nature.

In the case of the human race, interbreeding between different peoples is going on all over the world; the crossing of species of men of all kinds is not only a fact of the present day, but it has taken place in various quarters of the globe as far back as history carries us. It was much rarer in early times than it is now, for the reason that the earth was not so thickly populated, nor were the means of travel anything like as perfect as today. When the various races and tribes of men were more distinctly separated; when great stretches of uninhabited wilderness or bodies of water isolated their habitats, and when the means of communication were extremely slow and limited, the several stocks were far more pure and unmixed. It is modern liberty, coupled with ease and rapidity of communication, enormous increase of population, and the various habitats becoming overcrowded, that afford the constant opportunity for race-crossing. The more pressing and evident these conditions become, the greater is the amount of cross-breeding among the peoples so situated. Under such conditions it is certain to take place, and just as certain to be followed by the appearance of half-breeds where it is going on. It matters little what races are thus brought into juxtaposition; crossing will occur to a greater or less extent. This will more frequently be done without the law of marriage than within it, although intermarriage, too, will be far more common under such circumstances. In the city of New York the Chinese men, here in this country from China, have often married white women, and the crossing of the Caucasians—using that term in its widest application—with Japanese has been very frequent in years past and is constantly on the increase in this day and generation. I have had the opportunity to study a few of their half-breeds, and in one family I have in mind, some of the children were of the Anglo-Saxon type, more or less resembling the father; while one boy at least more strongly exhibited the Japanese in his general morphology and traits, or, as they say among breeders, favored his mother who was a pure-blooded individual of the latter nationality. No one will suppose for a moment that the enormous stock of people, which for years past have been pouring into the United States from the Old World, invariably remained distinct, for such is by no means the case. They not only cross, in marriage or otherwise, with people who were born and bred in America; but they intercross among each other, and even with Indians, Chinese, and negroes; this is going on far more extensively than most people are aware. In conversation with a very intelligent man of fine education and family connections in Germany, I learned that he very much preferred a good-looking negress to any white woman he had ever known.

There are no end of half-breeds produced by the crossing of the whites and the North American Indians on the plains. During the Indian campaigns in that country, it was a very frequent occurrence for both officers and men to keep Indian squaws, and in not a few instances they married them. I have seen not a little of their progeny, and it always struck me that they made neither desirable men nor women, the poor qualities of the two races being intensified and the good ones subordinated.

In this country but a small percentage of the half-breeds—the outcome of the crossing of whites and negroes, whites and Indians, and whites and Chinese—results through the institution of marriage. The great mass of them, especially in the case of the whites and the negroes, are the outcome of chance crossings and the children are illegitimate. On the other hand it is through intermarriage that we have a growing offspring in the United States from the representatives of the various European nations that have made America their home. Many checks occur here, however; for example, the Israelites usually marry only within their own race; so, too, with the Scandinavians and some of the others. Religion may have something to do with it. Catholics are more or less clannish in this respect, and, everything else being equal, Catholics select Catholics as mates when marrying.

In all such hybrids we can see, with greater or less distinctness, the laws of heredity carried out. Hybrids, the results of the crossing of individuals representing different races of men—as in the case of whites and negroes—often exhibit hereditary characters and traits in the most interesting manner possible. Sometimes, however,—where they are inherited from remote ancestors,—they may be very obscure as to their origin; then, too, they may be so mixed that we can tell but very little about them. There is no trait, habit, organization, disposition, anatomical or physiological character that may not be inherited down a line of related individuals from generation to generation. Pathological conditions or predispositions may be passed down in a similar manner, as may also deformities or at least abnormalities. Certain talents, gifts, abilities, inclinations, and idiosyncrasies often pass down through families with a similar certainty, sometimes cropping out in individuals in the most peculiar and unexpected way. In their main trend, however, all of these are governed by laws apparently as immutable in their operation as the most familiar laws in all nature. The matter of chance never enters the result in the case of any individual, be he white or black. In the main trend, again, men breed true to their race, their stock, and the lines of their family ascent. In investigating the attainments, accomplishments, and achievements of any line of pure-blooded and unmixed negro stock, we shall no more chance to find members in it who are, or have been, distinguished biologists, physicians, or artists, than we shall meet with semi-transformed, cannibalistic savages, fetish-worshippers or natural criminals, when we come to make similar researches in any first-class Anglo-Saxon pedigree.

Any number of people can be found in this country today who will deny that there is any interbreeding going on between the whites and the blacks, and who affirm that the numerous mulattoes we see are due to the effects of climate. Such people are, of course, absolutely blind to what is going on about them. They are ignorant; they do not care to see. Take the city of Washington, for instance; I can distinctly remember when mulattoes in the streets of that place were, comparatively speaking, rare exceptions, while now they are to be seen there simply in scores upon scores. Some of them are so white that it takes a very keen eye to detect the African blood in them. Some are handsome creatures with good figures, but handsome and fine-physiqued only in a sense.

These half-breed negroes in the United States—in fact, all that class of people having negro blood in them at all—are extremely objectionable factors to add to our nation, or risk in the building up of our civilization. They are often—indeed, in a large proportion of instances—worse than the negroes themselves; certainly a large number of them are no better. They are dangerous from whatever point we may elect to view them, as they may possess all the vicious and sensual traits of the negro, without the color of the latter's skin as a warning flag to the unwary. In any question at issue they will invariably choose sides with the colored race, and from their keener wits and higher intelligence they are capable of giving a greater amount of trouble. Then, too, mulattoes have better opportunities to contract white alliances in marriage, and thus insidiously perpetuate their savage blood. This is most deplorable; for, as I have frequently remarked, the negro has absolutely nothing of the slightest value in his organization that can be added to our own; while, on the other hand, nearly everything about him, mentally, morally, and physically, is undesirable in the highest degree. He is, as a rule, deeply imbued with criminal tendencies and his hybrids are equally so.

Mulattoes have no higher sense of our civilization than has the black stock from which they are derived. I have found them equally superstitious, treacherous, mendacious, and unreliable. The better class of hybrids command place and position in this country; many regard them as *colored* doctors, *colored* lawyers, *colored* clergymen, *colored* poets and authors, and so on; whereas, as a matter of fact, they are nothing of the kind,—they are *hybrids,* nothing more nor less, and often with a very minute tincture of the African blood in them. Some of them are so like Caucasians in face and figure that the *average* European would never suspect the negro blood in them; it would only be a person well versed in the negro character, and

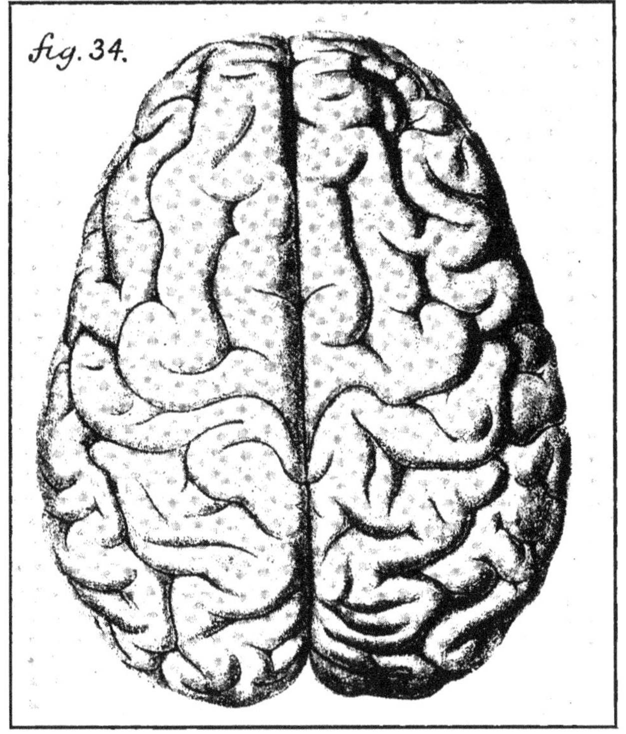

FIGS. 33 AND 34.

Fig. 33 is the superior aspect of the cerebrum of a male negro, and Fig 34 of the cerebrum of a Bosjes woman. Both reduced and copied by the author from the work cited in Figs. 31 and 32 *antea*. Taf. I and V It is very interesting to compare the convolutions here shown with those in Figs. 31 and 32.

possessing knowledge gained by long contact with the race, that could make the correct ethnical diagnosis.

But surely these hybrids are not negroes, although they are very convenient types to juggle with in this country for the admirers, among the whites, of the negro race in the United States, as well as for the negroes themselves, and to deceive the thoughtless into believing that the negro is making such vast and rapid progress among us. As a matter of fact, what he is doing is only through hybridization and crossing with the whites whenever the opportunity offers.

Men like Thomas—who is about one-sixteenth part negro—prejudice this entire question; I refer especially to this author's last work, "The American Negro; What he Was, What he Is, and What he May Become. A Critical and Practical Discussion by William Hannibal Thomas." He has shown the negro race in its true ethnological light. He supports all that I have said above in regard to the characteristics of hybrids; he deplores the presence of the negro and his kin in this country; he advocates his intellectual upraising and civilization with the same pen with which he points out its utter futility and impossibility. These several inconsistencies and incongruities he clinches by the last paragraph in the book, when he gives it as his opinion that "The future American negro will part, undoubtedly, with many of his racial characteristics as he approximates in color and conduct the white race. Even now many persons of negroid ancestry are so fair in color that they readily pass for white people, and marry among that class without exciting the slightest suspicion as to their mixed race identity. Furthermore, white

American marriages are constantly contracted with every variety of the colored races, and the fruit of such unions is certain to exert, hereafter, a considerable influence upon many existing social perplexities. The inevitable outcome of a perfect blending of our heterogeneous peoples would be the development of a composite type of American people of incomparable strength and beauty, who, if they clung fast to their best ethical instincts, would attain such heights as would make our country what it was ordained to be,—the cradle of world-wide liberty, the citadel of human fraternity, and the seat and center of universal righteousness."

I can conceive of no greater calamity that could happen to the people of this country than this. We have here at least a certain proportion of the population who can call themselves true Americans,—a race that, although it came from the Old World, is a composite stock of great antiquity, and one that has arrived at a stage of civilization unexcelled by any other race in the entire range of history. This civilization speaks for itself, and it is not necessary for me to dilate upon it. And it is this civilization, the building up of which has taken thousands of years, that Thomas would now jeopardize by the injection into it of a poison so foul that, whenever or wherever it mixes with it, rottenness is the only result.

Has Thomas ever seen a case of atavism in this country, resulting from the very interbreeding he so extravagantly proposes? Permit me to give an account of one that a few years ago came under my personal notice. A young American artisan of the better class and of excellent type, born of parents born in this country, and untainted by any mixture with African blood, meets a young and very pretty girl in Virginia, and in due course marries her. At the end of a year a boy child is born to them; but, horror of horrors! it is found to be as black as coal, and with hair as kinky as the veriest young Congo that a negress of that race ever gave birth to in Africa. Imagine the state of mind this at once threw the unhappy husband into! His poor young wife pleaded with him that he was the only man who had ever embraced her, and that the very suggestion of receiving the approaches of an African were most repugnant and disgusting to her. But the husband knew there must be a cause for it, as he was present in the room when the black child was born, and he quietly went to work to investigate his wife's antecedents. After no end of trouble and expense, he finally ascertained that her great grandmother was a plantation slave who had borne several children to her master. It was in this stock, through crossing and recrossing with other whites, that this young wife saw her pedigree, and her first child was simply a reversion to the black ancestry on her maternal side, which had inherited the African characteristics, and among them the black skin and kinky hair. I have heard of several other well-authenticated cases of this nature.

This is what Thomas would make general throughout the country; that Europe may point the finger at the American and say: Go to! You have negro in your blood, and you come of a mixed race who were slaves and eaters of human flesh. If you want to know something of your pedigree, read J. Cameron

Grant's "The Ethiopian," and the ceremonies attending the erection of the Juju House in Gnongo, from whence your black blood came; it runs thus: "The king of Gnongo ruled a small but very powerful and very populous country, and was the terror of all his neighbors to the North and West by reason of the number and ferocity of the slave-raids that started from his dominions, and were almost invariably successful. The whole religion of these people necessitated attacks upon their neighbors, for its basis was constant human sacrifice, and the simple law of self-preservation taught the Gnongos, for their own safety, always to keep at hand a goodly supply of the necessary victims. The true history of the place would be a dismal record of ruthless and brutal doing to death of human beings, often apparently for no reason whatever except to satisfy a ghoulish craving for the sight of human blood flowing fresh, or blackening, clotted and nasty in the open, in the town, in street, in square, in court-yard—nay, upon the very household utensils themselves.

"On this, the third day, were to be erected, with all the proper ceremonies, the six main uprights of the new Juju House. The reason, or even the simple mythology of these acts, it is hopeless to expect; one might as well hope to learn the mythology of the monkeys; though verily, I believe, the daily annals of the collection of the higher quadrumana would be more sane and cleanly, and far less blood-thirsty than those of the baser, lower bimana.

"But now it was time for things to begin, and as etiquette, dangerous to evade, constrained all to take part in the ceremonies fasting, so far as a solid meal was concerned, all real eating and drinking had to be deferred till the proceedings of the day were concluded.

"There appeared to be no regular commencement; but, seemingly by a kind of general impulse, drums began to be beaten, horns blown, and trade muskets discharged in the air. Then cows' horns, filled with powder and tamped with clay, were fired off with a thundering report and considerable danger to the neighbors; and, with the exception of the king, who practically never appeared in public, and of his immediate attendants, the whole population of the town flocked to the spot where the ghastly preparations were already well advanced.

"The priests and the warriors and women gathered in a great circle around the pits; the slaves who had carried the victims from the town, bound hand and foot to poles and rolled in cheap calico, at a sign came forward, and laid them two and two beside each excavation, one man and one woman to each. Cutting the lashings that secured them to the poles, they took these away. Then one of the priests began a sort of exhortation to the people, telling them that the king had graciously given orders for the erection of a new Juju House, which would be for the general benefit; then, after animadverting upon the crucifixions of the young women that had taken place two days previously for the prevention of famine and drought, he referred to the head-cutting of the day before, and declared that the auguries drawn from the positions in which the heads had fallen had been most favorable; that the posts of the Juju House were about to be set up in accordance with them; that the heads would be fixed upon the building and would bring great luck;

and, to prevent and minimize occurrences of such evil omen for the coming year, those women who had borne twins in his majesty's dominions during the year gone by would now be buried alive in the hole in the center of the house, over which, when a proper dwelling-place had been provided, a most powerful Juju would preside. He ended by saying that the king had given orders for a great feast to conclude the three days' proceedings, and that his royal bounty had provided for his people a more than usually liberal dole of rum and palm wine. He finished amid the frantic applause of the crowd, and more discharging of muskets and banging of drums.

"Now the warriors got into some sort of order in front and began to chant a monotonous song or hymn, to which the women marked a rude time by grunting at regular intervals and slapping their arms, breasts, and thighs.

"While this hideous anthem was being sung, the executioner and his assistants seized the victims two and two as they lay, male and female, and binding them face to face, pitched each couple into the long holes lying ready excavated beside them. This done, he and his daubed and painted assistants, in all their disgusting paraphernalia of charms and bones, began to dance about the pits, rattling hollow calabashes full of small nuts and seeds, and partially drowning the groans and screams of agony that proceeded from the wretched beings below.

"But now arose the cry of 'Rice-pounders! Women! O women, bring your rice-pounders! Let the family be fruitful and the year give many slaves! Women! O women, bring your rice-pounders!'

"These words were shouted and yelled by the warriors, but promptly taken up by the whole crowd, which, wild with excitement, began to stamp and dance with gyratory motion about the spot occupied by the executioner and his assistants.

"Several scores of women had rushed off to the town at the first words, and were now streaming back, each one armed with her rice-pounder of hard, heavy wood, about three inches in diameter and six feet long, shod with iron at the lower end. As they came up they were speedily arranged in rows round the pits, and at a given cry from the warriors and the crowd of 'Now, O women, pound the sacred rice to feed the gods!' they commenced pounding away with their formidable rammers at the wretched creatures below.

"The piercing shrieks that immediately rent the air soon ceased, and presently save for a low groan or two, no sound rose from the blood-stained mortars except the monotonous beat-beat of the horrid pestles.

"But while the women pounded, the people and the executioners yelled and danced till the excitement attained a frantic pitch. Then, suddenly closing in, the crowd seized the great pillars lying on the ground, hoisted them up by main force of arm, and, planting each one in the center of the gory mass below, filled in the loose earth and stones about them.

"Not till the earth was packed hard around the pillars and level with the surface of the surrounding soil did the women cease their ghastly labour. Then they stopped, exhausted, and rolled about, many of them apparently afflicted with a species of epileptic frenzy. [Just such a frenzy as we see the negro women exhibit at their religious camp-meetings and church services in the United States at the present day.]

"At once each became the center of an admiring circle, for their frenzy was a good omen, a sign that the sacrifice had been accepted with pleasure by the gods, whose spokeswomen they had now become, for the time being at least.

"After a while things quieted down; the crowd once more became attentive, for the final ceremony was at hand. As already mentioned, another pit had been excavated in the center of the pillars, now so firmly erected. Alongside this center hole, a dozen or more miserable women were dragged. These were the unfortunates who had given birth to twins during the previous year in the king's dominions, and so brought evil upon it. One of the priests gave the people his views upon the subject, views that will hardly bear reproduction in these pages; and then the executioner, carrying an iron bar about two feet long, and followed by his assistants rolling a short, thick log, threw the women down, one after another, and, deliberately smashing their arms and legs in two places, doubled them up behind them, and flung the poor creatures into the hole.

"Not a sound broke the silence save the screams of the unfortunate victims of this horrible cruelty, and as soon as the last of them had been pitched, shrieking, into the pit, the earth was filled in over them while they were still alive, and with a wild shout the whole body of spectators rushed in and commenced stamping it flat with their feet. In a very short time all trace of the excavation had disappeared, and the whole space enclosed by the uprights, and even several

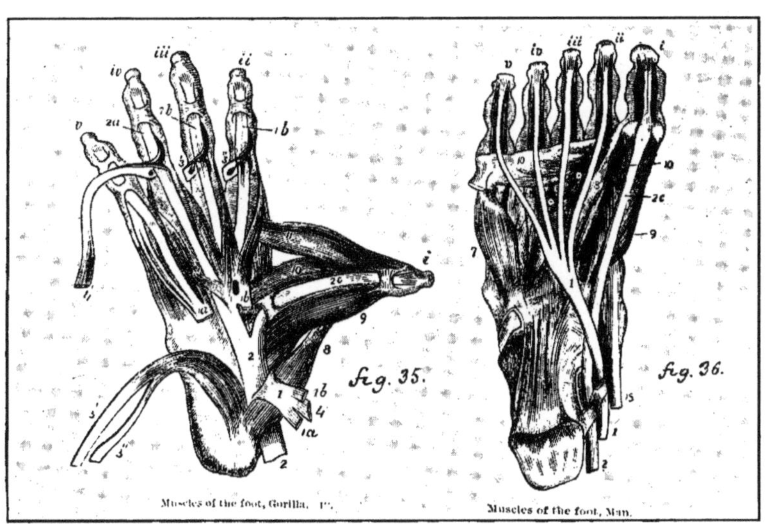

FIGS. 35 AND 36.—MUSCLES OF THE FOOT IN GORILLA (FIG. 35) AND MAN (FIG. 36).

Plantar aspect, and much reduced. (By the author, after Sir Richard Owen. "Comparative Anatomy of the Vertebrates," vol. iii.).

feet beyond them, was tramped smooth and flat and as hard as a threshing floor.

"No one passing could have guessed at the terrible crimes which had been committed, for hardly a splash of blood upon the pillars gave evidence of them.

"With firing of muskets, blowing of horns, and general congratulations and jollity, yelled and chanted, of the goodness of their king and his liberality, the crowd returned to the town, the women to prepare the evening meal and make such festive arrangements as were demanded by the king's orders, the men to talk over the day's celebration, plan future schemes of blood and rapine, and discuss the next slave-catching expedition, all separating later on to secure betimes the royal dole of drink.

"I have described the day; the night I will leave to the reader's imagination and to its fitting veil of darkness." (Pp. 33-42.)

A few years ago, *The Evening Star,* of Washington, D. C. (Dec. 5, 1895), reviewed the volume from which I have just so copiously quoted; and as this review, or rather what is said in it, is just as true today as it was the day it was written, I here reproduce some of its most pertinent paragraphs. They run thus:—

"The cannibalism of the black secret society known as the Human Leopards, in the country near Sierra Leone, disclosed by the recent trial, brings forcibly before us the difference between the East African and the West African habits of eating human flesh. The Sherbro cannibals waylaid and killed their victims and afterwards feasted on their flesh. The cannibalism of the east coast is of a very different kind. The flesh of the old people—the grandfather and grandmother of a family—is dried and mixed with condiments; and a portion of this is offered, with a dim sort of sacramental meaning, to travelers who become guests of the family. To refuse it would be a deadly insult. To accept it is a passport to the privileged position of a friend of the house. Many of our travelers in East Africa have eaten thus sacramentally of the ancestors of some dark-skinned potentate.

"The cannibalism of the west coast is, as has just been seen, of a more horrible kind. The Sherbro case seems to be connected with fetishism, the worst developments of which are peculiar to that country; but there is a hideously genuine appetite for fresh human flesh still existing among the negroes of West Africa. The cannibalism manifests itself in a refinement of gluttony which has its mild analogy in the tastes of Europeans. Young boys are brought from the dark interior, kept in pens, fattened upon bananas, and finally killed and baked. To these Thyestean feasts come not only the savage chiefs of the interior, but also, it is whispered, black merchants from the coasts.

"Men who appear at their places of business in English territory in broadcloth and tall hats, who ape the manners of their white masters, are said to disappear annually into the interior, where, we are told, they may be seen, in naked savagery, taking part in the banquets on plump boys, in which they delight. Be this as it may, somehow the native of the west coast and its Hinterland is unlike the East or South African native in the deep-lying savagery and the extraordinary facility for returning to it, which are his leading and very unpleasant characteristics. The subject claims the attention of the anthropologist, and certainly suggests a curious reason for questioning the relationship of the black man and the ape or gorilla, seeing that the race of monkeys seems to be singularly free from anything like cannibalism."

It is possible that we still have in this country a few negroes who have taken part in just such ceremonies in Africa as are here described; beyond all doubt we have hundreds of descendants living among us, whose near ancestors, negroes in Africa, took part in the erection of Juju Houses where such practices were indulged in. There are hundreds of hybrids of these people, crosses between the blacks and whites in this country, who come from such stock. There are millions of negroes in the South who, if taken back into Africa, would in very short time revert to all these customs, so superficial is the veneer of their pseudo-civilization gained in America.

Our white race has no such chapters in its history; but if we are to assimilate, by a general crossing, this cannibal race, as has been proposed by Thomas and others, *their* history becomes in time linked with our own record, and in the future no American will be able to say that he has no such blood in his veins, for there will be no means of detecting the mixture in intermarriage. It has been stated that the hybrids become sterile in the second, third, or fourth generation; but this would not affect the question, for, assimilation once commenced, the blood of the inferior race must all be taken up eventually; and so great is the number of negroes in this country that there is plenty of their blood to effect complete adulteration of the entire white population of the United States.

I have satisfied myself that not only is hybridization of the two races largely in progress, but that cases of atavism occur all the time. It is the aim and highest ambition of the negresses to have children by white men, for the reason that such children, by the superior intelligence coming from their white fathers, will command better positions when they grow up than the pure blacks, and in so doing will powerfully further the interests, political and otherwise, of the African population in this country.

CHAPTER VII.

Effects of Fraternization upon Morals, Ethics, and Material Progress.

Animals of all kinds are invariably affected by their environments. Man forms no exception to this; indeed, in the case of man, I am strongly inclined to believe that he is more susceptible to his surroundings than any other organized being or class of beings. This is due, in the highest races, to the sensitiveness, plasticity, and moral composition of his organization. As we descend through the scale to the lower races, this becomes less and less evident, being least observable in those races most nearly related to the anthropoids. Negroes are, of course, affected more or less by the environment in which they live, but more by climatic conditions than by reactionary effects on their organizations, due to the presence of peoples more highly civilized than themselves. A race without morals has it within its power only to mimic the qualifications of the higher race, just as parrots mimic the human voice; they neither know the meaning of the words they utter, nor are they in any way mentally advanced through the accomplishment. These conditions are often much improved in hybrids, when those hybrids are produced by the crossing of the lower races with representatives of either sex in the higher.

In large parts of the United States, especially in the so-called "black belt," all these conditions, and others which have been referred to in previous chapters of this book, are ever in operation. In some of the regions in this belt the two races are about equal in numbers; in others the whites are more numerous; while in still others the negroes far outnumber the whites. Where the blacks are in proportion relatively very few, the harm done to the higher race is comparatively insignificant; the harm only increases in degree as the blacks increase in numbers. However, the crossing of the two races goes on wherever they are brought in contact for any length of time. Proportionately, there are but few negroes in New York City, and the black women are constantly sought by white men of the various planes of society for carnal gratification. Lighter colored hybrids are produced and they are making their appearance in considerable numbers. As I have before said, negresses are well pleased to have children by white men, and for reasons already given. If the offspring happens to be good-looking, cleanly in habits, and not especially repulsive, they make better arrangements; and if light colored, with regular features, fine figures, and sensuous and attractive, they are often selected by white men of position. Such matings are usually made where scandal is least likely to flourish. Children may or may not follow, depending upon the means adopted to prevent such calamities.

All this is very degrading, injurious, and harmful to both races, though in very different ways. In the case of the whites, it aids the adulteration of the higher stock by a baser material,—a practice harmful under any and all conditions; whereas in the case of the negroes—the majority of whom believe that procreation and nature's method of insuring it are about all that life means—it fosters the idea that they are ethnologically the equals of the whites; consequently they become dissatisfied with the social plane they occupy, and are restive under what they deem to be the barriers placed in their road to wealth and political power. It is impossible for them to appreciate the fact that nature is the author of such restrictions and limitations and not their Anglo-Saxon superiors. Brains, ability, and the power of achievement are the factors that are principally responsible for the status of the individual and of the nation, and not that either simply possess human form and the power of speech,—a notion that appears to dominate the mind of the manumitted slave.

As we pass southward to the mid-Atlantic cities, where the negroes are far more numerous than the whites—as in Baltimore and Washington—not only is the crossing between the two races more evident, but there likewise exist harmful influences of a widely different nature. Long contact with American civilization has had but the effect of making the better class of negroes admirable mimics of the whites in dress, social requirements, and conversation, while it has in no way improved them morally or physically. American civilization has but endowed the hybrids with the most superficial veneer of refinement; and, as a matter of fact, the pure negro in this country is, in his real nature, just as much of a savage today as he was three hundred years ago. Were the bulk of the blackest ones in the South taken back to their native haunts in Africa, they would resume all of their savage practices and customs within a brief space of time. This makes all the more forcible the ethnic argument for sending them there, and giving them the opportunity to work out their own destiny; of the practicability of this, however, more will be said further on.

Coming back to Washington, we find that, though the negro has benefited but superficially through his long contact with our civilization, he has by no means been lacking in the harm he has worked with our own race in morals and ethics. This injurious influence has been of such an insidious nature, and so varied in its character, that it is not always apparent to the observer. Moreover, it requires careful, just, and far-reaching comparison in order to measure the moral standard of a race at intervals in its career, in that we may ascertain the differences in it. So far as it appears, no such comparisons have been made in the case of the unadulterated population of whites in the city of Washington; but it is as true now as it always has been that, by contact with a naturally criminal race, a superior and sounder race will, in time, slowly but surely, morally deteriorate through sheer force of circumstances. The crime of the one people is almost certain to involve the acts of the other; transitory acts in time become habits, and habits define the characteristics of the whole people. As long ago as 1891 I pointed out that the negroes in Washington constituted but one-third of the population; yet they furnished the great bulk of criminal cases of all kinds. The police report, ending June 25, 1890, exhibited the following terrible record, sustaining what I have just stated: Assaults on policemen, 162,—by whites, 75, by colored 87; assaults on special officers, 25,—by whites 9, by colored 16. "Last year three

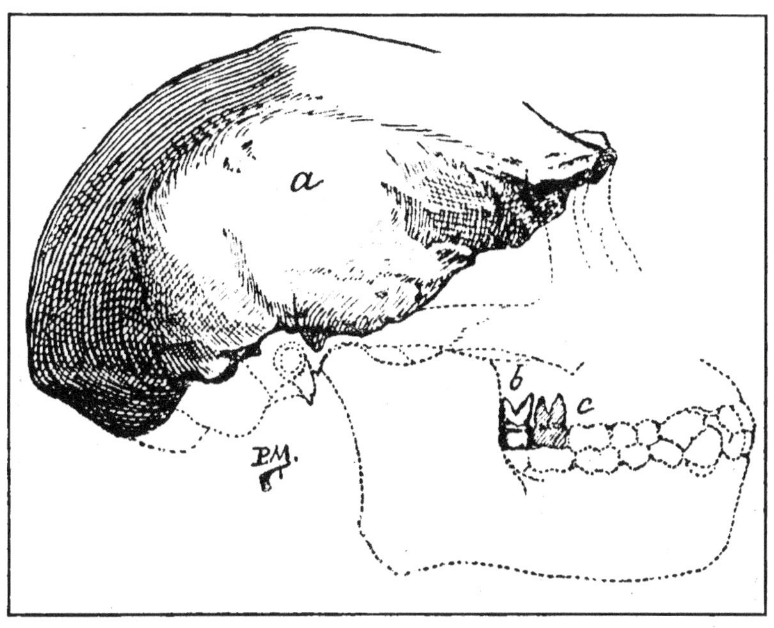

FIG. 37—RIGHT LATERAL VIEW OF THE CALVARIUM OF *Pithecanthropus erectus,* WITH FACIAL PARTS OF THE SKULL AND LOWER JAW RESTORED IN OUTLINE. (From Sergi, after Dubois and Manouvier.)

According to Sergi, "The *Pithecanthropus* of Java, it is true, is an animal with some human characteristics; but, in my opinion, it is not man nor the intermediary type; it is a higher type of the other anthropomorphic species." ("The Mediterranean Race," pp. 201, 202.) (By the author, after Dubois.) See also Deniker, *Races of Man,* pp. 359-361, where a fuller account of the skull of *P. erectus* is given.

policemen were killed by negroes, two when attempting to arrest them, and there is scarcely a year that this does not occur." (*Science,* New York, August 14, 1891.) In *The Star,* a Washington newspaper, of December 24, 1888, it was shown that there were then in jail, awaiting trial or sentence for murder, 16 persons,—2 white and 14 colored. Two years afterward (March 26, 1890) there were on the calendar 18 murder trials, the greater proportion by far having been committed by negroes. That brief article was more than prophetic in its statements; and now, many years later, hundreds of newspapers all over the country are printing accounts of crime that sustain what I then stated, and further stated in the Washington *Analostan Magazine* for March, 1891; in *The Daily Picayune* of New Orleans, February 16, 1891, and elsewhere. In the New Orleans paper I remarked that "In 1882 I watched several hundred negro children as they poured out of one of the large colored public schools in Washington, D. C. Later, in 1890, the same sight was presented at exactly the same place, but a most marked change was perceptible. In 1882 the vast majority of the children were black, the mulattoes being the exception; in the second instance, more than 50 per cent. were mulattoes, and many others so white that it would be difficult to pronounce with certainty upon them." (See also "Hybridization," in *The Religio-Philosophical Journal,* Jan. 17, 1891.)

The "problem" is now far graver; the number of negroes far greater, and the means of ridding ourselves of the black more difficult. At the nation's capital, as everywhere else in the country, they continue to furnish nine-tenths of the crimes on the court calendars. As an element they are more dangerous than ever in the matter of assaulting white women. Their notions of national and municipal politics are just as rotten and debased as they have always been. They are just as much given to mendacity as they were when in Africa. And they still exhibit, as a race object-lesson before our growing generation, all that is most lewd, degrading, objectionable, ignorant, and superstitious; in short, the bestial side of the genus *Homo.* The negro—the pure negro—in this country is no more responsible for his organization and character than is any other animal. A vulture will eat carrion when surrounded by every kind of cleaner food; it is the nature of the bird.

A number of years ago I was at the voting polls of a State election in the southern part of Maryland. Negroes went up there in numbers to deposit their votes. Every vote they deposited had been bought for a trifle by the representatives of the political parties at the time. There are those who say that the members of our own race are to blame for this, because they buy the votes, which is just as criminal as the sale of them, perhaps more so; for the higher race should set the better example. However, it illustrates what I have already stated in a former paragraph. Were it not for the presence of the negro in such numbers in such places, the whites would not have the inducement to resort to these practices. One never sees scenes of that kind in New York City, where but comparatively few negroes appear at the polls, and where the votes cast at a general election run into myriads.

As a rule, the youth of the American negro are liars by nature; they are nearly all predisposed to gambling, and the majority of them will steal. So far as example goes, in these respects they set a bad one to the youth of our own race in this country. Moreover, the young blacks are distinctly lewd and sensuous in their inclinations, and at an early stage develop a desire to possess white women, traits which they, in reality, never outgrow, and which are a constant menace to the gentler sex of our people everywhere. This influence is extremely bad, and the knowledge of it reacts disastrously upon the minds of our daughters and wives throughout the country, as I shall presently show. To develop a fine, pure-minded, clean and cultured race, it is essential that it should ever have before it all that is refining and beautiful, all that tends to elevate body and mind, all that inspires to cultivate art, science, literature and learning; and certainly not be brought into the atmosphere of another race, who have all the factors of degradation and ignorance in their organization. People may think that the latter have no influence upon the higher race; but this is a profound error. Anything and everything in the environment of any animal is certain to affect it in one way or another. The same axiom applies, with equal truth, to a race or group. With respect to the superior people, their morals and ethics are bound to suffer. A few rotten apples may spoil the entire barrel, and the greater the number of rotten ones, the sooner will general corruption and decay take place. It is all nonsense to talk about the better race redeeming, and eventually elevating, the lower one to the plane of the former, for nature's laws work in no such manner. In this country the highest civilization and the cleanest and soundest white people flourish where the negro exists in comparatively few numbers. But to carry this argument further would be to introduce odious comparisons. Washington, our nation's Capital, has in these particulars a terrible load to carry, and the amount of black venom that has been injected into her veins requires all the force of her Caucasian constitution to tolerate. As beautiful as that growing city is, it could be far more so were it not for the presence, in its every place and thoroughfare, of the low African stock that constantly attacks its vitals. Baltimore is another city profoundly affected by the same malady; and Dr. William Lee Howard has well said, in an article on the subject, entitled "The Negro as a Distinct Ethnic Factor in Civilization":—

"The attitude of complacent moralists, the preaching of far-distant ascetics, and the Sunday-school advice of the New England maiden who would take the African to her bosom, would be amusing were it not for the serious conditions underlying the misunderstood facts.

"The truth is that the negro of today, untrammeled and free of control, is rapidly showing atavistic tendencies. He is returning to a state of savagery, and in his frequent attacks of sexual madness, his religious emotionalism, superstition, and indolence, is himself again—a savage. This animalism, this innate character of the African, will demonstrate itself more and more as he is allowed the liberty of his sway of ancestral sexual impulses, and as long as moralists and sociologists of the 'suppressive school' continue to remain purblind to the negro's dominant physiologic and psychologic organism."

Further on he very truly says: "It is unscientific to attempt to study the adjustment and laws of society without a thorough knowledge of the structure of its individual parts. It is useless for philanthropists, preachers, and editors in the North, or any other part of the country where the African is not understood or studied, to talk about school and college education controlling his hereditary racial instincts. His individual parts are not known to such people. Only he who knows life from the monad to *cell-complex man* can intelligently discuss the negro question. To understand the ineradicable racial traits of the African, one must know the structural life and habits resulting from a certain biologic basis. We must penetrate beneath superficial ideas, throw aside prudish philosophy, and open our eyes to anatomical and physical facts if we wish to render justice to civilization. Silence regarding sexual matters must give way to vocative statements, for it is by these unavoidable statements that we must be guided in dealing with the negro question." (*Medicine,* June, 1903, p. 433.)

The time has arrived—or ought to have arrived—when man, or the intelligent part of mankind, can largely control his or its own environment. So far as we know, nature has no pity and no designs in such matters. With her, the laws are simply operative in accordance with the conditions present and involved. Certain effects are bound to become evident if certain states and conditions exist. Nature would evince no emotion were this planet to become as cold as an iceberg, solid to the core, and with a surface as smooth as a billiard-ball without so much as a grain of dust upon it. With her, biologic law would then simply cease; physical law alone would still remain active. In other words, it remains entirely with ourselves to control our environment; and were there a consensus of opinion upon the point, followed by a consensus of action, we would have it in our power to render the negro race harmless in the United States in very short time. Sociologic adjustment would follow quite as quickly, and natural laws would still continue as unceasingly in their action. That mankind would be enormously benefited in the long run, and the white race in this country be the distinct gainer, cannot for a moment be doubted.

But let us pass for a while still further south in this region south of Washington and Baltimore, into our subtropical realm, into the so-called "black belt," to see how our Caucasian brethren are faring in that quarter. The dangers attempted to be portrayed in the leading paragraphs of this chapter are there vastly intensified and increased. The bulk of the white population throughout those states are slowly awakening to the horrors of the situation that now confronts them. Negroes are massed everywhere, and, being no longer under control, menace all that is decent in the developing nation: menace morals, menace progress and development, menace legal and political stability, and threaten, in no uncertain manner, the very existence and purity of the American race and its career. Ask any intelligent Southern man or woman, and he or she will tell you something of the state of affairs existing there, even if such people do not grasp the danger in its fulness as the biologist and anthropologist does. Read some of the paragraphs that Ellen Barret Ligon, M.D., of Mobile, Alabama, has printed in her article on "The White Woman and the Negro," which appeared in the November (1903) issue of a Springfield, Massachusetts, magazine called *Good Housekeeping.* After pointing out the nature of our American civilization in the South and our duties in preserving it; after touching upon the calamities which follow an attempt to inaugurate social equality between the negroes and the whites; after indicating the true attitude of the Southerner toward the colored race; after arraigning the negro hybrids for boasting of the white blood in their veins, and reminding them that they are still negroes, and after rejoicing that the negro in the South is manumitted, this writer proceeds to say: "Those at a distance cannot realize the situation the people of the South are facing, nor the conditions arising from living in the midst of hordes of negroes. One or two negroes may be to some tastes picturesque; but to be in the midst of a whelming black flood, rolling its waves against the bulwarks of our civilization, overflowing our public highways and public conveyances, and threatening our homes, is the condition which the men and women of our own race should investigate and realize, before they devote themselves to that strange philanthropy which is so tender of heart for the black brother or sister, and criminally ignorant of, and careless about, the terrible dangers that threaten the women and children of their own race, and which they may be so largely instrumental in precipitating.

"The all-pervasiveness of the negro, not by ones and twos, but by the million, with his 'equality' insolence, his odoriferous person and his criminal tendencies, is a factor for danger and discomfort that must be held in check by the most far-seeing intelligence. There is no community, where the blacks exist in any numbers, where they have not made themselves offensive to the whites—Washington, for example—and there is no other part of the country where this offensiveness, when short of actual criminality, is borne so forgivingly as in the South. They put on extra police force that their daughters, in going to and from school, may be protected from infamous remarks made to them by passing negro men; city districts must have extra guards that negro fiends may not enter homes and knock sleeping women senseless that they may be violated afterwards. This happened in the same city over and over again for two years, in spite of extra guards. Several of the women died. One wretch was at last caught; the tolerant people decided that he was a degenerate, and sent him to the insane asylum to be cared for by the State. Yet there are people at a distance, unknowing the conditions in the South, who throw all their sympathies with 'the poor, downtrodden negro.'

"It is time they knew better. Let all the world listen while the South calls on you to hear: The white woman is the coveted desire of the negro man. The despoiling of the white woman is his chosen vengeance.

"The white woman must be saved!

"The vital point in the race question today is the safety of the Southern white woman, and all the help-

FIG. 38.—PAN CHIMPANSE. (Reduced.)

(By the author, after D. G. Elliot: "A Review of the Primates," vol. iii, Pl. VIII.)

lessness of womanhood appeals to the manhood of the world to protect her with every possible safeguard. 'Social equality' is battering on the walls that protect her, and for what purpose? To make a breach where the negro may climb up and over. And who is to be helped by this invasion? Not the negro, for it puts him in a false position, and the white race will certainly be no better for the mixture.

"All philanthropical claims can be fully met, mentally and morally, without taking the negro, even the best negro, into the home circle. It makes no difference that social equality is asked only for those who are worthy. The social recognition of one good negro stimulates in thousands of black devils resentment at not being similarly treated, and rouses them to fresh insults and outrages aimed at the Southern white woman. Negro equality is a theory; negro outrages and insults resulting from the inculcation of the doctrine of equality are hideous facts."

This lady knows whereof she speaks, and she possesses the courage of the heroine, putting her thoughts to paper and print without a spark of false shame or fear. We cannot sufficiently admire her candor and her appeal. Her words, her description of actual conditions, should be sounded throughout the length and breadth of this country; with that view I take pleasure in reproducing here still more from her admirable invocation: "Today, because the negro has been taught 'you are the social equal of the whites, you have the right to whatever the white man has a right to,' the object most desired by him is the forbidden, the unattainable white woman. In that over-and-over repeated story of the outrages in the South, it is almost invariably a white woman or white child that has been the victim, and a negro the criminal. The Southern white man knows that his wife is not safe in her home, nor his child in her bed, except for the vigilance and surveillance of the law.

"When one American woman was carried off by bandits the entire nation, even the government, was roused with indignation and anxiety. Almost daily in our own country beasts worse than bandits despoil the tender and the helpless. Good, conscientious, mistaken women are sympathizing with the black man, because they have not heard the little child's voice crying in the night and found their baby girl out of doors in her own blood, mangled and torn; nor seen some white woman's body with skull crushed and bruised breast, nor even heard the obscene infamies that, in wanton insolence, are spoken to the white girl or woman by the passing black."

Proceeding, this Southern lady exhibits the record for all kinds of crimes in the South and the increase of certain diseases. Eighty-five per cent. of the crimes committed in the Southern States are committed by negroes. Insanity is increasing among them to a fearful extent, especially among the mulattoes. Tuberculosis has a similar showing; the blacks there are especially prone to that disease, forming an immense nidus to propagate the malady, and pass it along to the most susceptible types among the whites. All this is a curse, adding death and disease to every other infliction brought upon us through the presence of this criminal, semi-savage race in our midst.

"Within the past year or so," says this courageous writer, "the horror has crept across the line, and what the North once viewed with incredulity and indifference from afar has lately become visible from its very doors. It can no longer be dismissed as a fable from Louisiana or Texas, for it has manifested itself in Delaware, Kansas, and Illinois. It has come too close to be ignored or pooh-poohed, or relegated to the limbo of malignant fiction. Suppose it were to be your daughter next?

"What are you going to do about it, Americans?"

This is a very fitting question wherewith she closes this burning appeal to our race; and it is the members of our own race—Americans—who are the real sufferers in this matter.

Yes, Americans, what *are* you going to do about it? We are not responsible for the acts of our forefathers in this country, nor are we pledged to abide, for a single instant, by the monumental blunders they made. It was an enormous mistake on the part of our ancestors, the bringing of the African negroes to this country; but the proposition that confronts us now is an entirely different matter. They are here; and instead of being slaves under control, they are free, —free to pollute our entire country. Are we to stand with our hands down our sides and see them do it? Are we to allow this miscegenation to go on?

As far back as he can look into human history, the Anglo-Saxon has no *cannibalism to conceal* from his offspring. Are we now to take up into our blood a race of human flesh-eaters, who would consume human flesh again with relish were they returned to the country from whence they came? Are we to make a hatchery of crime and disease simply because we are afraid to act? Are we of the North to remain deaf to the earnest appeal from the mothers and daughters of our own race in the South for aid in this matter? What, in the name of all that is brave, and manly, and honorable, has come over this American nation? Are we already so foully adulterated by the black scum that we can no longer be moved through the dictates of honor, and through the highest instincts of manliness, to listen to and to heed the distress and danger of thousands of our own women?

Are we, as a nation, after all our effort, with all our civilization, and with everything before us, to have no better record for the future than this: that we proved a curse rather than a benefit to mankind? It is a nation's highest duty to so acquit itself in its career that its national record will not only redound to its own credit, but that, in the general trend of humanity's progress, it will exhibit a high regard for the interests of mankind in general.

In this race question one thing is certain: our mothers and daughters in the South are becoming thoroughly awakened to the dangerous side of the freed negro's character, in so far as it concerns *them;* what is quoted above demonstrates this fact.

To rid ourselves of what is criminal, we must first recognize the source of the crime. With respect to the negro this has been done. To rid ourselves of disease and unsanitary conditions, we must first recognize the disease and the class of people who are giving rise to it, and whether it be curable or incurable. With respect to the negro this has, again, been done. Finally, to sustain a high standard of morals and refined ethics, we must rid ourselves of the source of the immorality, and of the cause of our retrogradation. With respect to the negro, this it evidently remains for us to do. Penal legislation by itself has never been known to eradicate vice or crime; isolation or removal have proved far more effective.

Through our experience, the safest of all teachers, we have come to know thoroughly the mental density of the negro; his ignorance and superstition; his mendacity; his innate predisposition for crime; his bestiality and sensuality, and his savage and cannibalistic history. A diagnosis having been made, every educated physician appreciates what is next to be done in the case. In the following chapter this diagnosis will be discussed; something will be said of the treatment that has thus far been instituted, and what may yet have to be done.

In closing this chapter, I have a word to say to those people of the North who, seeing nothing beyond the comfortable homes in which they live, complacently remark, upon reading Mrs. Ligon's appeal in the foregoing paragraphs, that such things, or state of things, may have been true ten years ago, at the time I quoted her, but that all this is now past history, and that the women of our race are, in these days, never molested in any such manner, anywhere in the South. Will the people, to whom I refer, read the following letter which comes to hand as this book goes to press, and which I have full permission to print in this chapter?

E——n, Georgia,
October 15, 1914.

Dr. R. W. Shufeldt.

Dear Sir:—A letter from Mrs. Annie Riley Hale suggests that I give you, from the centre of the black belt, where I was born and reared, a few personal experiences. It is said women prefer the concrete to the abstract, and I am wondering if the circumstances under which this is written would not best describe or visualize a condition you wish to emphasize in my section. Briefly, then, I am writing under the nervous tension of expecting to be strangled at any moment, as there is a negro man in the house with me, and I am—alone. *I* picked up my pen, intending to give you a few facts on the "negro peril," with a furtive glance over my shoulder, and a sensation of a hand at my throat; and it occurred to me, "Why not put this in words?" Why not, indeed!

To make my meaning clearer: Out of pity for a hungry, vagrant negro, *I* have just fed, clothed, warmed, sheltered, and put into my home to work [a negro of this class], and I am in a panic of fear, knowing he may spring at me like a tiger, should I relax my vigilant watch. This, then, is the exact situation throughout the whole black belt: Vigilant watch and constant fear on account of the horror that crouches in or near every Southern home.

The little town from which *I* write is the most nature-favored region of the world—the Piedmont plateau of the South, elevated on Titan's rocky shoulders, nearly 800 feet above the sea level, and endowed with a climate of almost endless summer. From the very prodigality of its blessings has come its curse: the overwhelming presence of the negro, brought here by the slave owner, who sought the richest and best agricultural section of the State! Below is the dead level of ocean deposit, once considered too unhealthful for whites to live in. Above is the infertile mountainous region; so the middle section of the South, with its warm, sunny slopes, from the Alleghanies to the Atlantic or Gulf of Mexico, became the preferred home of our race who tilled the soil with slave labor. The result: tragedy in the 20th Century, where barbarism now strikes sharp on civilization and Christianity!

No white woman dares walk alone and unprotected on the country road, or even in the Southern village, when the shadows fall. She must, in her lonely plantation home, forever keep a watchful eye on the loaded gun—her only defense in her husband's absence. And this in the days of telephones and telegraph and all the marvels of our age, only twenty-four hours from New York, and much less from Washington City! Our women living in as deadly peril as they were in the time of the scalping knife and tomahawk!

Does the average white man of the North, who knows the South only as he views it from a palaçe-car window, doubt this statement? I will only say: Let him buy or rent a lonely plantation home, miles away from town police, in any section of the South where the negro race predominates; let him leave his wife and children unprotected there, and then state to the world the result if he can, or dare.

....

Name and address withheld; but the writer is known and vouched for by Mrs. Annie Riley Hale, who has visited her, and personally verified every statement she makes.

This does not look like past history.

Such cases, however, or such condition, as my correspondent has just cited above, are by no means confined to the "black belt;" for, only a few weeks ago, a negro assaulted a white woman a short distance from my home in Washington, and within half a pistol-shot from where the present book was being written.

The Washington Times, of the 24th of September, 1914, gave the following brief account of the above:—

"Attacked by a colored man, as she was walking on the Park drive near Rock Creek Park, Mrs. Catharine Lee, who lives at 3402 Nineteenth Street northwest, and conducts the fruit and refreshment stand at the Harvard Street entrance to the Zoo, was saved by the screaming of her two children.

"Throwing Mrs. Lee to the ground, the man held his hand over her mouth so that she was unable to make an outcry. The children cried out at the top of their voices, and the colored man fled. As soon as the matter was reported to the police, a squad of officers scoured the woods on the edge of the Zoo, but the man was not found. He is about nineteen years old, light-brown skin, and was roughly dressed.

"Mrs. Lee is suffering severely from shock."

Should anyone wonder that President Wilson believes in the segregation of the whites and the negroes in Washington, as pointed out in the newspapers lately?

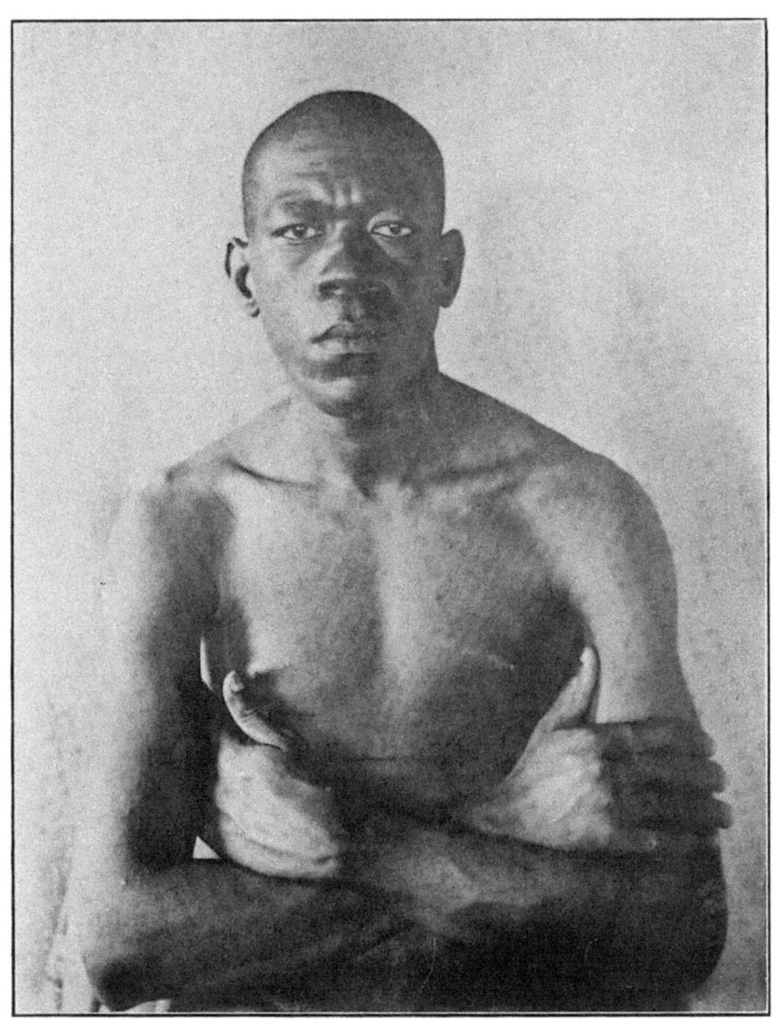

FIG. 39. PURE AFRICAN NEGRO. (New York City.)

Male. Born in Demarara, British Guiana. Parents unmixed. Africans. Age, 24; height, 5 feet 11 inches; weight, 165 lbs. Came to the United States when eighteen years of age. Victim of syphilis. (From life, by the author.)

CHAPTER VIII.

Criminality of the Negro: Lynch Law.

As the development of the body in man and in all other animals has been a matter of evolution, so, too, has been the growth and development of all the psychological attributes, using the latter term in its most far-reaching sense. This being true, it becomes evident that the lower the position held by any particular race of mankind in the scale of morphological development, the lower will all the passions, instincts, morals, emotions, and aims be found in that race. To this universal rule and all its variations and refinements, the typical negro forms no exception, and it is equally applicable to every grade of hybrid produced by crossing the negro with other races.

In the negro, all passions, emotions, and ambitions are almost wholly subservient to the sexual instinct, and that quite apart from the procreative instinct. They seek solely for the gratification of passion and for the erotic pleasure it affords them. In other words, negroes are grossly animal, that is, animal in the sense of quadrupeds; nor should we expect anything different from this. Civilization and progressive civilization are altogether meaningless to them; posterity has practically no interest for them. The negro lives in the present; and being essentially without morals—and as a rule equipped far above the average man for unlawful indulgence—he gives that side of his nature full sway when no restrictions of any kind are present to hinder.

Thomas says, in his previously quoted work: "He [the negro] is regarded as a creature of lascivious habits, personal vanity, and physical laziness. All who know the negro recognize, however, that the chief and overpowering element in his make-up is an imperious sexual impulse, which, aroused at the slightest incentive, sweeps aside all restraints in the pursuit of physical gratification. We may say now that this element of negro character constitutes the main incitement to the degeneracy of the race, and is the chief hindrance to its social uplifting." (Pp. 176, 177.)

My study of the negro, as he exists in the United States, has convinced me that he is so bestial by nature that he holds in no regard whatever such decency as may be observed by the mothers, daughters, wives, or sisters among his race. He revels in lewd conversation, in erotic practices, and in unlawful pursuits; especially does he delight in encouraging the approaches of the whites among the women of his kind. On the other hand, negresses, although not altogether given to making advances of this character, readily accept the embraces of white men.

"So lacking in moral rectitude are the men of the negro race," says Thomas again, "that we have known them to take strange women into their homes and cohabit with them with the knowledge of, but without protest from, their wives and children. So great is their moral putridity, that it is no uncommon thing for step-fathers to have children by their step-daughters, with the consent of the wife and mother of the girl. Nor do other ties of relationship interpose moral barriers; for fathers and daughters, brothers and sisters, oblivious of decent social restrictions, abandon themselves without attempt at self-restraint to sexual gratification whenever desire and opportunity arises. That such licentiousness is prevalent is not surprising, when we reflect that animal impulse is the sole master, to which both sexes yield unquestioned obedience. Not only is negro immorality without shame, remorse, or contrition, but their unchaste men and women are perfidious, malevolent, and cowardly in their relations, and with reckless obliviousness to consequences eagerly gloat over each other's frailties and readily betray the indiscretions of their companions in guilt. Moreover, the contradictions of the freedman's nature are such that, while imputations of personal impurity are resented by the known impure, there is a common disposition to question each other's morals, and rarely is either male or female accorded a clean bill of approval. Soberly speaking, negro nature is so craven and sensuous in every fibre of its being that negro manhood with decent respect for chaste womanhood does not exist." (*The American Negro,* pp. 179, 180.)

In the present chapter, thus far, I have presented enough, I think, to illustrate what an intensely sensuous and lascivious race the negro race is,—utterly lacking in chastity among themselves, and in these particulars highly dangerous to the whites who chance to reside in the same region with them.

The very important question now arises: Is there any remedy for all this, in so far as the redemption of the American negro is concerned? My firm conviction is that there is none,—absolutely none. It is impossible to improve the morals of a people when they have no morals to improve. Every one, knowing anything of the typical negro, knows full well that he is an utterly non-moral being; and to endow the whole race of them in this country with a sound morality, would be just as impossible as to change the color of his skin and take the kink out of his hair.

Says Thomas: "The extent of the crime instinct in the negro is indeterminate for the reason that accurate data are unobtainable. In so far as he has been held to an outward observance of moral restraints, it is obvious that fear of bodily harm has been the chief influence which has kept him in check. That his nature is surcharged with latent ferocity is shown by abundant evidence of atrociousness, committed on weak and defenseless objects. Indeed, there is good ground for believing that, were the negro once convincingly assured of personal security, all the malignity of his slumbering savagery would immediately find expression in the most revolting acts of physical lawlessness. His passions are easily excited, and his feelings readily inflamed to the point of reckless vindictiveness, though a natural unsteadiness of character renders him fickle and unstable in purpose" (pp. 208, 209).

By nature the negro is, in fact, capable of committing any known crime, in so far as his intelligence will permit him to be the author of it. For the lack of such intelligence, and often for the lack of sufficient amount of courage, there are fortunately limitations to some of the heinous criminal acts he might otherwise be guilty of and be forever committing. But lacking in courage, intelligence, forethought, and the necessary staying powers, the criminal negro is perforce restricted to certain of the coarser and grosser crimes in the calendar not requiring these several prerequisites. His murders are clumsy and brutal; his thefts of all kinds are usually paltry and liable to be easily detected. Except for the purposes of spite or to cover other crimes he rarely resorts to arson; while in the refinements of criminality in other directions he is fortunately helpless.

However, all things considered, and notwithstanding the enormous amount of crime of all kinds committed by negroes in the United States, the one above all others for which he is held especially responsible by the American descendants of the Anglo-Saxon race is that of his assaults upon white women. These heinous, devilish, fiendish cases are often associated with the murder of the victim after the assault, and they have become so common in many parts of the country where negroes abound that a species of terror has come to prevail and haunt the minds of all the white women who reside within the same region. Indeed, matters have come to such a pass in these respects that no white woman, no white girl, and in fact no white child, can, with any safety, venture out alone in those districts and places where the negroes have more or less sway. For if not directly accosted, they may be subjected to insulting glances, to indirect insulting remarks, or to direct assault and violence. Such assaults may occur anywhere and at any time,—city or country, night or day. A case took place many years ago on "L" Street in Washington, D. C., during the early part of the afternoon. The victim was a little girl not more than twelve or thirteen years of age, and her father was an officer in the military service of the United States. Her mother had sent her upon a little errand, and when on her way back a burly negro accosted her, saying that he had just been talking to her mother at the house, and that she had said, if he met her daughter, he was to take her to a candy-store before she came home to buy her some candy. The child believed the story and followed him a few squares to where they crossed the Georgetown Tubular Bridge, in the very heart of the town. Here he suddenly seized her in his arms, made a leap, and was instantly in some shrubbery that grew beneath the bridge. Out came his great clasp-knife, at which the child screamed fearfully. Some men overhead, hearing her cries, landed by her on the jump, but not, however, before the negro had ripped her clothing with his knife and severely choked her; then, making a dash for a nearby lumber yard, he escaped among the high piles of timber before any one had realized what had happened. The father and I hunted for that negro until long after dark, and he would, undoubtedly, have been shot on sight. The would-be raper was never discovered in this case. Fortunately he did not have time to mutilate the child, a common practice among negroes when they assault little white girls.

Such is the class of cases which for years past have terrified Southern mothers; which have filled fathers, husbands, and brothers with apprehension throughout the great "black belt." Owing to the peculiar nature of the crime, they cannot well communicate to their little daughters—or even to those of maturer years—these apprehensions, without putting ideas into their minds which, in many instances, would be harmful.

In other words, there is an ever-present danger for them, against which a warning becomes extremely necessary but impracticable upon many accounts. It is this state of affairs, so little appreciated by the people in the Northern part of the United States, which has induced the women in the South, those occupying the best positions in society, to represent this sad condition of affairs in the pages of our magazines.

But what has it availed? Nothing, absolutely! The negro is not responsible for his animal nature any more than for the opportunities he takes to gratify the normal impulses which are a part of him. It is not a case of changing the spots on the leopard, although some, indeed many, think this to be the case. For example, a writer in *The New York Evening Telegram* of January 28, 1904,—a paper of wide circulation,—claims to have discovered a treatment for the negro which will have the effect of turning his skin white! Just as though all savagery, cannibalistic tendencies, thievish propensities, mendacity, and the rest were in *the skin* of this animal! Such an expedient might, if effective, prove to be of value politically; but it would be worse than useless biologically, for the danger sign—his color—would be removed, and the opportunity would be greater for this semi-metamorphosed race to mix its cannibalistic blood with that of the unsuspecting Anglo-Saxon in the United States. Whatever the inventor may think of this skin-bleaching invention, it can, of course, be nothing more than one of those cheap nostrums now so frequently put on the market solely for gaining money, but absolutely valueless.

I do not believe that, throughout the country as a whole, the number of assaults upon white women by negroes are diminishing in number or in their fiendish brutality; in some sections they even seem to be on the increase, the number of such cases being greater each year. It seems to me that the cases average at least one a day for the entire country; they are well exemplified by the following one from *The New York Herald* of January 31, 1904:—

"ROANOKE, VA.—When George J. Shields, a well-known young business man, reached his home, in the heart of the city, at the luncheon hour today, he found his three-year-old daughter Mildred lying on the reception-hall floor with two ugly wounds in the head. Following blood-stains from the dining room to an upstairs chamber, he found his wife in a clothes closet with her throat cut from ear to ear and her head horribly hacked. Mrs. Shields managed to gasp: 'A large black negro man came through the kitchen and attacked me in the dining room.'

"Excepting this, there is no clew to the criminal. Mrs. Shields had been assaulted, after which her assailant dealt her several blows on the head with a hatchet, fracturing the skull, dragged her upstairs, where he cut her throat with a razor and threw her into a closet, fastening the door on the outside.

"The dining-room floor bore evidences of a terrible struggle. The physicians entertain little hope for the recovery of either mother or child.

"Ever since the discovery of the tragedy, a large crowd of citizens has been in the vicinity of the city jail, watching to see if the police carry anyone into the building. At eight o'clock tonight, this crowd num-

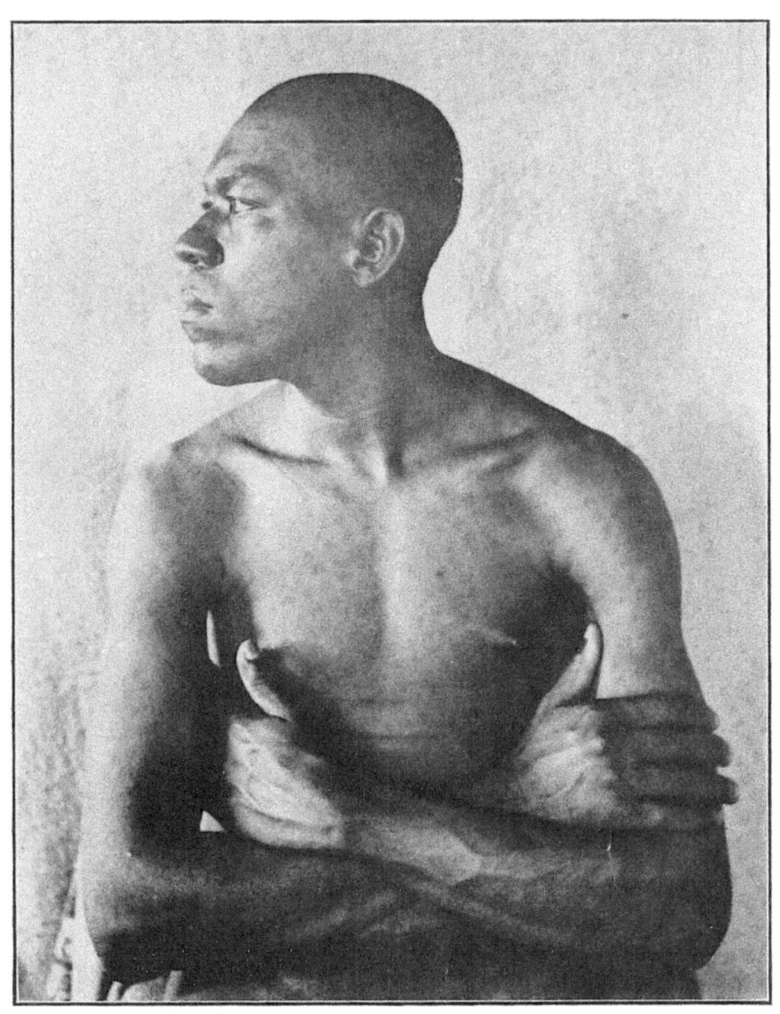

Fig. 40.—Same Subject as in Fig. 39. Profile.

bered more than a thousand men. Mayor Cutchin has ordered Captain Francis, of the Roanoke Blues military company, to assemble his men as a precautionary measure. By order of the Mayor, all the saloons were closed at eight o'clock tonight."

Further on in the present volume will be found a number of cases of this kind, so that the reader may become informed as to their brutality, and the various circumstances under which they have occurred.

In a large proportion of cases, if the negro assaulter and murderer is captured by the infuriated mob, a lynching takes place; in other words, the culprit is summarily taken out and hung.

My readers may remember the typical example of one of the lynchings that took place in the State of Texas some years ago. The criminal in this case was an unusually black and brutal negro by the name of Henry Smith, and his victim was little Myrtle Vance (aged three years, eight months, and a day), whom he outraged and murdered at Paris, where the infuriated people of the place burned him on the first of February, 1893, on the day of his crime. The details of that crime and the horrors of the lynching that followed are altogether too terrible to record here.

With respect to lynching, Thomas, in his work "The American Negro," says: "It is not the number of negroes lynched that makes such acts execrable, for the annual summary executions are less than two hundred, but the fact that such lawless methods deny to the accused the exercise of his highest privilege,—a free and impartial trial before a legally constituted tribunal. Were this phase of lawlessness directed solely against criminal assaults on women, it might have a color of justification; but while that is the offence for which negroes are mainly lynched, there are not infrequently summary executions of them for murder, arson, and theft.

"Lynching may be correctly described as the infliction of summary punishment for alleged offences, without authority of law; and there is among sane minds common agreement that such lawless violence is an execrable usurpation of ordained legal functions. As a mode of punishment for the freedman criminal class, there is never, under any circumstances, excuse or justification for resorting to it. It cannot be said that it is to be approved by the best sentiment of any community; yet when inflicted upon negroes for the commission of certain crimes, the perpetrators are assured of absolute immunity from punishment. No negro is likely to be legally acquitted in the South of the charge of criminal assault, or, in fact, of any heinous offence, when a strong presumption of guilt exists. No negro charged with criminal assault upon a white woman ever has been acquitted. Hence, there is justification for the assertion that, so far as the white people are concerned, the impulse to indulge in mob brutalities arises from their low sense of accountability to law; that their lawlessness is the sequence of freedom from those restraints which obtain in law-abiding communities.

"Lynching is resorted to merely to appease and gratify an instinctive brutality on the part of a lawless element of the white race. No man can foresee the final result of such disorders. Nevertheless, it is evident that, if current individual usurpations of authority continue, all legal morality and social obedience will cease, our civilization will be erased, and barbaric methods will take the place of law and order. What the South needs is an enforcement of equitable law. Its mobs now exercise a tremendous discretionary power of such far-reaching consequences as should make men pause in their madness.

"The question has been raised again and again as to why the national government does not take cognizance of local disorders, and use its authority for the suppression of lynching. But one familiar with the genius of our social organism will readily understand that constitutional limitations effectually intervene. The Federal government is limited to national interests. It is inhibited from taking cognizance of the acts of individual citizens, except as they may become trespassers upon national rights. Under existing conditions, then, national functions can neither deal with white lawlessness nor cope with black criminals, and no enactment by the Congress of the United States touching this matter would have the slightest standing in the Federal judiciary. We do not doubt but that Congress has the constitutional right to enact a law for the trial and punishment of lynchers by United States Courts, when the victims of mob violence are aliens or non-resident citizens. In such cases the responsibility of the Federal government for individual protection seems to be established. On the other hand, the state is supreme within its own domain, and has full and complete control over its citizens. No writ or process of law can issue, and no action can be begun in a Federal court against a citizen of a state unless the plaintiff is a resident of another state, or unless the alleged offence was committed against the United States. Personal wrongs are to be corrected and personal rights defended by the state within whose jurisdiction cause of action lies. If that state will not act on the complaint of its citizens or is powerless to enforce its decrees, the individual sufferer has no relief, so long as public sentiment is against him."

Thomas continues along this line of argument, into which I do not care to further follow him, although I concur in much that he says; and while I am, of course, morally opposed to lynching, I fear that it will be practised in the "Black Belt" so long as the blacks remain in this country and continue to assault and murder our people,—this whether they are responsible for their nature and ignorance or not, and all the law to the contrary in so far as the mob is concerned.

Touching upon this point, Thomas continues: "We are concerned chiefly with the cause which instigates sectional lawlessness, and our message to Southern civilization is to exterminate by *law* its lawless white element; at the same time to *exterminate,* at all hazards and at any cost, the savage despoilers of maiden virtue or wifely honor, and do it so thoroughly that the inexorable, remorseless certitude of punishment will make the lives and persons of the women of the South as safe in field, forest, and public highway as in their private homes. Our interest in the public welfare has prompted us to draft a measure for the correction of these evils, and one which we are gratified to know has received the approval of many of the leading publicists of the country. Its chief merits are the adequate safeguarding of all the rights of accused persons, the infliction of a penalty that would effectually deter others from committing like crimes, and the removal of all incitement to lawless usurpation of authority or justified excuse for its exercise. The punishment which we suggest for persons convicted by due process of law of criminal assaults upon women is an untried remedy, and the most that can be urged against it is that a heinous crime has a harsh punishment. Nevertheless, in the present abnormal condition of public morality, a measure of this kind cannot do otherwise than exert a wholesome influence on white and black society.

"It is proposed that, when any male person of the age of fifteen or upward shall be charged with an attempt to commit an assault on a female person of any age or condition, with intent to violate her chastity and have carnal knowledge of her under duress and against her will, or upon the commission of such act, such person shall undergo an examination before a court of competent jurisdiction, and upon conviction thereof, by due process of law, shall undergo emasculation, and be further subjected to such restraint as the nature of the case and the welfare of the community justifies."

The propositions here made are too puerile to be worthy of sober consideration at my hands; they are simply idiotic and impossible. It would doubtless be a righteous thing, if it could be done, to emasculate the entire negro race in this country and effectually stop the breed right now, thus preventing any further danger from them and their crossing continually with the Anglo-Saxon stock; but would it prove an effectual remedy?

No! When a respectable white woman, in any plane of society, has been brutally assaulted and outraged by a negro, it will be of little satisfaction to her, or to any of her relatives, to know that the brutal raper had simply been operated upon by a surgeon. The fact that the bestial creature *lives* after he has accomplished the crime is what neither the woman herself, nor any of those who care for her and are connected with her, can possibly endure. If the emasculated brute is ever at large again, what is to prevent him from in time wreaking his vengeance upon that woman, or upon one of those who took part in his mutilation? Thomas's idea is simply ridiculous from whatever viewpoint we may regard it.

As an example of what women think upon this question, we quote an account of a lynching from *The New York Evening Journal*:—

"For the first time since the crime and its terrible sequel, Mrs. Labouisse, who was formerly Mrs. S. Osgood Pell, of New York, and who, before her marriage, was Miss Isabel Audrey Townsend, was able today to tell her story of the crime. She has been confined to her home in a high state of nervous excitement, but in consequence of the publicity that the affair has received, she made the following statement to the press:—

" 'I am glad that the negro was hanged,' she said; 'he deserved his fate. Until I knew that he was dead, I had no peace of mind. There was no mistake as to his identity or the crime that he attempted to commit.

" 'I went into the woods with my nurse-girl, Margaret, and my baby, to gather mushrooms. After a short time the young negro came to me and told me that my horse was loose. I told him to go get him, but the negro said that the horse would run away if a stranger approached him, and asked me to go with him. The nurse was suspicious and begged me not to go, but I laughed at her, for the man's manner was perfectly respectful. When we reached the horse, I saw that the traces were cut, and then we started back. Suddenly he stopped and asked what he was going to get for his work.

" 'Come to the house tomorrow,' I said, 'and Mr. Labouisse will reward you.'

" 'I don't want Mr. Labouisse,' he said, 'I want you!'

" 'As he said this the negro let go the bridle and turned toward me. I gathered up my skirts and dashed toward the road. He ran after me. I ran as fast as I could, but the thick brush and trees obstructed my passage.

" 'Suddenly my foot caught on something and I fell. Before I could rise the negro had caught me. The moment I felt his grasp upon me I screamed as loudly as I could. I must have been a long way from the nurse, for she did not hear me, or at all events did not come to my assistance. The negro still held me on the ground, and I was left alone to fight the desperado.

" 'He drew a large knife and, holding it to my throat, threatened to kill me if I did not cease screaming and struggling. It was, of course, impossible for me to stop, so he drew down the knife and poised it above my heart.

" 'Stop!' he cried, 'or I'll kill you!'

" 'How long we struggled after that I do not know, but I paid no heed to his threats and was strong enough to fight the wretch off. As soon as he went away, I hastened back to where I left baby and Margaret. The nurse became greatly excited and frightened when I told her.

" 'We had walked about three hundred yards when we came upon Louis Allen, an old negro, chopping wood with his two sons, about fifteen years old. He brought his wagon, drove us home, and then told the people what had occurred. When the negro was brought before me a short time afterwards, there was not the slightest doubt in my mind as to his identity. After I recognized him, the men took him away. I don't see how they could possibly have acted otherwise than they did.'

"As soon as the news of this crime became public, John H. Lang, a prominent real estate dealer, William Trautmen and S. M. Thornton drove out to the Adams house. They saw Sam sitting on the fence. As they approached he got down, passed through the house, and ran into the woods. He had one hundred yards start, and, after they had emptied a magazine rifle and a shot gun at him, he was halted and taken to the Labouisse house.

" 'When we got there,' said Mr. Lang, 'we took the negro before Mrs. Labouisse.

" 'Do you know this negro?' I asked.

" 'Yes,' she answered; 'he is the one who attacked me an hour ago.'

" 'Are you certain?' I asked her, for in Pass Christian we are not given to lynching the wrong man.

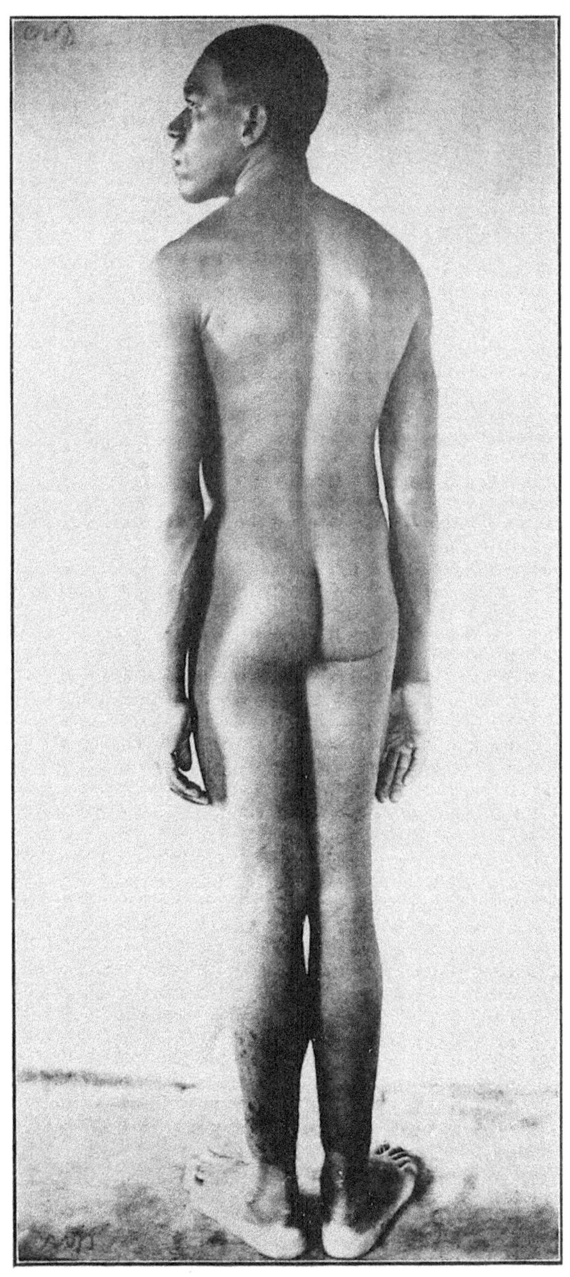

FIG. 41.—SAME SUBJECT AS SHOWN IN FIGS. 39 AND 40.

Photo from life by the author. Note the prognathous jaws, the length of the arms, and the comparatively slight development of the gluteal region.

" 'Yes,' replied Mrs. Labouisse; 'I am certain that is he.' Then she called out her nurse and old man Allen. They identified him, too. Mrs. Labouisse lost control of herself.

" 'Let me kill him! Oh, let me kill that negro brute!' she cried in a terrible voice that we who heard it shall never forget. We hurried Adams away toward the jail, and the servants calmed Mrs. Labouisse.

"A meeting was called at the Knights of Honor hall, in Pass Christian, and Adams was sentenced to death. The constable was advised by others to get Adams out of the county that night, and it was while he was being taken away that he was captured and strung up. When the rope was thrown around his neck, a voice said: 'Adams, you have ten minutes in which to pray and repent.'

" 'I don't want to pray none,' said the doomed man.

"For five minutes everybody waited, and then the same voice asked again: 'What have you to say before you die?'

"Adams shifted his weight lazily from one leg to the other. By the light of a single lantern in the midst of a tragic group his face could be clearly discerned. His black forehead drew itself into a frown, as if he were thinking. Suddenly his face cleared, as if he had found what he had sought.

" 'Ah wish,' he said, 'that when you all gets through with me you'd jes' give my shoes to my pa!'

"And with this anticlimax, the negro was hanged."

Does anyone for a moment suppose, even in the event of emasculation rendering this negro impotent, that it would have a particle of influence in deterring other ignorant negroes, who would never hear of this case, from doing likewise?

With the surgeon's knife actually pressing upon him; with the blazing fagots so near him that he could actually feel the heat, he would nevertheless seize his victim if it lay within his power to do so. Ninety-nine times out of a hundred cases, similar to the one just quoted, the negro, having gotten his nearly exhausted victim down, and by threats with his murderous knife deprived her of nearly all her remaining strength for struggling with a brute of many times her vigor, would in the end compel her to yield. And in the case of any chaste woman, if she survived the terrors of the shock, the injuries inflicted, the shame, and other feelings more easily imagined than described, she would very naturally demand that her assaulter be deprived of his life at once, so she would at least have the satisfaction of not running the risk of ever seeing him again.

Some Views and Opinions by the Way.

It is remarkable to hear these negroes and their hybrids express their views upon the future of the negro in the United States and to hear the arrogant opinions they entertain. Well do I remember listening to G. W. Murray addressing the House of Congress when he was a Congressman. It was a deplorable sight to see a man of that kind sitting there and having the right to help frame the laws for the United States. Here is what that negro thought of his race and its future some twenty years ago. I take it from *The Evening Star* of Washington, D. C., October 29, 1893. [This is the view of a full-blood negro, a quarter of a century ago, or rather less] :—

"The only colored man in Congress comes from South Carolina. His name is George Washington Murray, and he represents 216,000 people. His district is the famous black district, which was represented by Gen. Robt. Smalls, and it is the biggest negro district of the Union. It is two hundred miles long, and it winds in and out like a snake, scalloping the Atlantic coast and cutting the State of South Carolina like a saw. It is the district set aside by the whites of that State for colored representation. It contains few towns, and only one-fifth of its population is white.

"There is no question about Geo. W. Murray's ancestry. Every feature of his cannon-ball head is modeled on African lines. His complexion is that of the ace of spades, and his features are of the pronounced negro type. He is by no means a bad-looking colored man. He stands about five feet eight inches in his stockings, and is broad-shouldered and strong-limbed. He has shown himself to be a man of nerve, and a politician of shrewdness. He talks well, but butchers the king's English in many of his sentences. He has had to fight for all that he has, and his education has been acquired in almost as remarkable a way as was that of Fred Douglass. I had a talk with him last night about himself and questions relating to his race. I first asked him as to his history. Murray replied: 'I was born in the district in which I live, just about forty years ago. My parents were slaves, and when Abraham Lincoln freed the negroes I was just eleven years old. I had no money and no one to take care of me, but I decided at that time that I would have an education and went at it. I learned my A, B, C's by asking other children, who went to school, what the letters were, and by practicing on every person whom I met I finally learned to read and write. I studied as best I could until I became able to read the newspapers, and I know that I could stumble my way through a congressional speech when I was fifteen. It was about this time that Geo. S. Boutwell, a Congressman from Maine or Massachusetts, made a speech, which I read. It made a great impression upon me, and I can quote one sentence from it now. It was on the Southern question, and I think it read as follows: "I know that there is pro-slavery desire and always has been and always will be until we, the Republican party, grind it into powder, trample it under foot, and freedom blows the dust out with the healing of her wings." This sentence made an impression on me, and I probably read it to some of our people, as the colored boys who could read always read the papers to others. Well, in this way I learned to read and write. Arithmetic always came easy to me, and I could figure out sums in my head long before I knew how to make the figures. When I was eighteen years old I had so far progressed that I began to teach school, and the first school I ever entered was as a teacher and not as pupil. After teaching several years I went to the University of South Carolina, and remained there at school until the government of the State prohibited the coeducation of the races and forced me out. I then went back to teach in the public schools, and was engaged in teaching and farming until I was elected to Congress.

" 'The negro naturally wants a farm of his own, and my people are buying lands on time and are improving them. Some of them own farms of from one to two thousand acres, and there is a colored man in Washington today who farms seven thousand acres of land in Georgia. He owns more than this, but he has this amount under cultivation. I own a little farm of my own, and there are thousands of colored men in the South who own land. We are advancing right along in the accumulation of property, and the time will come when our people will be a commercial and business factor in the United States. I believe that our success depends upon our education and enrichment, and I look for the time when the negro will stand even with the white man as a property owner.'

"How about property rights in the South? Are those of the colored people respected?

" 'Yes, I think so,' was the reply. 'The Southerners are anxious that the negroes should own property, and they encourage them to save and invest their money. They treat them fairly so far as any of these things are concerned, but they do not give them a fair show in a political way.'

"How about the Ku-Klux?

" 'There are no Ku-Klux in the South, and there is very little terror arising at the polls. The whites are able to accomplish their ends without the use of shotguns. They don't need them.'

"How about the feeling between the negroes and the whites; will there ever be a war between the two races?

" 'I think not. The negroes appreciate the fact that such a war would result in their destruction, and the fight that they intend to make is along business and educational lines. We propose to educate ourselves and to save our money, and when we become the equals of the whites in property and in business you will see that we have better recognition.'

"Do you think that the negro is the equal of the white in natural ability?

" 'I do,' replied the African Congressman; 'history has shown that the sons of Ham are as strong as the sons of Shem and Japhet in every way. It was once thought that the negro could not advance in learning beyond a certain point, but the colleges know that the negro is the equal of the white, and, in many cases, superior. I think that we will gradually equal and eventually distance the whites. The reason for this is that we have got to start from the bottom. We have nothing, and we must fight for every inch. We are very ambitious, and we will not stop until we get to the top.'

"What will be the future of the two races? Will the negro ever unite with the whites?

" 'I believe,' said Mr. Murray, 'that there will eventually be a mixed race in this country, made up of negro and white blood. When the negro becomes rich and educated the objection to him will wear away, and there will be intermarriage between the two races. At present the negro has no objections to such marriages. They think that the only ground of marriage should be that of love. The objection comes from the whites, and this will disappear as the negro equals them in property and other things.'

"Do not a large number of your people object to colored men marrying white women? You remember the howl of indignation that went up from the colored people of this country when Fred Douglass married a white woman.

" 'Yes,' replied Mr. Murray, 'I do, and the indignation against Mr. Douglass was so strong because he, to a large extent, represented the colored people of the United States, and the fact that he married a woman of white blood was considered by our people a slap at the women of his own race. They thought it meant that he could not find a colored woman good enough for him, and hence had to take a white one.'

"How about negro colonization, Mr. Murray? Will such schemes ever succeed?

" 'No,' was the reply. 'The negroes have never been in favor of such colonization, nor have such schemes ever been engineered by people who have not wanted to make money out of it. There was a movement about fifteen years ago to take the colored people to Kansas, and there have been propositions to send them to Brazil and other places. The negroes are in the United States to stay, and if they could have free transportation to Liberia, or to Africa, they would not take it. I do not think the people of the South want to get rid of the negro, and I think if we are let alone that we will work out our destiny to the satisfaction of every one.'

"Speaking of the future of the colored race, Fred Douglass is one of those who believe that the two races will eventually come together. He says that the color line will eventually be obliterated, and that the only salvation for the negro is in union with the white. Douglass is about three-fourths colored himself, and his second wife is as white as any woman in the United States. She was his private secretary when he married her, and is, I am told, very fond of her husband. She is twenty years younger than he, and lives with her husband near Washington. Fred Douglass is rich. He is said to be worth in the neighborhood of 200,000 dollars. He got $7000 as marshal of the district, and he has for a long time received $100 a night for his lectures. His books have paid him well, and he has so invested his money as to be well fixed. He is now seventy-six years old, and he has failed within the last three or four years. He has lost weight and strength, but intellectually he is now as strong as ever, and his last letter in reply to Senator Ingalls was as strong a paper as he has ever written.

FIG. 42.—PAN KOOLOO-KAMBA. (Du Chaillu.)

(By the author, after D. G. Elliot: "A Review of the Primates," vol. iii, Pl. VIII.)

"I saw Blanche K. Bruce on the floor of the U. S. Senate the other day. He looks hardly a day older than when he walked up to be sworn in on the arm of Roscoe Conkling. He is now devoting his time to his estate in Mississippi, and to lecturing. He has made money in both pursuits, and he told me not long ago that he was dividing up his Mississippi property into small farms, and was selling it on installments to the colored people. He has built a church and school-house on the plantation, and he believes, with Mr. Murray, that the future of the negro lies in his education and in the accumulation of property.

"Ex-Senator Bruce now lives in Washington, in a fashionable part of the northwest. His wife is a beautiful woman, nearly as white in complexion as many of our Washington society ladies. He met her while the two were at college together at Oberlin. He married her while he was in the Senate, and the event was one of two senatorial weddings which took place at Cleveland, Ohio, one summer. Mrs. Bruce was a teacher in one of the Cleveland public schools. She had been very well educated, and she is, in fact, as accomplished a lady as you will find anywhere. She dresses well, looks well, and has great natural refinement. The last time I saw her was at one of Clara Barton's receptions, and she was assisting Miss Barton to receive her guests."

Before this contribution appeared in *The Star,* United States Senator John J. Ingalls had published a long article on this subject in *The Chicago Tribune,* May 28, 1893. The article was entitled: "Always a Problem," and Senator Ingalls sent me a marked copy of the same inviting my attention to it. I very much regret that the contribution is too long to incorporate in this place, as it is pregnant with valuable facts on the history of the African negro in America. Senator Ingalls, however, did not believe that race union would ever take place, and in the aforesaid article said:—

"Frederick Douglass is perhaps the widest known and most distinguished representative of the negro race. He is an eloquent, accomplished, and dignified gentleman. His father was a white man and his mother a slave. It is perhaps not invidious nor uncivil to affirm that the distinction of Douglass is not on account of his African blood, but in spite of it. The intellectual traits, qualities, and characteristics which have given him renown are due to his Anglo-Saxon reënforcement. He once said to me that he believed the white and black races were not inherent but causal, and that there was a temporary prejudice that would be obliterated, so that they would eventually coalesce and the race question thus be effaced and disappear. There are no indications at present that this prophecy will be verified. Instead of vanishing, the repugnance appears to be more distinct and emphatic. Mr. Douglass bravely acted upon his theory, but his example has not been followed nor seriously approved.

"Whether justly or unjustly, African blood is regarded by the Caucasian as a taint to be abhorred. The discovery of an unsuspected negro strain by the heroine is the tragic motive of one of Howell's most powerful novels. Whether this sense of degradation is peculiar to Americans and due to slavery is disputed. Certainly the revulsion in Europe is not so marked as here, but in the most cosmopolitan capitals the negro is not *persona grata*. Black is not a badge of inferiority, because Cubans, Brazilians, Spaniards, and Hindoos are of dusky hue; but the African is not considered an equal or kindred race. No white man ever wanted to be a negro. Probably every educated and intelligent negro would prefer to be white.

"That the condition of the African has been improved in many respects by freedom and education needs no arguments; but his progress has been toward segregation. The great gulf fixed between the two races has widened and deepened since emancipation. As dependents and subordinates the blacks were associates of the whites. As political equals they are strangers. Their children are no longer playmates. They are taught in separate schools; they worship in separate churches; they are buried in separate cemeteries. If possible, the barrier is more insuperable at the North than at the South, and the proscription more contemptuous and intolerant. Wherever the negro appears in considerable numbers, the irritation is violent. Their settlement in any locality depresses the value of real estate and repels white occupation. Immigrants avoid contact with them and shun the South as an infected region. Places of trust, honor, and emolument are shut against them inexorably. With confessed majorities in many districts, and the balance of power in others, they have no positions of high rank in the State or National government. Although more than two hundred thousand enlisted in the Union armies, no full-blooded negro holds a commission in the army or navy, and in the militia their organization is distinct. The learned professions, business, commerce, and manufactures are open to all, but except with his own people the African has no function. His occupations are menial. In their employments he finds toleration and is content. The rights and communities conferred by the three constitutional amendments have given him no protection against the stronger edict of public opinion. Surrounded by opportunities which he cannot share, and by advantages from which he is excluded, the future offers no prospect of release from a bondage whose imperceptible manacles are forged and riveted by the tyranny of nature."

Much of what Senator Ingalls says, in what I have just quoted from him, has been entirely reversed in recent times in this country. Through juggling with politics, and receiving the advantages bestowed by politicians for political ends, some few negroes in the country and a large number of bastards or those descended from bastards (or half-bloods born out of wedlock, of negro mothers by white men) have been placed in all sorts of positions, from the Assistant Attorney General of the United States, down to a corporal in the army.

As an incident of our "negro problem," of the very highest significance, I cite the following account from *The Washington Times* of Thursday, November 12, 1914 (pp. 1 and 2), and it appeared in hundreds of other newspapers in all parts of the country. It is the most extraordinary attempt to blackmail the President of the United States that ever occurred at the White House, and a superb example of the aspirations of the modernized mulattoes and negroes in the United States at the present time. This incident is so full of significance and importance for the future, that I publish *The Times* account in full, omitting only the unessential headlines and comments. It runs as follows:—

"Warm words passed today between President Wilson and a delegation of colored men, who called at the White House to protest against the continuation of segregation at the Treasury and other departments of the Federal Government.

"Declaring that never since he has been in office has he been addressed in such an insulting fashion, the President told William Monroe Trotter, of Boston, a colored man, secretary of the National Independence Equal Rights League, that if ever again he consented to receive representatives of the league, that body would have to select another spokesman.

"The delegation will hold a mass meeting at the Asbury Methodist Episcopal Church here next Sunday, to protest against what the members declared on leaving the White House, was an 'entirely disappointing' expression from the President as to his position on the matter.

"The delegation is the same which sought unsuccessfully before the recent elections to see the President, and then threatened to advise all colord voters of the country to vote against the Democratic ticket.

"The President granted the delegation fifteen minutes for the interview; but these uncultured negroes knew no better than to extend the time to a full hour, keeping the Secretary of Commerce and others waiting outside for them to end their 'talk.'

"In the meantime, the members of the delegation, after delivering their set speeches and hearing the

President's reply, attempted to cross-examine him. He answered several of the questions put to him by the secretary of the league; but as these grew more objectionable in character, the President showed his indignation.

"Previously, however, he had told the delegation that, while he believed that segregation in the departments was for the best interests of both races, in order to overcome racial friction, and wished in every way to assist the colored race toward its independent development, he would investigate any individual cases of discrimination which they might, from time to time, present to him.

"The President refused to regard the matter from a political standpoint, and indicated his indifference toward the previously conveyed threats of the league that it would oppose all Democratic candidates in the future. The problem, he declared, was a human one, and one which the best thought of the Administration had decided to be best solved by segregation, but segregation under such circumstances that the colored civil-service employees would have equal advantages in the way of working conditions.

" 'What the President told us,' said Secretary Trotter, as he left the White House, 'was entirely disappointing. His statement that segregation was intended to prevent racial friction is not supported by facts. For fifty years colored and white employees had worked together. It was not until the present Administration came in that segregation was drastically introduced, and only because of the racial prejudices of John Skelton Williams, Secretary McAdoo, and Secretary Burleson.

" 'It was a warm session, boys,' declared Trotter, winking his eye at the newspaper men as he left the White House.

"Others in the delegation included the Rev. Byron Gunner, of Hillburn, N. Y., president of the league; Thomas Walker, chairman of the Washington branch of the league; M. W. Spencer, of Wilmington; the Rev. E. E. Ricks, pastor of the First Baptist Church of West Washington, and F. Morris Murray, of Virginia, all colored.

"Addresses were made by Trotter, Gunner, Walker, and Spencer, although the principal and, from the President's standpoint, the only objectionable remarks were uttered by Trotter.

"They presented copies of resolutions adopted by the Massachusetts legislature, and letters from Congressmen Thatcher, Mitchell and Gallivan, of Massachusetts, all Democrats, protesting against the separation of the races in the Government service.

"Trotter told the President that segregation 'means a charge by the Government of physical indecency.'

"He declared that the public was so against the Administration because of its attitude on segregation that the voters protested at the last election.

"President Wilson expressed great regret that the colored men should consider such a question a political one, and he practically told them that if the colored race was dissatisfied with what his Administration was doing, they could register their disapproval at the next election.

"The President pointed out to the delegation that the race is making progress in the United States, and that it should not consider segregation here in other than a friendly light.

"The delegates protested specifically against segregation in the Treasury and Postoffice Departments.

"Mr. Trotter's speech to the President follows:—

" 'One year ago we presented a national petition signed by colored Americans in thirty-eight States, protesting against the segregation of employees of the National Government whose ancestry could be traced in whole or in part to Africa, as instituted under your Administration in the Treasury and Postoffice Departments. We then appealed to you to undo this racial segregation in accord with your duty as President and with your pre-election pledges. We stated that there could be no freedom, no respect from others, and no equality of citizenship under segregation for race, especially when applied to but one of the many racial elements in Government employ. For such placement of employees means a charge by the Government of physical indecency or infection, or of being a lower order of things, or a subjection to the prejudices of other citizens, which constitutes inferiority of status. We protested such segregation as to working positions, eating tables, dressing rooms, rest rooms, lockers, and especially public toilets in Government buildings. We stated that such segregation was a public humiliation and degradation, entirely unmerited and far-reaching in its injurious effects, a gratuitous blow against ever-loyal citizens, and against those, many of whom aided and supported your elevation to the presidency of our common country.

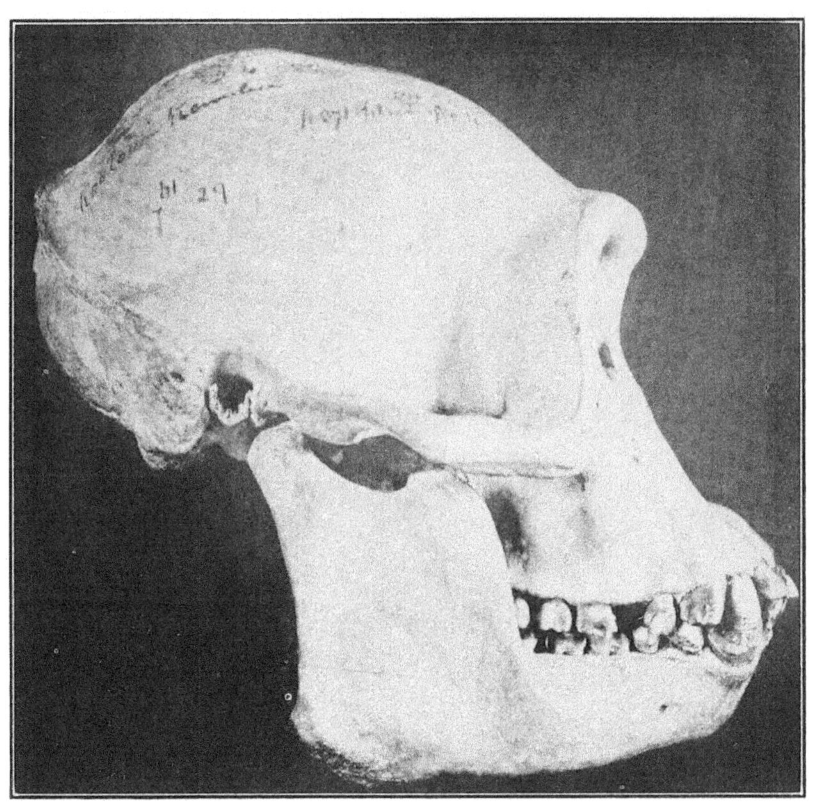

Fig. 43.—Right Lateral View of the Skull of Pan Kooloo-Kamba (Reduced about one-third.)

By the author, after D. G. Elliot. ("A Review of the Primates," vol. iii, Pl. XXXVI.) Possesses the prognathous jaws as in many negroes.

" 'At that time you stated you would investigate conditions for yourself. Now, after the lapse of a year, we have come back, having found that all the reforms of segregation of Government employees of African extraction are still practised in the Treasury and Postoffice Department buildings, and to a certain extent have spread into other Government buildings.

" 'Under the Treasury, in the Bureau of Engraving and Printing, separation not only in the dressing rooms but in working positions, Afro-American employees being herded at separate tables, at eating tables and in toilets; in the Navy Department there is herding at desks and separation in lavatories; in the Postoffice Department there is separation in work for colored women in the alcove on the eighth floor, of colored men in rooms on the seventh floor, with forbidding of entrance even into an adjoining room occupied by white clerks on the seventh floor, and of colored men in separate rooms, just instituted on sixth floor, with separate lavatories for colored men on the eighth floor; in the main Treasury building in separate lavatories in the basement; in the Interior Department, separate lavatories, which were specifically pointed out to you at our first hearing; in the State and other departments in separate lavatories; in Marine Hospital service building, in separate lavatories, though there is but one Afro-American clerk to use it; in the War Department, in separate lavatories; in the Postoffice Department building, separate lavatories; in the sewing and bindery divisions of the Government Printing Office on the fifth floor, there is herding at working positions of colored women and separation in lavatories, and new segregation instituted

12

by the division chief since our first audience with you. This lavatory segregation is the most degrading, most insulting of all. Colored employees who use the regular public lavatories on the floors where they work are cautioned and are then warned by superior officers against insubordination.

" 'We have come by vote of this league to set before you this definite continuance of race segregation, and to renew the protest and to ask you to abolish segregation of Afro-American employees in the Executive Department.

" 'Because we cannot believe you capable of any disregard of your pledges, we have been sent by the alarmed American citizens of color. They realize that, if they can be segregated and thus humiliated by the National Government at the National Capital, the beginning is made for the spread of that persecution and prosecution which makes property and life itself insecure in the South; the foundation of the whole fabric of their citizenship is unsettled.

" 'They have made plain enough to you their opposition to segregation last year by a national anti-segregation petition, this year by a protest registered at the polls, voting against every Democratic candidate save those outspoken against segregation. The only Democrat elected governor in the Eastern States was Governor Walsh, of Massachusetts, who appealed to you by letter to stop segregation. Thus have colored Americans shown how they detest segregation.

" 'In fact, so intense is their resentment that the movement to divide this solid race vote and make peace with the national Democracy, so suspiciously revied [sic] when you ran for Presidency, and which some of our families for two generations have been risking all to promote, bids fair to be undone.

" 'Only two years ago you were heralded as perhaps the second Lincoln, and now the colored leaders who supported you are hounded as false leaders and traitors to their race. What a change segregation has wrought!

" 'You said that your "Colored fellow citizens could depend upon you for everything which would assist in advancing the interests of their race in the United States." Consider that pledge in the face of the continued color segregation! Fellow-citizenship means congregation; segregation destroys fellowship and citizenship. Consider that any passerby on the streets of the National Capital, whether he be black, can enter and use the public lavatories in Government buildings, while citizens of color who do the work of the Government are excluded.

" 'As equal citizens and by virtue of your public promises, we are entitled at your hands to freedom from discrimination, restriction, imputation, and insult for race in Government employ. Have you a "new freedom" for white Americans and a new slavery for your "colored fellow-citizens?" God forbid!

" 'We have been delegated to ask you to issue an executive order against any and all segregation of Government employees because of race and color, and to ask whether you will do so. We await your reply in that we may give it to the waiting citizens of the United States of African extraction.' "

The Washington Post next morning (Nov. 13, 1914) gave the matter almost a column in fine print, and stated that during the interview the President said, addressing himself to Trotter, the negro spokesman, "that he (Trotter) was the only American citizen who had ever come into the White House and addressed the President in such a tone and with such a background of passion."

The ill-mannered negro then brought in something in regard to votes, etc., whereupon "This mention of votes caused the President to say that politics must be left out, because it was a form of blackmail. He said he would resent it as quickly from one set of men as from another, and that his auditors could vote as they pleased; it mattered little."

The next day (Sunday, Nov. 15, 1914) an immense mass meeting of negroes took place at the Second Baptist Church. W. Monroe Trotter was the chief speaker, and he, negro-like, denied that he had been insulting or impertinent to the President, implying that the President did not know what he was talking about! Then, continuing his address, he declared, in strong Afro-American terms (not American) that "For the first time in history a President had pronounced his Administration's policy as one of racial discrimination. Our delegation wanted him to stop departmental segregation or say where he stood. Now, at last, after two years' silence, he has told."

It is not necessary for me to comment upon what is so clearly set forth between the lines. In fact, this negro's previously prepared address to President Wilson was an open insult from start to finish; threatening, and pregnant with blackmail from one end of it to the other.

Negroes and half-bloods in other parts of the

country immediately took up the cudgel and rushed into such papers as would print their grievances; for instance, in holding forth in the *New York World* on "The Colored Vote," Alexander Walters, President of the "National Colored Democratic League" (New York, Nov. 14, 1914), takes occasion to make an exhibition, negro-fashion, of his particular brand of Ethiopian political astuteness and says: "More than a half-million negroes are voting today, and they too must certainly be a factor in the defeat of the Democratic party this year, for nearly all of them voted the Republican ticket."

This negro seems to be quite oblivious of the fact that probably half of these voters were half-bloods and not "negroes," and that negro votes, in most districts where the voting takes place, can be purchased by the score at the price of a drink of whiskey or a twenty-five cent piece; this I have witnessed with my own eyes in Maryland. Further, this negro seems to be crassly ignorant of the fact that American politics are not a species of jugglery and a privilege, the sole use of which is for blackmailing purposes or to simply defeat the opposing party. He continues by saying: "Is it not time that our Democratic friends be awakened to the fact that the black man is a factor in American politics?" A question which most properly may be answered in Irish fashion by another question, to wit: Is it not time that the American people were awakened to the fact that the black man, with all his history, should not only cease to be a factor in American politics, but that, for the welfare of this American people, he be, with his entire race, removed to some other quarter of the globe?

This negro terminates his howl in the *New York World* thus: "Another thing which has caused us to be discredited in the eyes of the world is, that out of this ten million colored citizens, not one is invited to a social function in the White House, and in this said-to-be the greatest democracy in the world! No wonder that America throughout the world is branded as a nation of Hypocrites."

Did one ever? And I wonder if this particular negro has it in him to be made to see *the* reason why pure-strain negro men and women are not "invited to social functions at the White House?" I fear not—any more than he can be made to see that such part of our *American* population as is composed of the highest elements of the Anglo-Saxon race, or its pure-strain descendants, are not "branded as a nation of hypocrites;" but that, on the other hand, thinking and observing people of broad minds and intelligence all over the world know only too well that we have a racial canker-worm gnawing at our vitals: the imported African negroes, and the race of half-bloods they have given rise to in this country. It is these "Afro-Americans" that would have their "uplifted," illegitimate descendants, born of wenches out of wedlock, foisted upon the "social functions at the White House," and placed in the most important governmental positions within the power of the President of the United States. It is the presence of *this* stock among us that is rapidly bringing our country into discredit and worse! The time is now surely at hand when this Alexander Walters can with profit discuss with William Monroe Trotter some of the reasons why negroes are not admitted to the "social functions at the White House;" even a half-blood might catch the idea here.

This entire incident is now past history, but it goes to show the exact attitude of the negroes and mulattoes in our midst on the question of their social and general standing in the country. As they become more numerous, and come into power through their increased numbers, they intend, *nolens volens,*—in so far as we are concerned,—to force themselves into American society *everywhere,* from the simplest of social gatherings to functions of all kinds in the Government, from the White House, down.

It is now a thoroughly established fact that these negroes are so dense mentally that they cannot appreciate their position, nor see that they are *not wanted. Any other* race, under such conditions, would gather up its belongings, emigrate to some other part of the world, and set up a government of its own.

Passing from this significant incident to other matters to be touched upon in this chapter, I may say that, very recently (November, 1914), I have communicated with many influential people in this country in regard to all possible aspects of the so-called "negro problem," and I have read extensively on the subject, including the best literature touching it during the past ten years or more. Some important correspondence has come to me of a similar racial problem in certain parts of Africa; but the discussion of this would be of but little value as throwing any serviceable light on what we have to deal with here. The conditions are, essentially, quite different,—those in the parts of Africa to which I refer being associated with the matter of labor, while here it is largely a social question, and one of miscegenation.

With respect to the question of expatriation or enforced removal of the negroes in the United States to some other country, I have not, up to the present time, put myself in communication with the heads of any government, which might be willing to have them come as colonists, as this is a question better handled *after* the present volume has appeared and been considered by the American public. However, in the next chapter I shall take up some of the initial features of this solution, and present some views upon it as have very recently come before me.

As Professor Franz Boas, of Columbia University—an eminent anthropologist—was known to me, I wrote him for a brief letter to publish in this chapter, on his recent studies of the negro. Unfortunately, he could not comply with my request for the reason, as he states in his courteous letter of September 29, 1914, that "I am afraid that you would not wish to include an expression of my opinion in your book, because I am not at all convinced that the miscegenation of races is a bad thing from a biological point of view. I know, of course, that half-bloods always grow up under very unfavorable circumstances, and for this reason are seldom up to the mark."

Such an opinion cannot possibly stand in the light of modern biology,—that is, when applied to the pure negro and the *white* races of the world. In the admixture, the higher race is sure to suffer in every possible way, while the half-bloods offer very unstable improvement or worse.

Doctor Josiah Morse, to whom I have also written,

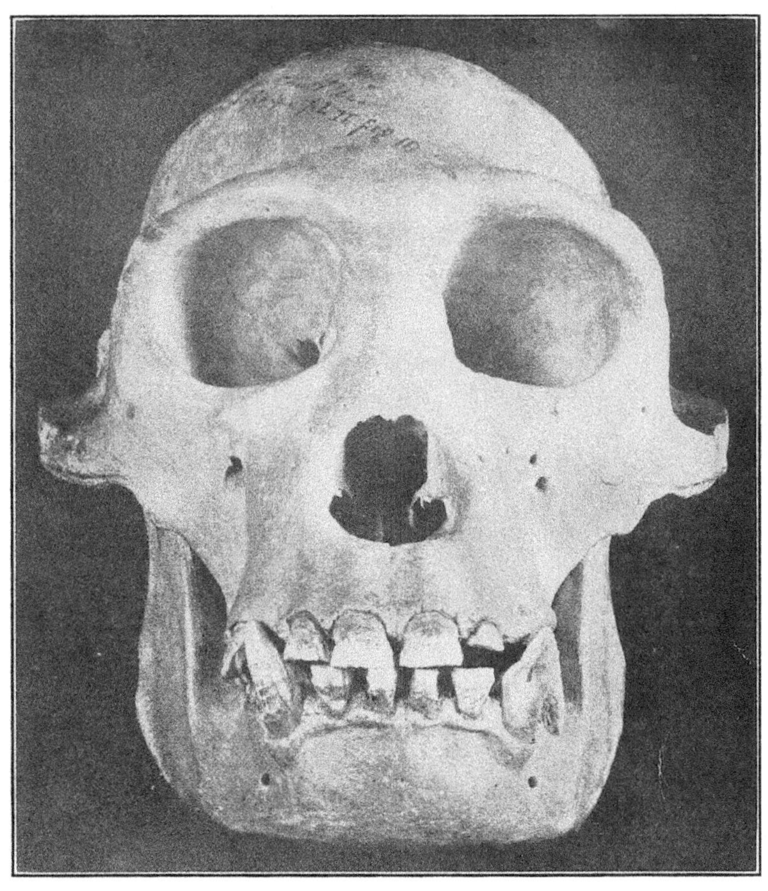

Fig. 44.—Same Skull as Shown in Fig. 43. (Anterior view; reduction the same.)

By the author, after Elliot. Note the highly developed supra-orbital ridges as in many negroes. Compare with Fig. 19.

has recently thrown some light on this point in his researches. The following quotation from *The Literary Digest* (Jan. 17, 1914), will make this sufficiently clear, and the reader will meet with no trouble in consulting the doctor's other papers on the subject elsewhere:—

"Is the negro race less intelligent than the white? Le Bon, the French psychologist, says that the two races are forever separated by a 'mental abyss,' while Boaz, the American ethnologist, sees no essential mental difference between them. Interesting tests of white and colored children in Columba, S. C., made by Dr. Josiah Morse, of the University of South Carolina, with the aid of what is known as Binet's 'scale of intelligence,' are described by the author in *The Popular Science Monthly* (New York, January). The results are somewhat unsatisfactory, altho interesting. So far as it is possible to select white and colored children from the same 'walks of life,' the former seem to be more intelligent, but 'poor white' children from the mills come out almost as badly in the test as the colored children, which does not look as if race had much to do with it. 'The Binet scale,' it will be remembered, is a set of simple questions and commands, classified by their adaptation to children of six to twelve years. The 'mental age' of the child is determined by the highest group of tests that he can pass successfully, only one failure being permitted. But if he can pass five tests in various higher groups, he has an additional year's credit. Comparison of mental age, thus determined, with the real age shows whether, and in what degree, a child is backward or forward. Says Professor Morse:—

" 'The same tests were given to both the white and colored children under practically uniform conditions, with the exception that some of the colored children tested were older than twelve years. The course of study in the colored school, which is a part of the public-school system, is essentially the same as in the white schools, and the quality of teaching is good. The children seemed to be at ease in the presence of the white examiner, and to do their best. No marked variation from the white children in the manner of responding could be noted. In almost every case the dress, cleanliness, and manners of the children indicated that they came from good homes. The replies were usually couched in fewer words than those of the white children. There was less tendency to enter into conversation, and it was soon found that they were more at ease when reacting to the tests than when an attempt was made to talk with them about other things. . . .

" 'The results of the investigation upon the white and colored children may be briefly summarized as follows:—

	Colored. Per cent.	White. Per cent.
More than one year backward	29.4	10.1
Satisfactory	69.8	84.4
More than one year advanced	0.8	5.3

" 'The number of white children testing at age is decidedly larger than any other group, whereas for colored children the largest group is the one testing one year below age. In the satisfactory group there is a difference of nearly 15 per cent. between the white and colored; nearly three times as many colored are more than a year backward, and less than 1 per cent. are more than a year advanced.

" 'The picture tests gave the colored children considerable trouble, probably due to difference in racial esthetics. The tests relating to time and money, distinguishing between morning and afternoon, enumerating the months, counting stamps, and making change, the drawing tests, both copying and reproducing from memory, were all too difficult. The answers to the questions of comprehension, to the absurd statements and to the problems of various facts, were often absurd or senseless; the best replies, however, compare very favorably with those of the white children. The definitions were often not better than terms of use, and frequently stated in the language of a younger child.

" 'In general, it may be said that the colored children excel in rote memory, *e.g.*, in counting, repeating digits (but not one was able to repeat twenty-six syllables), naming words, making rimes, and in time orientation. They are inferior to the whites, however, in esthetic judgment, observation, reasoning, motor control, logical memory, use of words, resistance to suggestion, and in orientation or adjustment to the institutions and complexities of civilized society.

" 'To what extent these differences are due to difference in racial intellectual ability, and how much to environmental influences, difference in physiological age, or other subtle factors, cannot be dogmatically stated. They are certainly not due to difference in school training. In order, therefore, to make the comparisons as just as possible, and at the same time ascertain the extent of the influence of environment, the white children were divided into two groups—city children and mill children. The economic, educational, and environmental conditions of the cotton-mill children are but little, if any, better than those of the colored children. The results of the comparison showed that the proportion of colored children who are satisfactory is less than that of the mill children, which in turn is less than that of the city children. Less than 6 per cent. of the city children are more than a year backward, 18 per cent. of the mill children, and 26 per cent. of the colored children. None of either the mill or colored children test more than one year above age, while 10 per cent. of the city children do. . . .

" 'Another table of statistics showed that the colored children made a better showing in the first five grades than in the first seven, but their inferiority to the whites existed throughout the school years, contrary to the widespread opinion that colored children are as well, if not better, endowed during the first school years. Again, according to the Binet scale, a larger number of white children are in a school grade below their mental ability than above, whereas the reverse is true of the colored children. A rough classification into three groups, according to color—dark, medium, light—showed that the darkest children are more nearly normal; the lightest show the greatest variation, both above and below normal.'

"The limitations of the study are freely admitted by Dr. Morse, who considers it but a crude beginning of a subject that will soon be opened up and made to yield interesting and profitable data. He comments:

" 'It need not be pointed out what radical changes

would have to take place in our educational theory and practice, as well as in our social philosophy, if it could be shown conclusively that races differ in mental capacity and aptitude just as they do in physical appearance. No final conclusions, however, are here offered, nor is any attempt made to settle once and for all the question of race superiority or inferiority. That requires investigation along many lines hardly opened up as yet. But this much we may surely conclude from the above study: that negro children from six to twelve and possibly fifteen years are mentally different, and also younger than Southern white children of corresponding ages, and that this condition is partly due, at least, to causes that are native or racial. That is, if MM. Binet and Simon had originally tested Southern negro children they would have worked out from the results a scale which would have been different from their present one in several respects, and which, when applied to Southern white children, would be found to be, for the most part, a year or more too young, tho possibly there would be some tests which would yield the opposite results.

" 'Perhaps some day each branch of the human family will have a Binet scale of its own. Then, by a wholesale interchange of tests, as we do now with professors, it will be possible to determine wherein a given people are proficient and wherein deficient; and later, perhaps, by adding co-efficients and credits, to settle mooted questions of racial rank. But this again belongs to the realm of speculation.

" 'Probably the point of greatest value brought out by this study is that perchance a key has been found in the Binet scale which will prove of the greatest service in the solution of problems in contemporary folk-psychology and race and social adjustment. Certain it is that these important human problems need the spirit, methods, and instruments of science applied to them. The Binet scale is the first instrument that has appeared.' "

Surely, in the light of Binet's "scale of intelligence," would any intelligent and well-read American on the subject favor the miscegenation which is now so rapidly going on in this country between the negroes and certain classes of the white population?

In regard to what Dr. Morse says on the subject of the limitations of the study of this negro problem as a whole, I have received the following contribution from Doctor James Bardin, of the University of Virginia, kindly prepared especially for this work:—

"One of the most striking things to be noted in the scientific circles of North America is the indifference of scientific investigators to the negro problem. The mere presence of the negro in this country offers a truly exceptional and, in some ways, extraordinary opportunity to study the problem of race from every angle. The problem in the South is one of extreme acuteness and importance, and any light that can be thrown upon it will be welcomed by all who are trying to do something practical toward ameliorating the situation. Throughout the entire world, race problems were never more prominent than at the present moment. Yet American scientists are doing practically nothing toward elucidating the one great race problem that they have constantly before them, despite the fact that by studying it and finding out just what it really is, they could illuminate indirectly practically all the problems growing out of race throughout the world.

"The sociologists, economists, historians, and religious workers are putting forth their best efforts in their respective fields to obtain accurate information about the relationships of the negro and white races to each other; in the South, a really tremendous amount of work of this sort is being done. These men realize that here at home they have a sort of gigantic laboratory in which can be observed the innumerable reactions resulting from a juxtaposition of dissimilar peoples. But the men who are devoting themselves to those sciences having a more or less biological basis are, on the contrary, doing nothing. This is particularly to be regretted, since from a biological point of view almost nothing is with certainty known about race. In one of the most recent works dealing with anthropology the following statement occurs, and sums up very adequately the prevailing ignorance: 'I shall not attempt to conceal the difficulties relating to the race problem. I know that the ordinary reader is supposed to prefer that all the thinking should be done beforehand, and merely the results submitted to him. But I cannot believe that he would find it edifying to look at half-a-dozen books upon the races of mankind, and find half-a-dozen accounts of their relationships, having scarcely a single statement in common. Far better to face the fact that race still baffles us almost completely.'[1]

"It is true, to a limited degree, that those who have the most manifest opportunity to investigate the

[1] "Anthropology," by R. R. Marett, M.A. (page 61).

biological field of our own race problems—that is to say, the medical men, police officials, charity workers, and the like, residing in the South—have contributed something toward clearing up the difficulties. But they have done so principally because the problem forced itself upon their attention in forms which demanded the acquisition of knowledge for practical reasons. A very few men devoted to pure science have done a little work—painfully little!—in this field. But aside from the most negligible contributions made by these, and the incidental contributions made to the scientific side of the problem by those carrying on practical work in certain phases, almost nothing has been brought forward upon the subject of the biological relationships of the whites and the negroes in this country.[2] There is not now being carried out on a large scale any investigation of the negro's relationship to public health. His anatomy is nowhere being adequately studied.[3] There is not now, and never has been, an institution anywhere in this country devoted to the study of these and similar problems.

"The principal factor, in the opinion of the writer, which has operated to bring about and perpetuate this indifference on the part of American scientists to this problem is, that there is a widespread, practically general misconception in regard to the fundamental nature of the negro problem as a whole. The problem is regarded as being almost entirely sociological.

---

[2] The literature in the Surgeon General's office contains very few contributions by American investigators.

[3] Practically all the work extant upon the comparative or "racial" anatomy of the negro has been done by the Italian or French anatomists.

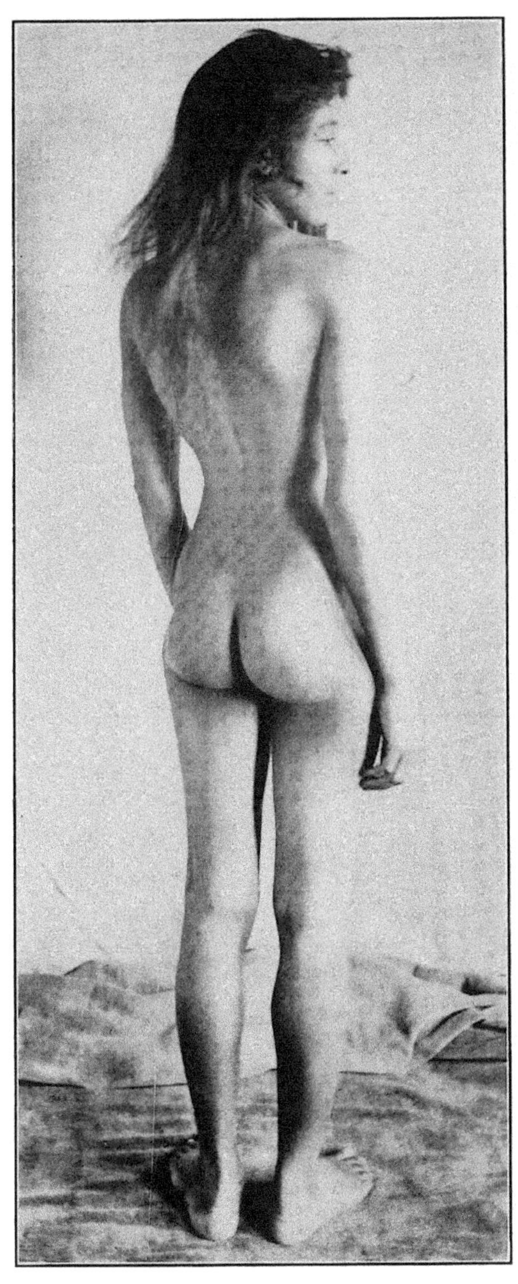

Fig. 45.—Type of Northern Mulatto. Female (New York City.)

(Photo from life by the author.)

The reason for this supposition is not hard to discover. The current interpretation of the anthropological and anatomical facts thus far brought forward by students of race questions tends to indicate that the physical and mental differences existing between dissimilar races are not sufficiently great to be of any vital importance in their relationships. It is obvious, of course, that the races differ markedly in certain anatomical details. It is also obvious that races differ somewhat in mental operations and performances. But it is almost universally believed at present that the mental differences are of such a nature that they are not essential. And it is concluded that the races are so nearly alike mentally that it is not difficult to bring them all to the same plane of mental development. It is inferred from this conclusion that the negro, if he is given the proper opportunities, will equal, or very nearly equal, the whites in his mental performances.[4]

"This conception has had the effect of discouraging work in the biological field. As long as it remains current and is generally accepted, no one is likely to concern himself particularly about it, because it seems to dispose of the whole question. And the problems of race, and particularly the problem of the negro, is regarded as one of adjusting the social relationships in such fashion that the undeveloped race will have a chance to become like the advanced race, mentally, and in every other respect, save the color of the skin.

"The situation, however, is not as well settled as the foregoing would lead one to infer. Despite the anatomical and anthropological evidence brought forward by Franz Boas, Mall, and others, it is not at all

[4] Cf. Boas: "The Mind of Primitive Man."

certain that the problem of the mental differences between the races has been solved, and can be disposed of in the statement that such differences are not great enough to be of vital importance. There is a great deal to be said for the contrary supposition. The work of a large number of sociologists and psychologists, particularly, tends to show that these differences are of vast importance. Gustav Le Bon, the French psychologist, is so convinced that they are of great significance that he has written a book to indicate their nature and importance.[5] And he has been engaged for a long time in writing, from the point of view of his theory of 'racial soul,' a re-interpretation of the entire sweep of history. A great many books are being written which assume and attempt to prove by one means or another that these mental differences are not only of great importance, but are absolutely irreconcilable. Furthermore, nearly everyone who has lived long in the South holds the opinion, based upon empirical grounds, it is true, that the differences are of such a nature that they preclude all possibility of bringing the negro into accord with the civilization of the whites in any ultimate sense.

"In sum, where there is so much smoke, there must be fire. And the investigator is confronted with diametrically opposed theories in regard to the mental capacities of the negro. The one, upheld by certain anthropological and anatomical evidence (most of which turns out to be *negative* evidence when it is closely examined), declares that while there are a few differences between the mental operations of whites

[5] Gustav Le Bon: "Race Psychology."

and negroes, these differences are too slight to be of any importance, and can easily be overcome. The main fact upon which this supposition is based is that no one has ever yet pointed out a structural difference between the brain of a white man and the brain of a negro. (Cf. Boas, 'The Mind of Primitive Man;' Hoffman, 'Race Traits and Tendencies of the American Negro,' and a paper by Mall, the title of which I cannot recall, refuting the conclusions of Bean, as set forth in his paper, 'On a Racial Peculiarity in the Brain of a Negro.') The other theory, supported by the observations of a few scientific psychologists, and by a great mass of empirical observations, unchecked by anthropological and anatomical studies, contends that the differences *are* great enough to be of first-rate importance. Which of these theories is the true one, no one knows.

"The evidence brought forward by anthropology and anatomy seems at first sight to be conclusive; but when it is subjected to a thorough examination, in the light of recent anatomical, physiological, and psycho-physiological discoveries, it is at once seen to be almost wholly irrelevant to the point at issue. It casts no light upon the real heart of the problem, mainly because it does not go deep enough. Every scrap of evidence thus far brought forward reveals nothing that the student of evolution would not expect, simply because the evidence deals only with those anatomical, physiological and psychological facts which the student of evolution would *a priori* assume to be common to mankind in general. And the fields of anatomy (such as the anatomy of the association tracts of the brain, and of the connection between basal and bulbar ganglia and the cerebrum), physiological (such as the question whether the ductless glands of the negro function like those of the white man), and psychological (such as the question of how the negro reacts to his social environment, and whether he possesses the same 'instinct'—using the word as it is used by McDougal—as the white man), which would be expected to yield some significant result have never been explored at all.

"The arguments advanced to prove the irreconcilable nature of the mental differences of the two races rest upon an even slighter scientific foundation. No one has ever yet demonstrated an essential structural difference between the brain of a negro and the brain of a white man. All the other evidence offered rests upon empirical data having no essential relationship to the point at issue. And in the last analysis, no one upholding this theory has been able to bring forward the slightest evidence of a scientifically accepted nature in support of his position.[6]

"The question, 'Are there radical differences between the mental operations of whites and negroes?' is, therefore, the true basis of the negro problem as a whole, and in all its special aspects. The problem is one of race psychology and anatomy, and not one of sociology, since the question lying at the root of the sociological problems has not yet been answered.

[6] To illustrate the worthlessness of most of the evidence submitted, there have recently been made by several investigators a series of Binet tests of negroes, for the purpose of detecting mental difference between the races. Not one of these investigators made the preliminary experiment of finding out whether the Binet scale will, in unaltered form, apply to the negro mind! As a consequence, any conclusions drawn from these tests will be valueless.

Until it is answered, and answered so conclusively that no one can ever ask it again, all other questions in regard to the negro's relationships to the whites cannot be answered, nor even understood correctly. We cannot interpret any sort of facts until we know whether they apply similarly or differently to the two races. And all conclusions drawn, and all hypotheses erected upon them, will be and can be nothing but more or less shrewd guesswork. The whole problem will necessarily remain in a state of chaos until this one fundamental point is settled.

"For this reason, it is the imperative duty of the South to have this question studied and, if possible, answered. The negro problem is day by day growing more complex and probably more dangerous. None of the measures being taken at present to meet the situation rest upon rational scientific knowledge, and they amount to nothing more than makeshifts and compromises. No one knows exactly what the situation is, and until this is known nothing can be done with certainty to ameliorate present conditions or to safeguard the future.

"There are more than ten millions of people of negro ancestry in this country. Numbers such as these make vain the hope that we shall ever get rid of the negro by peaceful emigration, or prevent him, by political and social restrictions, from exerting a massive and intestinal influence upon our social institutions. We have not in the past taken pains to find out what this influence is. We should, however, regard it as an imperative duty to find out. There should be established in the South, liberally endowed and competently manned, an institution whose purpose will be to study this phase of the problem, which is the fundamental phase. Until this is done, and something which will stand the test of rigorous scientific criticism is brought forward by way of answer to the question, 'Are there radical differences between the mental operations of whites and negroes?' the negro problem will continue in its present state of chaos and hopelessness, and our ignorance concerning its real nature will, every year that passes, multiply our dangers and add to our already too heavy burdens."

In the *Popular Science Monthly* for October, 1914 (pp. 368-374), Doctor Bardin contributes a most excellent article on "The Psychological Factor in Southern Race Problems," which, I regret to say, is perhaps too long to reproduce entire in the present chapter; so we must be content to quote only a few selected paragraphs from it. Among other things, the Doctor says:—

"On conventional ethical grounds, the hypothesis of human equality cannot be assailed. The Christian world, particularly that part of it which really thinks, is essentially altruistic, and this altruism demands that all men be given the fullest and most equal opportunities to get the best out of life. But it is seldom realized that this is an ideal, not a working formula; that it is, further, an ethical ideal, not a scientific one. Out of this misconception of the ideal of human equality have sprung many grievous and oftentimes dangerous fallacies, chief among which are two: (1) that all men possess the same potentialities for culture; and (2) that a so-called 'higher culture' may and ethically should be substituted for a so-called 'lower culture' whenever opportunity presents itself.

"As has been said, each of these ideas has a basis in ethical principles. But both are fallacious when scientifically considered. Each assumes too much, and each tries to make out of an ethical ideal the scientific working formula for the uplifting of backward peoples. Neither takes into account that culture and civilization are as much the products of evolution as a white skin or a black skin.

"Culture, in its broadest sense, is a phenomenon of race. Even in our more or less homogeneous western European and American culture, racial differences are to be observed; if this were not true, why should we take the trouble to call some people Germans and others Spaniards, some Danes and others Italians? Yet, despite these evident differences, western European and American culture is a definite, characteristic thing, and underlying it we recognize a common stock of traditions and general ideas, which have come down through the ages 'in the blood,' so to speak. The white-skinned peoples of western Europe and America all have approximately the same origin, in that, through the remote mixing of a few strains of blood, the modern racial types were set; and since then the peoples of western Europe have given evidence of their biological kinship by displaying approximately similar reactions to similar environmental conditions and to the influence of general ideas and movements of thought. Whatever variations have appeared in the physical and psychical types among the various peoples are due to differences in the mixtures of the original strains of blood, with the accompanying differences in the contributions of hereditary mental predispositions received by the respective peoples, plus subsequent adaptations to environmental conditions. But behind all the differences lies a common kinship of blood and of tradition, which has operated to produce the unit we call western European culture; and this racial kinship is the principal reason why it is not difficult for one group of western Europeans to adopt without revolutionizing it the culture of another group. Furthermore, as a powerful factor assisting in the formation and growth of this western European culture, and aiding constantly in keeping it homogeneous, is the fact that several strains of blood, particularly in the higher levels of society, where most of the productive thinking is done, are incessantly mixing, and there are being interchanged incessantly, through heredity, the mental predispositions peculiar to the groups thus crossing. The people of western Europe and the white portion of American population, for the most part, are a sort of 'blend' of similar racial stocks, presenting similar though not identical biological characteristics; and the varieties of this 'blend,' expressed in such terms as 'English,' 'Dutch,' and so forth, are due to differences in the numerical relationships of the contributing stocks forming these peoples. So, too, western European culture is a sort of 'blend' of cultures, and the varieties of this 'blend' parallel the varieties in the physical characteristics of the various peoples.

"The same statements apply to any other group of people presenting a special, characteristic type of culture. The Chinese are an example; they differ among themselves in certain respects; they are a 'blend' of races, and their present culture is a 'blend'

Fig. 46.—Same Subject as Shown in Fig. 45. Full Face.

(Photo from life by the author.)

of cultures. Yet Chinese culture is definite, peculiar and recognizable, and it is essentially Mongolian, just as our culture is essentially European. Behind the differences among the various groups in China lie their common Mongolian blood and their common store of traditions, the influences of which have moulded them into what they are today. Exactly the same statements apply to the Negroes. They have, physically and mentally, definite and easily recognizable characteristics, indicative of a common origin different from our own, and expressed in a similarity of Negro cultures throughout the world.

"The fact of race as a physical and mental phenomenon is evident to everyone. The peoples of the world differ, and often differ fundamentally; and these differences are ineradicable as long as the strain of blood remains unimpaired. On the physical side, this principle has long been an axiom. 'Can the Ethiopian change his skin?' asks Jeremiah. We cannot, do what we will with environment, change to any appreciable extent our anatomical make-up. A Chinaman's skin will remain yellow, a Negro's skin will remain black, no matter what we may do to alter them, so long as the races remain pure. The only way we can modify the color of the skin or the facial angle or the texture of the hair in any great number of individuals is by crossing with another race. And the product of this crossing, should it become permanent, is a different race.

"From the point of view of psychology, on the other hand, we have assumed that this principle is not true. We know that we cannot change a Negro's physical characteristics, so as to make him like ourselves, by bringing him to live among us. But we believe we can change his mental characteristics. In other words, while we are certain that we cannot change the Negro's facial angle, we are equally certain that we can change his mental angle and make it like our own; while we consider it absurd to think that we can do anything to make the Negro's physical skin become white, we believe firmly that we can make the physical analogue of his skin exactly like our own.

"But is this a fact? Racial psychology says no. Mental characteristics are as distinctly and as organically a part of a race as its physical characteristics, and for the same reason: both depend ultimately upon anatomical structure. Racial mental-set, racial ways of thinking, racial reactions to the influence of ideas, are as characteristic and as recognizable as racial skin-color and racial skull-conformation. This does not mean that mental characteristics and superficial anatomical characteristics necessarily bear any relationship to each other, as has sometimes been assumed; that is to say, the shape of the head, the weight of the brain, the cranial capacity, the length of the arms, the arrangement of the muscles in the calf of the leg, do not determine mental characteristics: physical and mental characteristics are, however, parallel expressions of the particular evolutionary process which has resulted in the formation of a race; each set of characters is the specific result, in different structures, of the evolutionary process. Ultimately, mental differences must depend upon anatomical and physiological differences; but these differences are differences in the structure of the brain itself. If we are to assume any relationship whatsoever between brain and mind (and such a relationship, whatever it may be, certainly exists), we must assume some anatomical and physiological differences in the brains if we are to account for mental differences.

"The more the races of men are studied, the more certain becomes the evidence to show that races have characteristic mental peculiarities, which would serve to distinguish species and varieties almost as well as physical characteristics. In practical life, in jurisprudence, in language itself, we empirically allow for these racial mental differences. But we have never taken the trouble to study them nor to understand their nature from a scientific point of view, and almost nothing is known about their potentialities.

"Taking as a fact these mental differences, let us for a moment consider the possibility of their modification. It has been pointed out that mental differences must ultimately depend upon material anatomical differences in brain-structure; if we deny this, we instantly remove racial psychology from the field of science to that of metaphysics, and controvert all the observed data of physiological psychology; there must be some structural differences between the brain of a Negro and that of a white man, though such differences are admittedly very hard to detect by present methods. We know that it is impossible for us to modify anatomical structures at will; we can undoubtedly change them (within narrow limits, by selection of characters already present and the accentuation of these), but we cannot make any two differing anatomical characters become exactly alike. Why, then, should we assume that we can modify at will the mental processes of a race, since these mental processes are expressions of a certain definite anatomical and physiological organization, which we know cannot be altered save by the crossing of bloods or by the laborious and infinitely slow processes of evolution?

"Yet, north and south, we wish to do this very thing, and to do it in its extreme form. For we are not merely trying to change the direction of the Negro's peculiar mental characteristics, and to improve them by selection among the elements already present—we are trying, on the contrary, to deprive the Negro of his own racial mental characteristics, and to substitute our own in their place, *at the same time keeping him anatomically a Negro.* That this is an impossibility follows after the former argument.

"It will undoubtedly be said, by way of refutation, that the Negroes of the Southern States have advanced and advanced considerably since they have been in this country. This is unreservedly true. But it is often forgotten that they have advanced as Negroes, not as anything else. They have adopted the form of our civilization and to a certain extent (due principally to the influence of language), the mould of our thought. But however much the form of the civilization and the mould of the thought resemble our own, the substance of both is different. The Negro has received much from us, and has profited greatly therefrom; but all that he has received he has modified in accordance with his racial mental-set, and his physical reactions to the influences of our civilization are entirely different from our own, and will necessarily remain so as long as the Negro is Negro. No matter how much we may educate him, no matter how much we better his position in society, he will remain a Negro psychically as long as he remains a Negro physically. We may cause him to absorb the full, rich store of our cultural elements, but by the time these elements have gone through the channels of his thought, they will be profoundly modified, and they will take on a different meaning in the Negro's consciousness from what they have in the white man's consciousness. Concomitantly, these cultural elements will modify the brain of the Negro; but this modification will not follow the same pathways, and will not give the same results as it would in the untutored brain, say, of a white child. The modifying forces acting upon the Negro's brain will have to start with an anatomical structure already formed and set by heredity, an anatomical structure different from that of the white race, which produced the modifying forces in question, and the final result in the Negro's brain will be determined and directed by this preëxisting anatomical make-up. So that the brain and the consciousness resulting from the absorption of our culture by the Negroes will be a brain and a consciousness different from our own to the same extent that the Negro differs from us in other respects, and both will be characteristically Negroid in nature, not European.

"It follows, therefore, that present ideals in regard to the 'solution' of our Negro problem (ideals, as has been pointed out and which it is well to reiterate, resulting from the confusion of ethical and scientific principles) are biologically fallacious and impossible of attainment. We can never make the Negro like the white man mentally. We can never have a bi-racial state based upon identity of ideas and political philosophies in both races.

"The Negroes will continue to progress, undoubtedly. But they will progress along the lines laid down by their evolutionary history. They will take our cultural elements and make them part of themselves; but they will modify these elements according to their nature, and when they have assimilated them, they will be our cultural elements no longer, but will be profoundly and permanently modified. The two races will continue to develop side by side, but the development can never be parallel—it must be divergent, even though its successive steps may perchance maintain approximately the same level, as long as the races remain pure. It will be like two men, thrown together by fortuitous circumstances, who start walking up the same slope toward the same hilltop; but because of differences in the nature of their interests, one goes east while the other goes northeast; each step will carry them closer to the top of the hill, but further and further apart.

"This fact, rather than ethical theory, should form the foundation of American thought in regard to the Negroes and the Negro problem. The Negro as an intellectual being should be studied as a Negro—not as a potential white man; and if we wish to help him, we should at least try to be sure that he is allowed to develop as a Negro in the freest, broadest manner possible, and to the full extent of his racial potentialities."

A few years ago, Mr. Arthur M. Allen published his paper on "The Race Problem" in the *Arena*

(Aug., 1906), and kindly furnished me with two reprints of it. What he said is, in many respects, as true today as it was the day it came off the press; it is, in any event, interesting from what it points out historically. Mr. Allen remarks that "The article by Professor Grimke on 'The Heart of the Race Problem,' reads like Theodore Tilton's *Miscegenation,* published during the war, and so offensive to the public that it has been practically suppressed. All these articles are based on the old idea of one race, and that all men, being children of Adam, were brothers and therefore equal.

"The progress of science has put Adam among the allegories of the past, and left us to solve the race problem by the scientific laws of natural history and zoölogy alone.

"Jefferson, although an Abolitionist, believed in deportation only. He had such a horror of race equality that he considered it *impossible,* and lamented that there had, at that time, been no scientific examination of the negro in the line of natural history.

"In 1850, Professor Agassiz, after long research, said that Caucasians and Negroes could never have been descended from the same stock, and, although men, could never have been brothers.

"This is the new doctrine of diversity of race; and when glamour and emotional conditions produced by the one-race theory have subsided, this will prevail, and solve this and other race problems.

"In 1901, Professor McGee, of the Smithsonian Institution at Washington, confirmed Professor Agassiz by saying that if there was any Garden of Eden, there must have been many original couples, for no two of the present races could have been descended from the same stock.

"The same evil English Tory influences, which originated and engineered the whole *negro equality* movement (miscalled Anti-Slavery), even though they succeeded so well that it is embodied in our Constitutional Amendments, have yet, ever since now almost forty years, in spite of every kind of failure of negro freedom, when *unsupported* by white proximity, constantly suppressed and destroyed all free thought, speech and action on this subject, and the one-race theory is being burned into the public mind as one of the unchangeable results of the Civil War.

"This is their *object,* for they *know* that if real race equality is a settled matter, democracy is destroyed and monarchy justified. This is the bedrock of the whole matter.

"There is now a great spirit of discontent abroad, due to the great amount of graft and corruption so universal at the present time, and when this spirit applies common sense and a *new* doctrine of diversity of races to our conditions, the problem will be quickly solved. Under this new doctrine all *mixed* races are *criminal* and should be prevented by law; and the three Tory amendments to the Constitution (13, 14 and 15) should be at once repealed. Professor Grimke's assertions (unproven) about the sexual evils of negro slavery seem trifling compared to the worse conditions since, and any of our large Northern cities are far worse today; and when he winds up with segregation and equality, he is the *antithesis* of Jefferson, our best-known Democrat.

"ARTHUR M. ALLEN.

"NEW BRIGHTON, N. Y. (Arena), Aug., 1906."

On the 21st of October, 1914, I called, by kind invitation, upon Senator James K. Vardaman, at the Senate Annex. Senator Vardaman's views on the negro question had apparently remained unchanged since the day he expressed them in his Message to the Legislature of Mississippi, in 1908, when he was Governor of that State.

In that Message, the Senator stated that "*I think that the greatest crime that was ever committed against any people was perpetrated against the white people of the South by the adoption of the Fourteenth and Fifteenth Amendments to the Federal Constitution.* These iniquitous measures were conceived in a spirit of hatred and ignorance, and brought forth in a spasm of venom and revenge. *They are known today throughout the length and breadth of this republic by all white men who think honestly and correctly, to be improper and out of joint with the better interests of the country.* To give the negro the right of suffrage, and place him on terms of absolute equality with the white man, was the *capital crime of the ages* against the white man's *civilization.* The effect has proven disastrous; and the perpetuation of the evil effects of the error can only work harm to both races. You cannot adjust laws suited to the government of the white man—'the heir of all the ages in the foremost files of time'—to this low-browed, civilization-veneered savage. And it is worse than a crime to undertake it. Indeed, it is the cultivation of crime and the encouragement of lawlessness to undertake it. In 1856, in a speech delivered at Boston, Mass., Robert Toombs uttered these undying words: '*I maintain that so long as the African and the Caucasian races co-exist in the same society, the subordination of the African is its normal, necessary, and proper condition, and that such subordination is the condition best calculated to promote the highest interest and the greatest happiness of both races, and, consequently, of the whole society; that the white is the superior, and the black the inferior, and that subordination, with or without law, will be the status of the African in this mixed society. Therefore, it is to the interest of both, and especially of the black race, that this status should be fixed, controlled, and protected by law.'* How faithfully he described the condition of affairs in the South today, and how completely the condition in the South vindicates the wisdom of his utterances! Unless 'this status' shall be 'fixed, controlled, and protected by law' it will be 'fixed' without the law, and in the process of the 'fixing' a spirit of lawlessness will be generated which will exterminate the negro, and well-nigh destroy the white man's civilization."

He further points out and apparently honestly believes what he says, when he asks and answers the question, "What shall we do with the negro? Certainly the system of education suited to the white child does not suit the negro. This has been demonstrated by forty years of experience, and the expenditure of more than three hundred millions of dollars in the Southern States. It was natural and quite reasonable, immediately after the civil war, especially by those who had made but a superficial study of the negro, to expect that freedom, equal educational facilities, and the example and precept of the white man, would have the effect of improving his morals, and make a better man of him generally. But it has not, I am sorry to say. As a race, he is deteriorating morally every day. Time has demonstrated that he is more criminal as a free man than as a slave; that he is increasing in criminality with fearful rapidity, being one-third more criminal in 1890 than be was in 1880. The startling facts revealed by the census show that those who can read and write are more criminal than the illiterate, which is true of no other element of our population. I am advised that the minimum of illiteracy among the negroes is in New England, where it is 21.7 per cent.; the maximum is found in the black belt—Louisiana, Mississippi, and South Carolina; there it is 65.7 per cent. *And yet, the negro in New England is four and one-half times more criminal, hundred for hundred, than he is in the black belt.* In the South, Mississippi particularly, I know he is growing worse every year. You can scarcely pick up a newspaper whose pages are not blackened with an account of an unmentionable crime committed by a negro brute, and this crime, I want to impress upon you, is but the manifestation of the negro's ambition for social equality, encouraged largely by the character of free education in vogue, which the State is levying tribute upon the white people to maintain. The better class of negroes is not responsible for this terrible condition, or for the criminal tendency of their race. Nor do I wish to be understood as censuring them for it. I am not censuring anybody; nor am I inspired by ill-will for the negro; but I am simply calling attention to a most unfortunate and unendurable condition of affairs. What shall be done about it? Surely something must be done. The white people of Mississippi cannot sit idly by without at least making an effort to arrest this destructive tendency. The State, for many years, at great expense to the taxpayers, has maintained a system of negro education, which has produced disappointing results, and I am opposed to the perpetuation of that system. My own idea is that the character of education for the negro ought to be changed. If, after forty years of earnest effort, and the expenditure of fabulous sums of money to educate his head, we have only succeeded in making a criminal of him, and impairing his usefulness and efficiency as a laborer, wisdom would suggest that we make another experiment, and see if we cannot improve him *by educating his hand and his heart.* There must be a *moral* substratum upon which to build, or you cannot make a desirable citizen. The negro, as a race, is devoid of that element. He has never felt the guilt of sin, and the *restraining influence* of outraged conscience is unknown to the real negro. *Slavery is the only process by which he has ever been partially civilized.*"

Senator Vardaman very well knows that, inasmuch as the negro now has the franchise, he can easily be induced to sell his vote at the polls for what money value he can receive for it, or he can use it at the White House, as Trotter did with President Wilson in a blackmailing way, to help the negro race along toward their goal of "equality" with the whites, socially and otherwise. How swiftly history in such matters paints upon the wall! (1908-1914.)

CHAPTER X.

Amplification of Some Previously Discussed Questions.

In one of the foregoing chapters of this book, the matter of lynching—in the case of negroes—for one crime or another, though usually for assaults upon white women, has already been referred to by me. A few paragraphs may, with advantage, be added to what was said there.

Whether sincere or otherwise, the legal profession in this country has, as a rule, held but one opinion in the premises with respect to lynching; so, in quoting this stock opinion, I can do no better than to reproduce what Mr. Justice Brewer, of the United States Supreme Court, had to say on the point a number of years ago, and which was reported in full at the time in *The New York Daily Tribune* (August 17, 1903). It is a hum-drum, cut-and-dried legal document, but it gives, nevertheless, an old American lawyer's opinion on this crime; and, as scores of old lawyers entertain precisely the same opinion today, I feel I am not laying myself open to the charge of digging up past history when I reproduce it for the purpose of making it stand for the legal view of the matter.

The *Tribune* published it thus:—

"The following article by Justice Brewer on the crime of lynching will appear in the current issue of *Leslie's Weekly*. In it Justice Brewer sets forth more fully the views he has already made public in regard to lynching as a blot on our civilization and what can be done to stay the epidemic of the crime. The full text of the article is as follows:—

" 'Our government recently forwarded to Russia a petition in respect to alleged atrocities committed upon the Jews. That government, as might have been expected, unwilling to have its internal affairs a matter of consideration by other governments, declined to receive the petition. If, instead of so doing, it had replied that it would put a stop to all such atrocities when this government put a stop to lynchings, what could we have said?

" 'No one can be blind to the fact that lynching is becoming altogether too common, and presents a serious question for the consideration of thoughtful lovers of their country. There have been two kinds of lynch-law, and it is well to distinguish between the two. In San Francisco, for instance, many years ago the better citizens became convinced that the officials were in league with gamblers and other wrong-doers —hence, crime was rampant, neither life nor property being sacred. Deliberately they came together, organized, and in effect took possession of the government, administering law promptly and severely, with the results—as claimed—that crime was checked and order reëstablished. Whatever may be said of such a movement, it is not like the lynch-law that now prevails. It was more in the nature of a revolution, by which the regularly elected officers were put out of office and a new government established. But the lynching which now attracts attention is the temporary uprising of a mob, called into being by the commission of some terrible crime, the perpetrator of which it seeks to punish.

" 'It is well to look the matter fairly in the face. Many good men join in these uprisings, horrified at the atrocity of the crime and eager for swift and summary punishment. Of course, they violate the law themselves, but rely on the public sentiment behind them for escape from punishment. Many of these lynchings are accompanied by the horrible barbarities of savage torture, and all that can be said in palliation is the atrocity of the offence which led up to them. For a time they were confined largely to the South, but that section of the country no longer has a monopoly. The chief offence which causes these lynchings has been the rape of white women by colored men. No words can be found too strong to describe the atrocity of such a crime. It is no wonder that the community is excited. Men would disgrace their manhood if they were not. And if a few lynchings had put a stop to the offence, society might have condoned such breeches of its law; but the fact is, if we may credit the reports, the crime, instead of diminishing, is on the increase. The black beast (for only a beast would be guilty of such an offence) seems to be not deterred thereby. More than that, as might be expected, lynching for such atrocious crimes is no longer confined to them, but is being resorted to for other offences.

" 'That lynching is a blot on our civilization no one questions, and European nations are pointing to it as evidence of a lower civilization. Shall we let this go on and thus practically admit that, in many respects, this is no longer a government of laws, but partly one of mobs? We seldom hear of lynchings across the waters; somehow or other it is an epidemic which prevails in America, but not in Europe. We all know that punishment of crime justly and promptly administered by legal methods tells of a higher condition of society than the wild outcries and hasty judgment of mobs. Take the case of the assassin of our late, much-loved President; how much more it speaks for our civilization that in an orderly way, before a legal tribunal, the assassin was tried, having the benefit of counsel, and thereafter put to death in accordance with the dictates of law, than if an angry mob had torn him from the officers of the law and tortured him to death!

" 'What can be done to stay this epidemic of lynching? One thing is the establishment of a greater confidence in the summary and certain punishment of the criminal. Men are afraid of the law's delays and the uncertainty of its results. Not that they doubt the integrity of the judges; but they know that the law abounds with technical rules, and that appellate courts will often reverse a judgment of conviction for a disregard of such rules, notwithstanding a full belief in the guilt of the accused. If all were certain that the guilty ones would be promptly tried and punished, the inducement to lynch would be largely taken away. In an address which I delivered before the American Bar Association at Detroit some years since, I advocated doing away with appeals in criminal cases. It did not meet the favor of the association, but I still believe in its wisdom. For nearly a hundred years there was no appeal from the judgment of conviction of criminal cases, and no review, except in a few cases in which, two judges sitting, a difference of opinion on a question of law was certified to the Supreme Court. In England the rule has been that there was no appeal in criminal cases, although a question of doubt might be reserved by the presiding judge for the consideration of his brethren. The Hon. E. J. Phelps, who was Minister to England during Mr. Cleveland's first administration, once told me that while he was there only two cases were so reserved. Does anyone doubt that justice was fully administered by the English courts?

" 'Opponents of this suggestion fall back on the ancient maxim that 'It is better that ninety-nine guilty men escape than that one innocent man be punished.' Maxims, like other things, are good in their places; but, like other things, may often be overworked. When criminal trials were conducted as they were in England a century and a half ago—defendant without counsel, trial with little publicity and the press an unknown factor—that maxim was good enough; but today, when a prisoner is guaranteed counsel, when trials are viewed by throngs of spectators, and the press makes public every detail, it seems well to as often consider President Grant's direction, 'Let no guilty man escape.'

" 'Further, laws have been passed requiring an immediate convening of courts and giving priority of hearing to certain civil cases deemed of public moment. Why may not direction be given to the presiding judge of the proper court, when such an atrocious crime has been committed as those giving rise to lynchings, to immediately convene that court and put the accused at once on trial? If this were done and no appeal were allowed, would not the community be more confident that full punishment would be promptly meted out?

If it be said that under the haste of such a trial some innocent men might be punished, a sufficient reply would seem to be that justice will be more likely done than when a mob takes the law into its own hands. If it were deemed necessary to guard against even a possibility of injustice, the statute might require that the testimony be taken down by a stenographer and at once presented to the Supreme Court; and if, in its judgment, not that some technical rules of law have been disregarded, but that an innocent man has been convicted, authorize it to stay the execution and grant a new trial.

" 'It is said, in extenuation of lynching, in case of rape, that it is an additional cruelty to the unfortunate victim to compel her to go upon the witness stand and in the presence of a mixed audience tell the story of her wrongs, especially when she may be subject to cross-examination by overzealous counsel. I do not belittle this matter; but it must be remembered that often the unfortunate victim never lives to tell the story of her wrongs; that if she does survive, she must tell it to some, and the whole community knows the fact. Even in the court-room any high-minded judge will stay counsel from any unnecessary cross-examination; and, finally, if any lawyer should attempt it, the community may treat him as an outcast. I can but think that if the community felt that the criminal would certainly receive the punishment he deserves, and receive it soon, the eagerness for lynching would disappear, and mobs, whose gatherings too often mean not merely the destruction of jails and other property, but also the loss of innocent lives, would greatly diminish in number.

" 'One thing is certain—the tendency of lynching is to undermine respect for the law, and unless it be checked we need not be astonished if it be resorted to for all kinds of offences, and oftentimes innocent men suffer for wrongs committed by others.' "

Here is another from *The New York Evening Journal,* August 10, 1903:—

"LYNCHING IS ANARCHY, SAYS ROOSEVELT.

"HATTIESBURG, MISS., Aug. 10.—Amos Jones, a negro, was lynched by a mob for shooting and mortally wounding Jailer M. M. Sexton.

"President Roosevelt has sent the following letter to Governor Durbin, of Indiana:—

" 'Permit me to thank you, as an American citizen, for the admirable way in which you have vindicated the majesty of the law by your recent action in reference to lynching.

" 'Mob violence is simply one form of anarchy, and anarchy is now, as it always has been, the handmaiden and forerunner of tyranny.

" 'All thoughtful men must feel the gravest alarm over the growth of lynching in this country, and especially over the peculiarly hideous forms so often taken by mob violence when colored men are the victims—on which occasions the mob seems to lay most weight, not on the crime, but on the color of the criminal.

" 'In a certain proportion of these cases the man lynched has been guilty of a crime horrible beyond description, a crime so horrible that as far as he himself is concerned, he has forfeited the right to any kind of sympathy whatever.

" 'The feeling of all good citizens that such a hideous crime shall not be hideously punished by mob violence is due not in the least to sympathy for the criminal, but to a very lively sense of the train of dreadful consequences which follow the course taken by the mob in exacting inhuman vengeance for an inhuman wrong.

" 'In such cases, moreover, it is well to remember that the criminal not merely sins against humanity in an inexplicable and unpardonable fashion, but sins particularly against his own race, and does them a wrong far greater than any white man can possibly do them. Therefore, in such cases, the colored people throughout the land should, in every possible way, show their belief that they, more than all others in the community, are horrified at the commission of such a crime, and peculiarly concerned in taking every possible measure to prevent its recurrence and to bring the criminal to immediate justice. The slightest lack of vigor, either in denunciation of the crime or in bringing the criminal to justice, is itself unpardonable.

" 'Every effort should be made under the law to expedite the proceedings of justice in the case of such an awful crime. But it cannot be necessary, in order to accomplish this, to deprive any citizen of those fundamental rights to be heard in his own defense, which are so dear to us all and which lie at the root of our liberty.

" 'It certainly ought to be possible, by the proper administration of the laws, to secure swift vengeance upon the criminal, and the best and immediate efforts of all legislators, judges and citizens should be addressed to securing such reforms in our legal procedure as to leave no vestige of excuse for those misguided men who undertake to reap vengeance through violent methods.

" 'We must show that the law is adequate to deal with crime by freeing it from every vestige of technicality and delay.

" 'It is, of course, inevitable that where vengeance is taken by a mob it should frequently light on innocent people; and the wrong done in such a case to the individual is one for which there is no remedy. But even where the real criminal is reached, the wrong done by the mob to the community itself is well-nigh as great. Especially is this true where the lynching is accompanied with torture.

" 'There are certain hideous sights which, when once seen, can never be wholly erased from the mental retina. The mere fact of having seen them implies degradation. This is a thousandfold stronger when, instead of merely seeing the deed, the man has participated in it.

" 'Whoever, in any part of our country, has even taken part in lawlessly putting to death a criminal by the dreadful torture of fire, must forever after have the awful spectacle of his own handiwork seared into his brain and soul. He can never again be the same man.

" 'Every violent man in the community is encouraged, by every case of lynching in which the lynchers go unpunished, to take the law into his own hands whenever it suits his convenience. In the same way, the use of torture by the mob, in certain cases, is sure to spread until it is applied more or less indiscriminately in other cases.

" 'The spirit of lawlessness grows with what it feeds on, and when mobs, with impunity, lynch criminals for one crime, they are certain to begin to lynch real or alleged criminals for other causes.

" 'The nation, like the individual, cannot commit a crime with impunity. If we are guilty of lawlessness and brutal violence, whether our guilt consists in active participation therein or in mere connivance and encouragement, we shall suffer later.

" 'The corner-stone of this Republic, as of all free governments, is respect for and obedience to the law. Where we permit the law to be defied or evaded, whether by rich man or poor man, by black man or white, we are, by just so much, weakening the bonds of our civilization and increasing the chances of its overthrow, and of the substitution therefore of a system in which there shall be violent alternation of anarchy and tyranny. Sincerely yours,

" 'THEODORE ROOSEVELT' "

Six days after the above opinion had been published in nearly every newspaper in the United States —and one would have thought that the practice of lynching would have been stayed for a week at least —the following news was published in the *New York Daily Tribune,* August 16, 1903:—

"WANTS BLACKS KEPT OUT.

"LAPORTE, IND., Aug. 15.—To prevent the settlement of any negro in Northwestern Indiana is the object of a movement begun by A. J. Bowser, editor of *The Chesterton Tribune,* in which he is finding much sympathy and support. The county jail at Valparaiso was under heavy guard last Sunday, and the streets were filled with crowds of angry farmers and Normal School students clamoring for the life of a negro tramp who on the previous day had assaulted and dangerously injured the wife of a farmer in Porter County. The councils of cool men prevailed, and no attack was made on the jail, but the intense excitement extended through the country districts, and did not subside for several days. This state of affairs led to the suggestion of Mr. Bowser.

"Had the negro never been in the country, no such practice as this would have come into vogue."

"BISHOP'S VIEW OF LYNCHING.

"CLEVELAND, Sept. 17.—Bishop William M. Brown, of the Arkansas Diocese of the Episcopal Church, formerly an Ohioan, was in the city today *en route* to Washington, D. C., to attend the Missionary Council of the Episcopal Church, and the Convention of the American House of Bishops. Speaking of the race problem, he expressed himself quite plainly.

" 'While I do not justify lynching, I can find no other remedy adequate to suppress the crime for which this has been made a punishment by the people of the South,' he said.

" 'I am a Northern man, and used to look with horror on lynching; but since I have been South, my eyes have been opened. Imprisonment does no good.

" 'I am of the opinion that it would be well to leave the solution of the negro question to the Southern people; they know best what to do.

" 'The enfranchisement of the negro has been a serious mistake. Very few of them have any convictions, and their votes are cast as a rule for the men who pay the most money.' "

Women who have been assaulted by negroes are invariably in favor of the destruction, sometimes even the torture, of the assaulter. The following, in connection with the case of Mrs. Labouisse, set forth in Chapter VIII, stands in evidence of this; it is from *The New York Times,* of November 10, 1903:—

"PASS CHRISTIAN, MISS., Nov. 9.—Mrs. Peter Labouisse, the young matron of New York who was assaulted last Thursday by Sam Adams, a negro who was soon afterward lynched, spent the day in this resort. Although not injured in the struggle, Mrs. Labouisse's nerves are still completely unstrung. She has remained in her room since the experience.

" 'It was only when I heard that that wretched creature was hanged that I began to experience a feeling of relief,' said Mrs. Labouisse today. 'I was so glad that the people had taken the law into their own hands. There was no doubt as to his identity. I don't see how they could possibly have acted otherwise than they did.' "

This case needs no further comment here. There is not one woman in five hundred who is strong enough to resist, in a lonely place by herself, the persistent attack of a burly, brutal and powerful negro. Unless aid comes quickly, the damnable fiend is certain to be successful, overpower his intended victim and accomplish his purpose.

Now, here are the opinions, in regard to the crime of lynching, of a judge of the Supreme Court of the United States; of a former President of the United States,—a man worthy of being listened to on any subject; an editor; an Episcopal bishop, and a young married woman who was the victim of an assault. These are not opinions of the past, but are, on the other hand, identical with those entertained by such persons at the present moment. Hundreds of people at this writing (November, 1914) agree with what Judge Brewer set forth; still other hundreds agree with what Colonel Roosevelt stated. The bishop and the editor would also have their following; and as to the poor, assaulted woman, there are thousands of her sex in the country today, any single one of whom would, without a second's hesitation, advocate the burning alive of the negro who had been successful in such an assault or in such cases of rape.

But all these opinions, all these lynchings, all the steps taken to impress upon the negroes the gravity of the crime, will have no more effect upon them in the future than it has had in the past. Assaults of negroes upon white women and lynchings will occur in the United States until the end of time, just so long as there are negro men and white women with us, and the whites and blacks are distributed as they are in the country at the present time.

As I have said in a previous chapter, I am in no way an advocate of lynching; but I am an earnest advocate of the following practice, although I know there is no hope of carrying it out in one case in ten, maybe more:—

When the negro is captured, he should immediately be taken to the nearest court-house, and a legal trial be given him at once, or just as soon as judge and jury can be assembled. Every possible step should be taken to make a correct identification of the prisoner, even by the woman herself, if she has survived his attack, or by such other evidence as may be forthcoming. If the negro's guilt is proven absolutely, beyond all manner of doubt, his execution should not be stayed more than a few hours following his trial, and this should be performed in the same manner as in the case of other executed criminals, duly tried in courts of law. In other words, I believe the trial for this crime should be immediate; identification certain; the penalty death, and execution to take place on the same day as the trial.

Do I believe that this practice and this procedure would exercise any deterrent effect with respect to the crime? No, I most emphatically *do not.* There are hundreds of negroes in this country today, any one of whom would rape a white woman with the noose of the rope about his neck by which he was to be hanged at the completion of his act, and the fagots aflame, by which he was to be roasted alive while being strung up, in plain sight. In other words: lynching never has and never will act as a deterrent in such cases, where the men are full-blooded negroes and their victims Anglo-Saxon women. With almost any other race it might and doubtless in some cases does act as a deterrent, but not with the pure

Ethiopian of the race we have in millions in the United States.

In this opinion I am fully borne out by the cases occurring every few days, in different sections of the country.

Why is it, then, that the negro man in the United States, whether he be a low, brutal one, or an "old, trusted servant," is not deterred by the only too frequent result of his crime? For the very reason that his sexual passions are so balanced psychologically, with respect to his mentality and will-power or the power of self-restraint, that when the opportunity presents itself (which is usually when he finds himself alone with a white woman), he quickly loses all control of his sexual passion, and the usual assault ensues. This is not the case with the men of other races, but it is the case with many other animals below man,—the negro excepted. I could give some curious instances of this, even of animals as high in the system as *rabbits* and other forms.

The legal handling of these cases as it should be done, and as I have given it as my opinion above it should be done, would have much to recommend it and practically nothing against it. It would satisfy the people and the victim as far as possible; it would snuff out, each time, one more of the kind that are a menace to any white woman with whom they may find themselves alone; and, what is very important, it would soon silence the criticism abroad that we are a nation given to torturing some of our criminals for certain crimes, without giving them even the benefit of a fair, legal trial.

What is the *radical remedy* for this incurable proclivity on the part of the majority of the pure negroes in this country? There is but one, namely, complete segregation of the two races,—so complete that the oceans will stand between them forever.

In order to emphasize the fearful extent of this most horrible and ever-present menace, it will be as well to take a glance at the number of negroes we have on our hands at this time. To present this information in the clearest manner possible, and at the same time have it bear the stamp of authority, I communicated with the Chief Clerk of the United States Bureau of the Census (Washington, D. C.), who very kindly sent me copies of the Bulletins of the Thirteenth Census of the United States: 1910. These are very complete documents, and present the populations of the United States from every essential viewpoint, up to include that year.[1] From this great body of information, however, it will only be necessary to present such matter as will give the reader an accurate idea of the number of these negroes which we have upon our hands, as compared with the total population of the United States.

One of the Bulletins referred to above is a "Reprint of Chapter II, pages 77-119, of the Abstract of the Thirteenth Census," and presents the following important data:—

"GENERAL SUMMARY: 1910 AND 1900.—Table 1 shows the number of persons of each color or race at

[1] It affords me pleasure to thank the Bureau of the Census for this assistance, and for the permission to use the maps, which occur in the above Bulletins, in the present work. The next census will not be taken until 1920, at which time the usual increase will be shown,—in so far as the negroes in this country are concerned,—unless it be influenced by some war, insurrection, or epidemic of a fatal disease.

the last two censuses, the total number of native and foreign-born inhabitants, and the number of whites distributed according to nativity and parentage.

TABLE 1.

CLASS OF POPULATION.	NUMBER.		INCREASE:[1] 1900–1910		PER CENT. OF TOTAL POPULATION.	
	1910	1900	Number.	Per cent.	1910	1900
TOTAL POPULATION	91,972,266	75,994,575	15,977,691	21.0	100.0	100.0
White	81,731,957	66,809,196	14,922,761	22.3	88.9	87.9
Negro	9,827,763	8,833,994	993,769	11.2	10.7	11.6
Other colored races	412,546	351,385	61,161	17.4	0.4	0.5
Indian	265,683	237,196	28,487	12.0	0.3	0.3
Chinese	71,531	89,863	−18,332	−20.4	0.1	0.1
Japanese	72,157	24,326	47,831	196.6	0.1	(2)
All other	3,175	....	3,175	....	(2)	....
Total native	78,456,380	65,653,299	12,803,081	19.5	85.3	86.4
Total foreign born	13,515,886	10,341,276	3,174,610	30.7	14.7	13.6
TOTAL WHITE	81,731,957	66,809,196	14,922,761	22.3	88.9	87.9
Native	68,386,412	56,595,379	11,791,033	20.8	74.4	74.5
Native parentage	49,488,575	40,949,362	8,539,213	20.9	53.8	53.9
Foreign parentage	12,916,311	10,632,280	2,284,031	21.5	14.0	14.0
Mixed parentage	5,981,526	5,013,737	967,789	19.3	6.5	6.6
Foreign born	13,345,545	10,213,817	3,131,728	30.7	14.5	13.4

[1] A minus sign (—) denotes decrease. [2] Less than one-tenth of 1 per cent.

"Of the population of the United States in 1910, 81,731,957, or 88.9 per cent., were whites; 9,827,763, or 10.7 per cent., were negroes; and 412,546, or four-tenths of 1 per cent., were other colored races.

"Of the total population, 78,456,380, or 85.3 per cent., were native and 13,515,886, or 14.7 per cent., foreign born, the latter consisting chiefly of whites.

"The native white population numbered 68,386,-412, and constituted 83.7 per cent. of the white population and 74.4 per cent. of the total population of the country. The 13,345,545 foreign-born whites constituted 16.3 per cent. of the white population and 14.5 per cent. of the total population.

"Native whites of native parentage in 1910 numbered 49,488,575, constituting 60.5 per cent. of the white population and 53.8 per cent. of the total population. Native whites of foreign parentage formed 15.8 per cent. of the white population and those of mixed parentage 7.3 per cent., the corresponding percentages based on the total population being 14 and 6.5, respectively.

"Of the total increase of 15,977,691 in the population of the country between 1900 and 1910, the whites contributed 14,922,761, the negroes 993,769, and other races 61,161. The increase in the native population was 12,803,081, and that in the foreign born 3,174,610, or about one-fifth of the total increase.

"The percentage of increase for the whites, 22.3, was a little less than twice as high as that for the negroes, 11.2. This difference is partly due, however, to the direct or indirect effect of immigration upon the increase of the white population. The native white population increased 20.8 per cent. and the foreign-born white 30.7 per cent. There was very little difference in the rates of increase for the three parentage groups of the native white population."

The above table graphically exhibits the fearful contract we have upon our hands, in the matter of *absorbing* this mass of savage people through the proposed plan of miscegenation. No full-blooded American, of pure Anglo-Saxon ancestry, actuated by pride of race, national and family history, in the light of his country's achievements, could for a moment favor such an infamous proposition.

In Tables 2, 3, 5, and others, further light is thrown on this subject; they are as follows:—

"White and Negro Population.—The number of whites and negroes in the total population of the

United States at each census from 1790 to 1910 is given in Table 2.

TABLE 2.

CENSUS YEAR.	NUMBER.				PER CENT. OF TOTAL.		
	Total population.	White.	Negro.	Indian, Chinese, Japanese, and all other.	White.	Negro.	Ind., Chi., Jap., and all other.
1910	91,972,266	81,731,957	9,827,763	412,546	88.9	10.7	0.4
1900	75,994,575	66,809,196	8,833,994	351,385	87.9	11.6	0.5
1890	62,947,714	55,101,258	7,488,676	357,780	87.5	11.9	0.6
1880	50,155,783	43,402,970	6,580,793	172,020	86.5	13.1	0.3
1870[1]	38,558,371	33,589,377	4,880,009	88,985	87.1	12.7	0.2
1870[2]	*39,818,449*	*34,337,292*	*5,392,172*	*88,985*	*86.2*	*13.5*	*0.2*
1860	31,443,321	26,922,537	4,441,830	78,954	85.6	14.1	0.3
1850	23,191,876	19,553,068	3,638,808	....	84.3	15.7	....
1840	17,069,453	14,195,805	2,873,648	....	83.2	16.8	....
1830	12,866,020	10,537,378	2,328,642	....	81.9	18.1	....
1820	9,638,453	7,866,797	1,771,656	....	81.6	18.4	....
1810	7,239,881	5,862,073	1,377,808	....	81.0	19.0	....
1800	5,308,483	4,306,446	1,002,037	....	81.1	18.9	....
1790	3,929,214	3,172,006	757,208	....	80.7	19.3	....

1 As enumerated.
2 Estimated corrected figures. See explanation in text.

"Table 3 gives the decennial increase, both absolute and relative, in the white and in the negro population for each decade from 1790 to 1910.

TABLE 3.

DECADE.	INCREASE.			PER CENT. OF INCREASE.		
	Total.	White.	Negro.	Total.	White.	Negro.
1900–1910	15,977,691	14,922,761	993,769	21.0	22.3	11.2
1890–1900	13,046,861	11,707,938	1,345,318	20.7	21.2	18.0
1880–1889	[1] 12,466,467	[1] 11,580,920	[1] 889,247	24.9	26.7	13.5
1870–1880	11,597,412	9,813,593	1,700,784	30.1	29.2	34.9
1870–1880[2]	*10,337,334*	*9,065,678*	*1,188,621*	*26.0*	*26.4*	*22.0*
1860–1870[2]	*8,375,128*	*7,414,755*	*950,342*	*26.6*	*27.5*	*21.3*
1860–1870	7,115,050	6,666,840	438,179	22.6	24.8	9.9
1850–1860	8,251,445	7,369,469	803,022	35.6	37.7	22.1
1840–1850	6,122,423	5,357,263	765,160	35.9	37.7	26.6
1830–1840	4,203,433	3,658,427	545,006	32.7	34.7	23.4
1820–1830	3,227,567	2,670,581	556,986	33.5	33.9	31.4
1810–1820	2,398,572	2,004,724	393,848	33.1	34.2	28.6
1800–1810	1,931,398	1,555,627	375,771	36.4	36.1	37.5
1790–1800	1,379,269	1,134,440	244,829	35.1	35.8	32.3

1 Exclusive of 325,464 persons (among whom were 117,368 whites and 18,636 negroes) specially enumerated in 1890 in Indian Territory and on Indian reservations.
2 Estimated corrected increase.

"The addition to the total white population in the decade 1900-1910 was considerably greater than during any other decade and indeed exceeded the total white population of the country in 1840. The increase in the negro population, however, was less than that from 1890 to 1900 and was much less than that from 1870 to 1880 as based on the returns.

"If, however, the irregularity in the increase for the decades 1860-1870 and 1870-1880, due to the defective enumeration of the population in 1870, be corrected to correspond with the estimated population of 1870, the increase of negroes from 1870 to 1880 becomes less marked, although still greater than that from 1900 to 1910.

"Assuming the estimates for 1870 to be approximately correct, each decade since 1790 has shown for the white population an absolute gain larger than that for the decade immediately preceding, and the percentage of increase for the white population has exceeded that for the negro population in every decade since 1790 except 1800-1810. In the 50 years 1860-1910 the white population increased 203.6 per cent. and the negro population 121.3 per cent.

"Black and Mulatto Population.—Table 5 gives a classification of the negro population as black or mulatto for the several censuses at which this distinction has been made.

"No data are available for 1880 or 1900. Of the 9,827,763 negroes enumerated in 1910, 7,777,077 were returned as black and 2,050,686 as mulatto. In 1850 the percentage of mulattoes was 11.2. It had advanced but little in 1870, being only 12 per cent., but since 1870 the proportion of mulattoes in the

TABLE 5.

CENSUS YEAR.[1]	NEGRO POPULATION.			PER CENT. OF TOTAL.	
	Total.	Black.	Mulatto.	Black.	Mulatto.
1910..............	9,827,763	7,777,077	2,050,686	79.1	20.9
1890..............	[2]7,488,676	6,337,980	1,132,060	84.8	15.2
1870..............	4,880,009	4,295,960	584,049	88.0	12.0
1860..............	4,441,830	3,853,467	588,363	86.8	13.2
1850..............	3,638,808	3,233,057	405,751	88.8	11.2

[1] No data for 1880 or 1900.
[2] Includes 18,636 negroes enumerated in Indian Territory, not distinguished as black or mulatto.

total negro population appears to have increased very materially, reaching 15.2 per cent. in 1890 and 20.9 per cent. in 1910. Considerable uncertainty necessarily attaches to this classification, however, since the accuracy of the distinction made depends largely upon the judgment and care of the enumerators. Moreover, the fact that the definition of the term 'mulatto' adopted at different censuses has not been entirely uniform may affect the comparability of the figures in some degree. In 1870, as in 1910, however, the term was applied to all persons having any perceptible trace of negro blood, excepting, of course, negroes of pure blood.

"POPULATION BY COLOR OR RACE, NATIVITY, AND PARENTAGE.—The population of the divisions and states in 1910 and 1900 is classified in Table 12 by color or race, and in Table 13 by nativity and parentage.

"The general geographic distribution of the principal race, nativity, and parentage classes of the population in 1910 is indicated in Table 11.

"Of the total white population in 1910, about two-thirds (54,640,209, or 66.9 per cent.) were in the four

TABLE 11.—PER CENT. DISTRIBUTION BY GEOGRAPHIC DIVISIONS: 1910.

SECTION AND DIVISION.	Total population.	White.				Negro.	Ind., Chi., Jap., and all other.
		Total.	Native.		Foreign born.		
			Native parentage.	Foreign or mixed parentage.			
UNITED STATES	100.0	100.0	100.0	100.0	100.0	100.0	100.0
THE NORTH	60.6	66.9	55.3	84.5	84.8	10.5	21.6
New England	7.1	7.9	5.3	10.9	13.6	0.7	1.4
Middle Atlantic	21.0	23.1	17.1	29.6	36.2	4.3	4.3
East North Central	19.8	21.9	19.7	27.0	23.0	3.1	5.4
West North Central	12.7	13.9	13.2	17.0	12.1	2.5	10.6
THE SOUTH	32.0	25.1	37.5	6.7	5.4	89.0	22.4
South Atlantic	13.3	9.9	14.8	2.3	2.2	41.8	2.6
East South Central	9.1	7.0	11.0	1.1	0.7	27.0	0.7
West South Central	9.6	8.2	11.7	3.2	2.6	20.2	19.1
THE WEST	7.4	8.0	7.2	8.8	9.7	0.5	56.0
Mountain	2.9	3.1	3.0	3.3	3.3	0.2	22.2
Pacific	4.6	4.9	4.3	5.6	6.5	0.3	33.8

northern divisions, and of the negro population, approximately nine-tenths (8,749,427, or 89 per cent.) were in the three southern divisions."

Table 12 of the Bulletin is altogether too extensive to incorporate here, as one may well imagine, for it presents the census for 1910 and 1900, compared with respect to color or race by divisions and states.

Without giving explicit figures, the maps I have borrowed from these Bulletins present this information in sufficient detail and clearness.

This very instructive Bulletin gives three other such maps as the one here shown in Fig. 47, exhibiting the "Percentage of Foreign-born Whites in the Total Population: 1910;" the "Percentage of Native Whites of Foreign or Mixed Parentage in the Total Population: 1910," and the "Percentage of Foreign-born Whites of Foreign or Mixed Parentage Combined in the Total Population: 1910."

These several maps show most clearly, beyond all doubt, that the immense number of white immigrants, annually flowing into the country, are practically entirely avoiding the Southern States of the whole southeast section of the United States; and the two

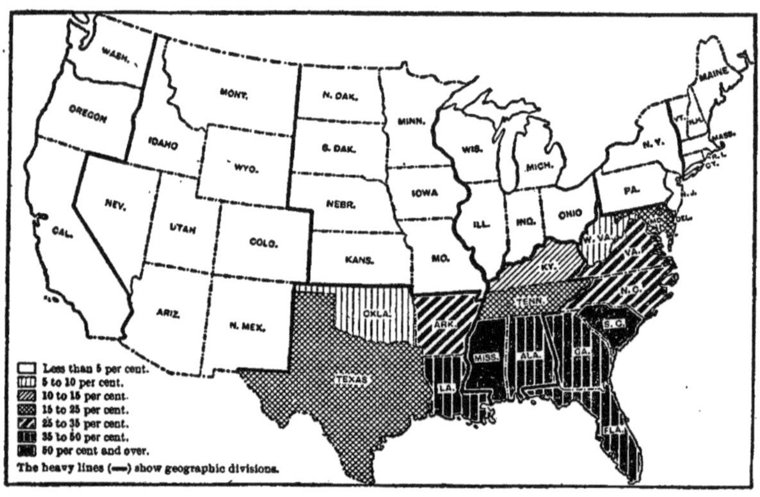

FIG. 47.—PERCENTAGE OF NEGROES IN THE TOTAL POPULATION: 1910.

other maps (page 85 of the Bulletin) go to show that this likewise applies to those of foreign and mixed parentage in the country. In other words, the foreign immigration, flowing into the United States, is carefully avoiding the States of Virginia, North and South Carolina, Tennessee, Georgia, Alabama, Arkansas, and Mississippi. So that the *white population* of these several States has the negro on its hands, and is, *at the present time,* that section of the country most interested in the solution of the "negro problem"—as any woman in the "black belt" will tell you!

In further support of this, a part of Table 14 is here introduced, giving the White and Negro Comparison for the per cent. distribution by divisions and States (1910-1900):—

TABLE 14.

DIVISION AND STATE.	White.		Negro.	
	1910	1900	1910	1900
UNITED STATES	88.9	87.9	10.7	11.6
GEOGRAPHIC DIVISIONS:				
New England	98.9	98.8	1.0	1.1
Middle Atlantic	97.7	97.8	2.2	2.1
East North Central	98.2	98.3	1.6	1.6
West North Central	97.5	97.3	2.1	2.3
South Atlantic	66.2	64.2	33.7	35.7
East South Central	68.4	66.8	31.5	33.1
West South Central	76.5	73.0	22.6	25.9
Mountain	95.7	94.3	0.8	0.9
Pacific	96.0	94.9	0.7	0.6
NEW ENGLAND:				
Maine	99.7	99.7	0.2	0.2
New Hampshire	99.8	99.8	0.1	0.2
Vermont	99.5	99.7	0.5	0.2
Massachusetts	98.8	98.7	1.1	1.1
Rhode Island	98.1	97.8	1.8	2.1
Connecticut	98.6	98.2	1.4	1.7
MIDDLE ATLANTIC:				
New York	98.4	98.4	1.5	1.4
New Jersey	96.4	96.2	3.5	3.7
Pennsylvania	97.4	97.5	2.5	2.5
EAST NORTH CENTRAL:				
Ohio	97.6	97.7	2.3	2.3
Indiana	97.7	97.7	2.2	2.3
Illinois	98.0	98.2	1.9	1.8
Michigan	99.1	99.1	0.6	0.7
Wisconsin	99.4	99.5	0.1	0.1
WEST NORTH CENTRAL:				
Minnesota	99.2	99.2	0.3	0.3
Iowa	99.3	99.4	0.7	0.6
Missouri	95.2	94.8	4.8	5.2
North Dakota	98.8	97.7	0.1	0.1
South Dakota	96.6	94.8	0.1	0.1
Nebraska	99.0	99.1	0.6	0.6
Kansas	96.7	96.3	3.2	3.5
SOUTH ATLANTIC:				
Delaware	84.6	83.4	15.4	16.6
Maryland	82.0	80.2	17.9	19.8
District of Columbia	71.3	68.7	28.5	31.1
Virginia	67.4	64.3	32.6	35.6
West Virginia	94.7	95.5	5.3	4.5
North Carolina	68.0	66.7	31.6	33.0
South Carolina	44.8	41.6	55.2	58.4
Georgia	54.9	53.3	45.1	46.7
Florida	58.9	56.3	41.0	43.7
EAST SOUTH CENTRAL:				
Kentucky	88.6	86.7	11.4	13.3
Tennessee	78.3	76.2	21.7	23.8
Alabama	57.5	54.7	42.5	45.2
Mississippi	43.7	41.3	56.2	58.5
WEST SOUTH CENTRAL:				
Arkansas	71.8	72.0	28.1	28.0
Louisiana	56.8	52.8	43.1	47.1
Oklahoma [1]	87.2	84.8	8.3	7.0
Texas	82.2	79.6	17.7	20.4
MOUNTAIN:				
Montana	95.9	93.0	0.5	0.6
Idaho	98.0	95.5	0.2	0.2
Wyoming	96.1	96.2	1.5	1.0
Colorado	98.0	98.0	1.4	1.6
New Mexico	93.1	92.3	0.5	0.8
Arizona	83.9	75.6	1.0	1.5
Utah	98.2	98.5	0.3	0.2
Nevada	90.7	83.6	0.6	0.3
PACIFIC:				
Washington	97.1	95.8	0.5	0.5
Oregon	97.4	95.4	0.2	0.3
California	95.0	94.5	0.9	0.7

[1] Less than one-tenth of 1 per cent.

This Bulletin also gives us a number of most instructive diagrams, showing at a glance the distribution of the negroes in the United States, and their relative proportions with respect to the white population, both in the urban and rural districts and places, etc. It is not necessary to reproduce any of these diagrams here; for, should the reader require such extended information, it can easily be obtained from the Bulletin itself, which, as I say, is almost exhaustive in this respect.

With this immense horde of negroes upon our hands, there comes up another question for consideration and one of the most vital importance.

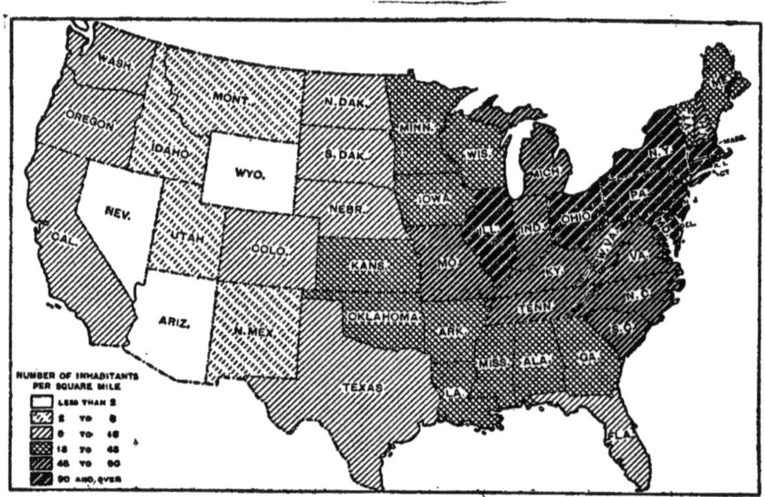

FIG. 48.—POPULATION PER SQUARE MILE BY STATES: 1910.

How is the hygiene of the country influenced by these negroes? There is a large literature now extant on this subject, much of which, during the last few years, I have read. It can easily be shown that the race, as a whole, is an extremely uncleanly one. To appreciate this fact, the investigator needs but to make a house-to-house survey of negro homes in any of our cities, in the rural districts, or on any Southern plantation. The great bulk of their homes or other habitations are filthy and disease-breeding. I would say that it was the case in at least 85 per cent. of them.

Few groups of diseases undermine the health of a nation more thoroughly than the so-called venereal diseases, and the negro in this country is the disseminator of these very diseases,—a fact due to his promiscuous carnal relations among all classes of women; to his lack of cleanliness; ignorance of infection and methods of prevention, and the renewal of his immoral practices before a cure is effected. This knowledge, now so abundantly spread before us, would alone be sufficient to segregate all the negroes in the Government departments and elsewhere, as well as in all hotels, sleeping cars, places of public comfort, and other resorts of any and all characters, built and maintained by the whites.

A few years ago, I read two excellent articles on this subject, compiled by Mr. Robert W. Wooley, now of the U. S. Auditor's Office (*Pearson's Magazine,* January and February, 1910), who based his facts, in regard to the matter of the negroes spreading the venereal diseases—and especially syphilis—on the published writings of the most eminent syphilologists and syphilographers in the United States. What Mr. Wooley brought to the notice of the American public on this question is simply appalling. And, notwithstanding this showing, such negroes and mulattoes as William Monroe Trotter, Booker T. Washington, and scores of others of their kind, cannot be made to see that this fact, as one among many, is sufficient to account for their being kept out of public places, and debarred from participating in the social functions given at the White House.

As I write these lines, Doctor James Bardin, of the University of Virginia, invites my attention to an address given by Dr. Robert Wilson, Jr., of Charleston, S. C., at the symposium on tuberculosis of the Southern Medical Association, which formally opened its eighth annual convention at Richmond, Va., on the 10th of November, 1914. Dr. Wilson said that, in the relation of the negro to disease, the South had a health problem of the very highest importance. He said that it was the clear duty of the South and justice to the negro to ascertain, by careful clinical and post-mortem study, if the commonly accepted belief that the negro is a menace to the health of the white race is true. He recognized that the negro had sowed the seeds of certain diseases in the South, and was particularly a carrier of the germs of malaria and tuberculosis. Special attention, he thought, should be paid to the relation of the negro to the spread of pellagra, since statistics from Southern States and cities show that he is more susceptible to this disease than the whites.

Doctor Wilson, with great propriety, might have been asked at the close of his address as to what his line of treatment would be, were he called into a case where the patient was suffering severely from the presence of a tapeworm. He probably would promptly answer: "Get rid of the parasite." I agree with him; and in its broader sense, this applies to the treatment of the "negro problem."

Since writing this brief reference to Dr. Wilson's address, he has very generously forwarded me the MS. of it entire. And as this contains so much on the matter here being discussed, and is so important a document for physicians everywhere, I am taking the liberty of reproducing the address here as it was delivered. Dr. Wilson said:—

"So many of the peculiar problems of Southern medicine are influenced in greater or less degree by the close association which of necessity exists between the two races in this part of the country, that I need offer no excuse for introducing the work of our section by a short discussion of some of the medical aspects of the negro. I appreciate thoroughly the magnitude of the subject and do not propose to attempt anything like a full and comprehensive treatment. I wish merely to point out very briefly the importance of the negro from the medical viewpoint, and to urge upon you the need of careful and accurate knowledge of his medical characteristics, indicating some of the lines of study which might prove profitable.

"While some work has been done, notably by Hoffman in his treatise on the 'Race Traits and Tendencies of the American Negro,' and in shorter publications by a number of writers, we are still very far from accurate knowledge based upon careful scientific work. Some of our conceptions are only unproved assumptions resting upon no more secure foundation than general impressions and current opinions. The negro is a large factor in our Southern life, economically as well as socially and politically, entering intimately into our domestic relations, coming into closest contact with us in practically every walk of life, and it is our clear duty to ourselves as well as to him to ascertain if the commonly accepted conceptions and beliefs be true, and to what extent he reacts upon the community at large.

"That the negro is a public health problem of the highest importance can scarcely be gainsaid. In the words of Sir Harry Johnston,[2] the negro 'is a hive of dangerous germs, perhaps has been the greatest disease-spreader among the other subspecies of *Homo sapiens.*'

"Coming from tropical Africa to America, he brought with him the diseases which afflicted him at home, to some of which he himself seems to have acquired no little degree of resistance, and sowed them in the Caucasian. Leprosy, hemoglobinuric fever, filariasis, uncinariasis, and yellow fever were probably introduced by the negro. Tuberculosis has found a fruitful soil in his tissues, rendering him a serious menace in our homes. Whether he is racially predisposed to tubercular disease, or whether, as I believe, his environment and habits will explain its prevalence, need not be discussed here; the important fact is that he has become a great carrier of tuberculosis. It is the general opinion that the negro is less susceptible to malaria than the white man. Hoffman,[3] however, adduces 'abundant proof that the negroes of today are far more liable to malarial and typhoid fever than the whites;' and Terry's[4] figures for the city of Jacksonville, covering the five-year period 1908-1912, show an average death rate from malaria per 100,000 of population among the whites of 1.72 as against 8.3 among the negroes. Von Esdorf[5] has pointed out that negroes are much more frequently

[2] Johnston, Sir Harry: "The Negro in the New World."

[3] "Race Traits and Tendencies of the American Negro."

[4] "The Negro: A Public Health Problem." Southern Medical Journal, June, 1914.

[5] Southern Medical Journal, June, 1914.

carriers of malarial infection than the whites, and it is highly probable that this is especially true of negro children in the rural districts. The important bearing which this must have upon the great problem of eradicating malaria should stimulate systematic research in order to ascertain the extent to which it is true.

"That the negro is a frequent carrier of filarial infection is, I believe, undoubtedly a fact. Some years ago I endeavored to ascertain the proportion of filaria-bearing negroes admitted to the Roper Hospital in Charleston, selecting for examination only those who gave no history of chyluria, and who presented no signs of elephantiasis. The investigation was cut short almost as soon as begun; but of about 35 cases examined, 18 per cent. were found to harbor the parasites. This work recently has been carried on upon a more extended scale and with more refined methods by Dr. F. B. Johnson, who has obtained some interesting results.

"With the ever-growing importance of the pellagra problem, the negro's relation to this disease must receive attention. The relative prevalence of pellagra among whites and negroes, the relations which exist between the habits and environment of the negro and the incidence of the disease are profitable subjects for investigation.

"In the following table is shown the death rate from pellagra for both whites and colored per 100,000 of population in three Southern cities, and in the three States in which the returns are tabulated separately for the two races:—

TABLE *I.*

Deaths from Pellagra per 100,000 of Population.

	Charleston.		Augusta.		Jacksonville.	
	W.	C.	W.	C.	W.	C.
1906	3.5	6.7	....	....	....	....
1909	3.5	33.9	....	....	....	....
1910	18.0	38.6	39.7	16.2	....	....
1911	28.5	76.6	105.4	32.4	16.6	9.6
1912	17.6	138.8	48.4	59.6	19.2	33.6
1913	35.2	149.0	32.1	59.0	27.2	11.6

	Kentucky.		Maryland.		North Carolina.	
	W.	C.	W.	C.	W.	C.
1910	2.8	2.7	....	....	5.3	4.2
1911	2.8	2.7	0.7	1.2	7.4	8.9
1912	4.2	6.7	0.4	1.2	5.5	5.9

The averages are as follows:—

Charleston	1908-1913,	Whites, 17.7	Negro, 73.9
Augusta	1910-1913,	Whites, 56.4	Negro, 41.8
Jacksonville	1912-1913,	Whites, 21.0	Negro, 18.2
Kentucky	1911-1912,	Whites, 3.5	Negro, 4.7
Maryland	1911-1912,	Whites, .55	Negro, 1.2
North Carolina	1910-1912,	Whites, 6.0	Negro, 6.3

"The high death rate in Charleston and Augusta may depend upon a heavy influx of negroes from the country, or possibly upon conditions which are peculiar to these cities. While these quotations are not extensive enough to be convincing, it is nevertheless of interest to note that in two of the cities, and all of the three States, the negro mortality from pellagra is in excess of the mortality among the whites. A comprehensive comparative study of the disease in the two races might throw important light upon some of its phases.

"In approaching the subject of syphilis in the negro, there is especial need to guard ourselves against preconceived notions. It is the prevailing opinion that practically every negro who has reached middle life is syphilitic, an opinion which finds support in the exceedingly lax moral standards of the race. This opinion may be true, but I have not been able to find any definite and exact data upon which it is based. Even if syphilis be as prevalent among the negroes as is commonly believed, they do not seem to suffer in the same degree as the whites from its evil consequences. Keyes[6] remarks that 'negroes, though utterly careless about treatment, are relatively immune to syphilis, and rarely exhibit syphilitic lesions.' Fox[7] concludes from his studies of skin diseases in the negro that while syphilis is more common than in the whites, it is 'probably not more virulent;' and Hazen[8] is 'convinced that syphilis is not more prevalent among them than among the whites.' David Livingstone[9] makes the following interesting observation: 'A certain loathsome disease, which decimates the North American Indians, and threatens extirpation to the South Sea Islanders, dies out in the interior of Africa without the aid of medicine; and the Bangwaketse, who brought it from the west coast, lost it when they came into their own land southwest of Kolobeng. It seems incapable of permanence in any form in persons of pure African blood anywhere in the center of the country. In persons of mixed blood it is otherwise; and the virulence of the secondary symptoms seemed to be, in all cases that came under my care, in exact proportion to the greater or

[6] "Syphilis."

[7] "Observations on Skin Diseases in the Negro."

[8] The Journal of the American Medical Association, August 8, 1914.

[9] "Missionary Travels and Researches in South Africa."

less amount of European blood in the patient. Among the Corannas and Griquas of mixed blood it produces the same ravages as in Europe. Among the half-blood Portuguese it is equally frightful in its inroads on the system; but in the pure Negro of the central parts it is quite incapable of permanence.'

"Sir Richard Burton[10] expresses similar views: 'As might be expected among an ignorant and debauched race coming in direct contact with semicivilization, the lues has found its way from the Island of Zanzibar to Ujiji, and into the heart of Africa. . . . The disease, however, dies out and has not taken root in the people as among the devoted races of North America and the South Sea Islands.'

"The observation of Livingstone, that the virulence of syphilis seems to vary directly in proportion with the mixture of European blood, may have an important bearing upon the prevalence and severity of the disease in the American negro. While it is rather difficult to separate the mulatto from pure negroes always, it might be done in our clinics with sufficient accuracy to make the results of some value.

"An examination of the vital statistics of the cities and States already mentioned may throw a little side-light upon this uncertain subject, although no definite conclusion can be drawn. Turn for example to Table II, showing the comparative death rates from disease of the arteries, including aneurism, and from organic heart disease, which are selected on account of their frequent association with syphilis; for, as Osler[11] states: '*The* infection with which aneurism is espe-

---

[10] Burton, Sir Richard: "Lake Regions of Central Africa."

[11] "The Principles and Practice of Medicine."

cially connected is syphilis,' and lues far more often attacks the aortic segments than those of the mitral ring.

TABLE *II.*

Deaths from Disease of Arteries, Including Aneurism, per 100,000 of Population.

	Charleston.		Augusta.		Jacksonville.	
	W.	C.	W.	C.	W.	C.
1909	73.9	64.6	....	....	....	....
1910	82.8	61.2	13.2	32.5	....	....
1911	57.0	73.2	14.9	32.0	9.5	9.1
1912	63.7	58.1	25.7	36.3	21.2	17.5
1913	32.4	97.2	....	....	....	....

	Kentucky.		Maryland.		North Carolina.	
	W.	C.	W.	C.	W.	C.
1910	....	....	15.9	12.6	1.3	18.3
1911	9.7	12.1	19.7	20.4	2.0	2.0
1912	12.6	17.6	26.3	23.3	2.2	1.9

The averages are as follows:—

Charleston	1909-1913,	Whites, 61.9	Negro, 70.8
Augusta	1910-1913,	Whites, 17.9	Negro, 33.6
Jacksonville	1912-1913,	Whites, 15.3	Negro, 13.3
Kentucky	1911-1912,	Whites, 11.15	Negro, 14.8
Maryland	1910-1912,	Whites, 20.6	Negro, 18.7
North Carolina	1910-1912,	Whites, 1.8	Negro, 7.4

"In Jacksonville and in Maryland the white death rate was higher than the negro; in other cities and States the negro death rate was higher, considerably so in Augusta and in N. Carolina. These statistics perhaps do not cover a sufficient number of years, neither do they include a sufficient number of cities, to be of very great significance; still they do suggest that the grave effects of syphilis upon the arteries are not as frequent in the negro as we might expect if the disease is as prevalent as we are accustomed to believe, or if the negro is equally susceptible to this particular manifestation of lues as the white man.

"In the following table the comparative death rates from organic heart disease are shown:—

TABLE *III.*

Deaths from Organic Heart Disease per 100,000 of Population.

	Charleston.		Augusta.		Jacksonville.	
	W.	C.	W.	C.	W.	C.
1909	151.5	417.8	....	....	....	....
1910	151.2	332.0	79.4	146.6	....	....
1911	160.6	513.0	87.8	216.4	119.6	179.8
1912	127.3	461.6	119.1	256.7	79.2	128.4
1913	70.4	314.3	80.9	140.7	75.7	105.2

	Kentucky.		Maryland.		North Carolina.	
	W.	C.	W.	C.	W.	C.
1910	....	....	124.3	336.4	14.3	30.7
1911	74.4	179.1	127.5	212.2	15.2	38.4
1912	80.3	187.7	135.5	208.4	16.2	35.9

The averages are as follows:—

Charleston	1909-1913,	White, 132.2	Negro, 407.7
Augusta	1910-1913,	White, 91.8	Negro, 190.1
Jacksonville	1911-1913,	White, 91.5	Negro, 137.8
Kentucky	1911-1912,	White, 77.3	Negro, 183.4
Maryland	1910-1912,	White, 129.1	Negro, 253.3
North Carolina ...	1910-1912,	White, 15.2	Negro, 34.9

"The excess of negro over white deaths from this class of cases is uniformly very great. The vital statistics tables do not enumerate the aortic and the mitral deaths separately, and consequently no conclusion can be drawn as to their relative frequency; but my impression, drawn from my experience in the hospital wards, is that the mitral lesions are largely in excess of the aortic among negroes. If this opinion be correct it will give support to the views expressed in connection with the statistics relative to arterial disease.

"Acute and chronic nephritis claim a large share of negro deaths, and everywhere the preponderance over white deaths is very marked, as will be seen by reference to the following table:—

TABLE IV.

Deaths from Acute Nephritis and Chronic Nephritis per 100,000 of Population.

ACUTE NEPHRITIS.

	Charleston.		Augusta.		Jacksonville.	
	W.	C.	W.	C.	W.	C.
1909	24.6	81.5	....	....	....	....
1910	39.6	90.2	30.88	48.87	....	....
1911	21.4	93.2	21.95	10.82	....	....
1912	21.2	116.2	11.17	105.34	25.36	24.46
1913	24.6	97.2	7.36	63.56	21.2	26.29

	Kentucky.		Maryland.		North Carolina.	
	W.	C.	W.	C.	W.	C.
1910	....	....	10.9	28.1	1.7	2.3
1911	4.9	14.3	11.9	30.6	0.9	2.6
1912	6.3	10.9	13.6	30.7	1.6	3.0

CHRONIC NEPHRITIS.

	Charleston.		Augusta.		Jacksonville.	
	W.	C.	W.	C.	W.	C.
1909	218.4	295.5	....	....	....	....
1910	190.8	364.2	114.7	108.6	....	....
1911	232.0	413.1	144.87	180.17	....	....
1912	194.6	355.0	201.1	192.36	156.55	223.22
1913	225.3	291.6	165.6	263.32	154.53	172.28

	Kentucky.		Maryland.		North Carolina.	
	W.	C.	W.	C.	W.	C.
1910	....	....	111.6	135.2	1.2	16.7
1911	56.2	87.5	104.8	148.4	10.8	20.0
1912	62.0	115.2	111.6	172.1	13.6	20.6

TABLE IV. (*Concluded.*)

The averages are as follows:—

ACUTE NEPHRITIS.

Charleston	1909-1913,	White, 26.2	Negro, 95.6
Augusta	1910-1913,	White, 17.8	Negro, 57.1
Jacksonville	1912-1913,	White, 23.2	Negro, 25.3
Kentucky	1911-1912,	White, 5.6	Negro, 12.6
Maryland	1910-1912,	White, 12.1	Negro, 29.8
North Carolina	1910-1912,	White, 1.4	Negro, 2.6

CHRONIC NEPHRITIS.

Charleston	1909-1913,	White, 212.2	Negro, 343.8
Augusta	1910-1913,	White, 156.5	Negro, 186.1
Jacksonville	1912-1913,	White, 155.5	Negro, 197.7
Kentucky	1911-1912,	White, 59.1	Negro, 101.3
Maryland	1910-1912,	White, 109.3	Negro, 151.9
North Carolina	1910-1912,	White, 8.5	Negro, 19.1

"His extremely high mortality from the combined cardio-vascular-renal diseases is one of the most striking features of the negro, medically considered. We are not yet in a position to assign a cause. Perhaps his apparent susceptibility to many of the acute infections is largely responsible, and perhaps his mode of living plays an important part. Possibly, too, we are in error when we assume that the negro is the physiological counterpart of the white man.

"If we are to solve these problems we must first break ourselves of the habit of taking things for granted, and accepting assumptions for facts. In studying the negro we should begin by separating, as far as possible, the mulatto from the pure stock. Careful and comprehensive clinical observations should be followed by laboratory and post-mortem investigation. Such combined study, carried on in our Southern schools and clinics, would, in the course of a few years, enable us to rest our knowledge of the negro upon a secure foundation of fact, and I believe would aid materially in the solution of some of our medical and public health problems."

Were any American physician to discover, in the locality where he practised, a family, five or six members of which had developed well-marked leprosy, what would be the first steps he would take in order to prevent the spread of the disease, to insure the protection of the community? There can be but one answer: We know the disease; and segregation of the patients, and, if possible, deportation to some island where many more of their kind are located, is the only safe and proper thing to do. Leprosy is no worse a disease than what the presence of the negro stands for in this country today, and especially in the South. The only trouble is: This Government is a bad physician in a case demanding—long demanding—prompt and very different treatment from that which it has heretofore received. We know that the parasite is gnawing at the patient's vitals, but our procrastination and moral cowardice prevent us from applying the proper treatment. That's all.

It is senseless to trifle with this matter; and it is a thoroughly proven fact that the negro in the United States is, among other things, a constant menace to the health of the white race by reason of his being a pronounced disseminator of some five or six of the most dreaded diseases known to man. Were all the negroes and mulattoes in the United States sent bodily out of it, there can be no question whatever but that the hygiene of the country would at once improve, and this improvement would rapidly enhance as time passed (November 18, 1914). We cannot eliminate syphilis if we maintain thousands of blacks among us who are spreading it. What progress can we make with the "white plague" when a large per cent. of its propagation is due to the *black race?* Can we expect strong, healthy women to be the future mothers all through the "black belt," if hundreds of them, nay thousands, are to have their nerves ever on the stretch, through the fear of assault from some negro among the hordes that surround them on all sides? Never!

Sometime during the month of September, 1912, I accompanied Dr. White and Dr. Henry P. de Forest, of New York City, through the exhibition rooms of the American Congress of Hygiene, which met in Washington, D. C. that autumn. In one room, among others of a similar character, was hung a chart giving data with respect to the extent of prostitution and the venereal diseases among the negroes of this country.

This showing greatly displeased the negroes of Washington and they demanded its removal,—a demand which was promptly complied with by the Exhibition Committee of the Congress. Seeing the chart on the floor, leaning against the wall in such a way that the data was completely out of sight, Dr. de Forest lifted it up and hung it again in its place with the written-upon side facing outward. No one interfered with him. The three of us copied each his third of the statistics given, which, when completed, went into Dr. de Forest's possession. On his return to New York City, where he is professor of obstetrics in the Post-Graduate Medical School, he wrote me a letter (October 1, 1912) from which I quote the following:—

"My dear Doctor Shufeldt:—

"I am sending you herewith the result of the combined efforts of Drs. White, de Forest and yourself on Saturday last. My new secretary is a word-reader, and was able to decipher what each one of us had written.

"It would be a good thing, I believe, if this chart, with a comment as to the reasons for its removal, was published in one of the Washington papers, and it certainly will be of value in your preparation of the new edition of 'The Negro.'"

The following is the copy of the chart and the "comment" which Dr. de Forest was kind enough to supply:—

"THE NEGRO, PROSTITUTION AND VENEREAL DISEASE.

"There are about 10,000,000 negroes in the United States. Eighty-seven thousand of these are in Philadelphia alone.

"Hospital experience enters at some time into the life of nearly every city negro. Hospital records show that practically all male city negroes indulge in promiscuous illicit intercourse and carry with them venereal disease.

"It is the exception in hospital experience for a male negro to fail to admit having been infected with both syphilis and gonorrhea. These occurrences are with him almost a matter of course. Almost never is treatment carried to the point of cure.

"The result of the general infection of the male city negro is the almost equally widespread syphilization of the female population. The vast majority of city negro girls have been violated long before maturity, and very few have escaped infection with both syphilis and gonococcus disease.

"The gravest problem to be faced in dealing with the city negro is not his or her industrial future or right to social equality with the white man or woman. It is the danger to the public of his or her contagiousness and infections from the standpoint of physical and moral disease.

"Illicit intercourse between the negro and the white is taking place to an extent that is hardly believable until the question is deliberately studied. It has been estimated that one-third of the American negroes have an admixture of blood. A scrutiny of the features and the color of the negroes that walk the city streets, forces home the conviction that nearly all carry the blood of the white race.

"(The above chart was one of a series of charts shown at the 15th International Congress of Hygiene and Demography, held at Washington, September 23d to 28th, 1912. It was one of a series of similar charts included in the section devoted to Sex Hygiene. The chart attracted a great deal of attention on the part of the colored population of the city, about 30 per cent., and although the statements therein contained are truthful, and would be substantiated by any physician in any of the Southern cities where there is a large colored population, so much political pressure was brought to bear that the chart was removed.)"

So much, then, for the presence of these millions of negroes in our country from the view of public hygiene. And yet, with all this widely known, there are among us not a few of my own race who at this writing not only favor but urge free intermarriage of the whites and the negroes in the United States, as the only solution of the problem that now confronts us, and which is becoming a more serious one each year that passes. Many such men and women are of a class holding positions of the highest order, and who perhaps have a claim to refinement, intelligence, education, and a distinguished ancestry. This is the marvel of it! There are biologists and those who accept the laws of organic evolution among us, who seem to be so blinded by their science that they cannot appreciate the fact that the mixing, through marriage, of the negro and white stock in the United States can only result in type elimination in the case of the first, and the destruction of the civilization of the second group.

Those who believe in the philosophy, permanence, and *morality* of the monogamic marriage, as now performed in America, seem to utterly ignore what the consequences would be, in a very short time, were any such condition established. It is bad enough as it is for far-seeing people, as history has already proven that it is not the typical black-skinned negroes in the United States who have ever contributed a line to literature worth the printing; a single cog in the machine of invention; an idea to *any* science; or, in short, advanced civilization a single millimeter since the first Congo pair was placed on this soil. It is, on the other hand, those whom the pure negroes delight in claiming *as negroes*—the half-bloods, the mulattoes—of every shade of mixture, who have been given places of position, trust, and responsibility in the community. It is principally these mulattoes who crave all the advantages that American civilization and society can extend, even to being invited in numbers to the "social functions at the White House."

Think of the ladies of the land and the "first lady of the land" engaging in conversation with a group of these mulattoes in the East Room of the White House! Think of how the whole question of birth and ancestry must be constantly and skilfully avoided by these ladies throughout the conversation engaged in during such a function! For, although the mulattoes present are in no way responsible for the fact, yet, is it altogether desirable that these ladies should freely mingle in a social way with such a class, when, in the case of any and every one of them, his or her pedigree goes back, in the very near past, to a mating out of wedlock of a negress and some white father possessing intelligence and an education above the average?

Then, too, all these mulattoes have at this moment *black* relatives living with their tribes in Africa, many of which, where not under restraint by the whites, are still cannibals of the most fiendish variety!

Does America want this to *become general throughout the land?* Morality shrieks *No!* And civilization shudders at the very thought of it.

Let me say to some of those gentlemen who have recently ignored my correspondence on this subject, and who are of the opinion that this is what we must naturally expect from the operation of the law of evolution,—that unfortunately they are largely correct in the premises; and I may add, in so far as it falls within the law of organic evolution for consideration, the question is to be relegated to that phase of it which pertains to the matter of very undesirable and faulty breeding. Evolution in nature is one thing; but the deliberate crossing of various stocks in domesticity (man included) is quite another thing. No intelligent breeder of sporting dogs, for instance, would think for a moment of crossing his refined breed of setters with the yellow pups of the street, with the view of perpetuating in the first-named a stock that it had required several centuries to bring about.

Many years ago, I listened to a lecture at the U. S. National Museum, delivered by the late John Wesley Powell, then Director of the Geological Survey, who said, in the course of his remarks, that in the higher civilizations of the present day, man made his own environment, and was largely responsible for the results of his evolution.

It has taken untold ages for the white peoples of the world to develop the kind of civilization now found in it; at the best it rests upon a very unstable foundation, with, I fear, but little in some of its parts to support its respectability, as the present war in Europe will vouch for (November, 1914). Surely, in so far as America is concerned, we would not expect to strengthen this civilization in any way whatever by the introduction of miscegenation with a black race, still closely linked to cannibal tribes in Africa, who are, at the same time, non-moral, unhygienic, ignorant, and basically savage? I think decidedly not; and I think so as an evolutionist. The American eagle has a lot of chestnut burrs in her nest; it is high time she settled down to the legitimate business of incubating pure stock, and toss the disturbing burrs over the edge of her aery.

Unfortunately, in the case of these negroes in the United States, the evils of miscegenation do not rest upon the question of marriage of the two races; for, as I have several times pointed out above, it is now being accomplished at a rapid rate without the aid of that institution. As Arabs, Jews, and Egyptians are in no way comparable with negroes, the argument used by many falls to the ground, when it is pointed out that Spaniards in Spain were unchanged in any way during the six hundred years that their conquerors, the Arabs, were in their country, or that the Egyptians and Jews were modified to any extent during the long bondage of the latter in Egypt. It was the chief pride of all of these people to preserve the purity of the race to which they belonged; but the negro is absolutely devoid of pride in such a matter. He has nothing to lose and everything to gain; and in the light of this, those negrophiles among us would have us come down to the level of this host of savages, or at least through intermarriage meet them half-way.

We actually enlighten the negro in this country in every possible way in regard to the physical charms of the women of our race; what wonder, then, that results follow which any intelligent anthropologist could predict? Were the gates thrown open today, there are thousands of our race who would stand aghast at what would happen. One hundred negroes to one would immediately seek white wives, and the same percentage holds true in the case of the young negresses,—they would delight in making alliances with white men. The truth of this statement I know from personal interrogation of many of the black race in all parts of the Union.

In many instances I have taken the trouble to trace the parentage of intelligent and fine-looking mulattoes in New York, Washington, Mobile, New Orleans, Baltimore, and elsewhere. In five instances, the fathers proved to be officers of the army, and among the others there were men from nearly every profession, trade, and calling in the country. In several cases, the mothers were as black as the blackest Congo negress that ever lived. I could give some very interesting details along these lines, which, if widely known, might to some extent dampen the ardor of those who confuse undesirable breeding—faulty eugenics—with the law of evolution.

The time has now passed when any negro in this country thinks for a single instant of looking up his relatives in Africa,—a desire that would have been an all-pervading one had that many Americans been forcibly taken from their country, and brought, as slaves, to another and far-off land. In this respect, the Africans in the United States have conducted themselves much in the same way as so many apes would have done under similar circumstances. Even now, with all their holdings and advantages, no one of them ever makes any effort to investigate the land of their fathers, or to search out their kin in fair Ethiopia. The great bulk of their millions, beyond the wearing of clothes, are not one whit wiser, better, or more useful than they were the day they were brought here as slaves; it is only the illegitimate mulattoes that show any improvement.

As Walker[12] says in "Our Home Colony:" "In the Anglo-Saxon civilization the Negro is out of place. It is impossible for an alien race, placed as is the Negro race, in America, to have independent thought or action.

"The Negro has no ideals of his own; nor can he have. Everything that pertains to his own ethnic type he despises, and this is done in most cases unconsciously.

"Hundreds of Negro women do for white men what they refuse to do for men of their own race. Some Negro men, called 'leading Negroes,' engaged in menial occupations, are so bereft of manly and independent traits that they persistently refuse to work for members of their own race. They give as their excuse: 'It would ruin my business to work for Negroes.' The Negro prostitute says the same thing.

"Rarely, indeed, will you find a young American Negro girl or boy striving to cultivate a Negro type. They are trying to turn Anglo-Saxon. Any person at all acquainted with the nature of the human soul can see to what license this thing must lead.

"Lynching is mild as compared with the remedy that will be applied by the whites when they realize the dangers a continuance of the present relation of the races has in store for them.

"The Negro race will be a menace and a source of discontent as long as it remains in large numbers in the United States. The time is growing very near

[12] Walker, M. F.: "Our Home Colony: A Treatise on the Past, Present and Future of the Negro Race in America," pp. 28, 29. This little pamphlet, published by *The Herald Printing Company,* of Steubenville, Ohio, is one of the best and clearest discussions of the negro problem in the United States that I have ever read.

when the whites of the United States must either settle this problem by deportation, or else be willing to accept a reign of terror such as the world has never seen in a civilized country."

The state of affairs with respect to the negro in the South, and many places in the North, to which attention has been invited in this chapter, is thus commented on by Mr. A. V. Snell, managing secretary to the Chamber of Commerce of Charleston, S. C., in a letter to Mrs. Annie Riley Hale, dated May 21, 1913. After giving the population of that city from 1900 to 1910,[13] Mr. Snell remarks: "You will see, therefore, that not only has the black population decreased in this city, but also in the county. On the other hand, however, for every negro that has left, there has been one white man at least and more. Charleston has infinitely gained in the last ten years. The negro here is shiftless and useless, ignorant and unsanitary.

"If you will compare the census you will find that our mortality and illiterate rate are due almost entirely to the negro. The worst of it is that his character is not so much improved by his contact with the white man as it is that it acts upon the white man, making him shiftless and generally careless, in all phases of life. The negro, in my opinion, is absolutely the worst drawback the South has, and no one can doubt that, if it were possible to move every colored man from the South today, replacing him by a white man, in ten years the South, with its rich soil and climate, its great possibilities, it would be the richest section in the United States, if not anywhere in the world. Our cities are dirty; our yards and

[13] Whites and Negroes from the U. S. Census Bureau Bulletin.

negro homes are a constant menace; our own kitchens run by negroes are, in most cases, a menace to the public health. I, therefore, believe that the population figures of Charleston show much more decided improvement than the total increase would at first glance. Very truly yours,

"(Signed) A. V. SNELL,
"Managing Secretary."

This opinion of Mr. Snell's is very generally entertained by many prominent men and women in Southern cities, as letters before me will vouch for, but which the limitations of space debar from reproduction here.

The well-known authoress, Mrs. Annie Riley Hale, of New York City, whom I refer to above, has been deeply interested in the negro problem in this country for many years past. She has lectured upon the subject throughout the Union, and contributed many forceful articles to the newspapers and leading magazines, some of which I have read with interest while engaged upon the present book. Mrs. Hale has kindly given me permission to publish the following letter, addressed to myself last month:—

"6 WEST 66TH STREET, NEW YORK CITY,
"October 7, 1914.

"DR. R. W. SHUFELDT,
"3356 Eighteenth Street, Washington, D. C.

"MY DEAR DOCTOR SHUFELDT: *I* am so glad to hear that you have completed your book on the American Negro, and that it is soon to be published. The years of study and the exhaustive research you have put into the work, should make it invaluable as a scientific exposition of a difficult and dangerous problem, and *I* sincerely trust it may vindicate the purpose of its writing, in arousing and warning the white race as to the real peril of the Negro in this country. Unhappily, the native American, North or South, is seemingly much less aware of the peril than thoughtful observers abroad. Zangwill, Frederic Harrison, William Archer, and Hon. James Bryce, among Englishmen, have each sounded a note of warning on the subject.

"As you know, it is a question in which *I* am deeply interested, and to which *I* have devoted much study, viewing the Negro from the sympathetic standpoint of the Southerner, yet differing radically from the bulk of Southerners in my attitude *toward the problem. I* decided long ago that there was nothing to the negro question in this country, except the sectional issue; and if we could divest it of its sectional complication, we should have a speedy unification of white sentiment in regard to it, which would make short work of 'the problem.'

"The only way to take the question out of its sectional setting, of course, is to take the negroes out of their narrow Southern environment, and distribute them equally to all sections of the country. In this way only could we ever obtain a *national* consideration of the problem, looking toward a *national* solution, having as its ultimate aim the welfare of the nation—and not simply one of section. Such is my faith in the efficacy of this plan, that *I* believe the *mere proposal* for such distribution, if made in good faith, would have the desired effect of securing the attention and ultimately the coöperation necessary for a plan of peaceable segregation of the negroes, which is the only possible road to a permanent settlement of the problem.

"The chief obstacle in the way of this plan at present lies in the economic stupidity and the unreasoning conservatism of the Southern whites, who blindly cling to the negro in the face of every good reason for giving him up. Thus the very people who have most at stake in a wise and peaceable solution of this problem, are doing most to block it; and while the South maintains this attitude, the outlook is not hopeful. The North is not greatly interested, quite naturally, so long as the South harbors nine-tenths of the negroes.

"One good effect, at least, your book should have, emanating as it does from a Northern man, the son of a Union Admiral, who fought for the freedom of the slaves; it should tend to stop some of the cant about 'Southern prejudice' against the negro, and to force the frank recognition of the fact that the so-called 'prejudice,' which prompts necessary precautions against racial fusion with the blacks, belongs to self-respecting white people in every section, and, as a matter of fact, is stronger in the Northern than in the Southern white.

"With best wishes for the success of your publication, and with my regards, *I* remain, very sincerely yours,

"(Signed) ANNIE RILEY *HALE*."

At the present time, all thoughtful and intelligent people throughout the country, who take any interest whatever in this most momentous of all unsatisfactory and dangerous condition existing in our country, do not hesitate to affirm that deportation of the negro is the only rational solution of the state of affairs now existing. The strange part of it is that such a plan meets with its most strenuous opposition in a very large number of representative men throughout the South. They do not desire that the negroes shall go, even though they are a menace to the lives and virtue of their wives, daughters, and other white women and relatives; even though they do spread disease and rot the Anglo-Saxon race; even though they do eat up the money which accrues from taxation for the means to attempt to educate them,—even though the time may come when they will force social recognition through their very numbers and acquired power.

Many men in the South, blinded by their greed of gain, shut their eyes to all this and say: "Let our young men keep black and mulatto mistresses if they choose to do so; let the diseases come,—we have doctors enough to take care of that. If they assault our women, we'll lynch them for doing so, that's all. And there is money enough in the South to pay for such education as they will receive. They say we are used to them, and we want them. We cannot spare their labor in the cotton fields and elsewhere, and they are needed as domestic servants everywhere."

Apart from such barbarous opinions as these, there are, on the other hand, many men and women throughout the South who entertain exactly the opposite opinions, and who well know that in a comparatively short time the black labor in the South can be entirely supplanted by white in every known activity, from the kitchen to the cotton plantation. This is especially true just now, as the great war in Europe has made available thousands of Belgian's and others, who would be more than glad to seize upon such an opportunity. Moreover, the blacks once away and out of the country, there are thousands of most excellent workers of all kinds among the whites in the North, foreign and otherwise, who would at once move down to fill the room left available by the negroes' departure. This part of the problem has long been relegated to the shelf containing the scare documents. As Mr. Snell says above, the city of Charleston, S. C. has already proved that the blacks can be replaced by white labor with immediate and profound advantage; and there are men in various sections of the South who, at this writing, employ a great deal of white labor in preference to negro labor, as, for example, such men as Mr. Lewis W. Parker, of Greenville, S. C.; Mr. J. W. McQueen, of Birmingham, Alabama; Mr. Jos. D. Morgan, of Nashville, Tennessee; Mr. D. A. Tompkins, of Charlotte, N. C., and others.

"The Negro should be taught he is an alien," says Walker, "and always will be regarded as such in this country; and that equal, social, industrial, and political rights can never be given them. It is doubtful whether or not the Negro as a race would ever turn to emigration as his salvation if left to take the initiative. He is not of a migratory race, and has never been found further than twenty degrees from the torrid zone unless under force. When forced from home he is loath to return, even when free to do so, and under immense oppression" (*loc. cit.,* p. 31).

As I have said above, there are in the South today (1914) many who are strongly in favor of the deportation of the entire negro element in that section of the country; such people are encouraged through observing recently the forming and operation of many "Immigration Commissions" in the Southern States, having for their object the importation of whites which may come from other parts of the world. Here would be the opportunity of the thousands of Belgian peasants, now without homes or means of support, due to the ravages of the German armies in Belgium in the war now in progress.

There are other thinking men in the South today who recognize another menace in the presence of the millions of negroes now living in the South. I have heretofore avoided the discussion of this particular menace in this volume, for the reason that it did not seem wise to introduce it for discussion, and it is only mentioned now in that no part of the "negro problem" will be left untouched by me.

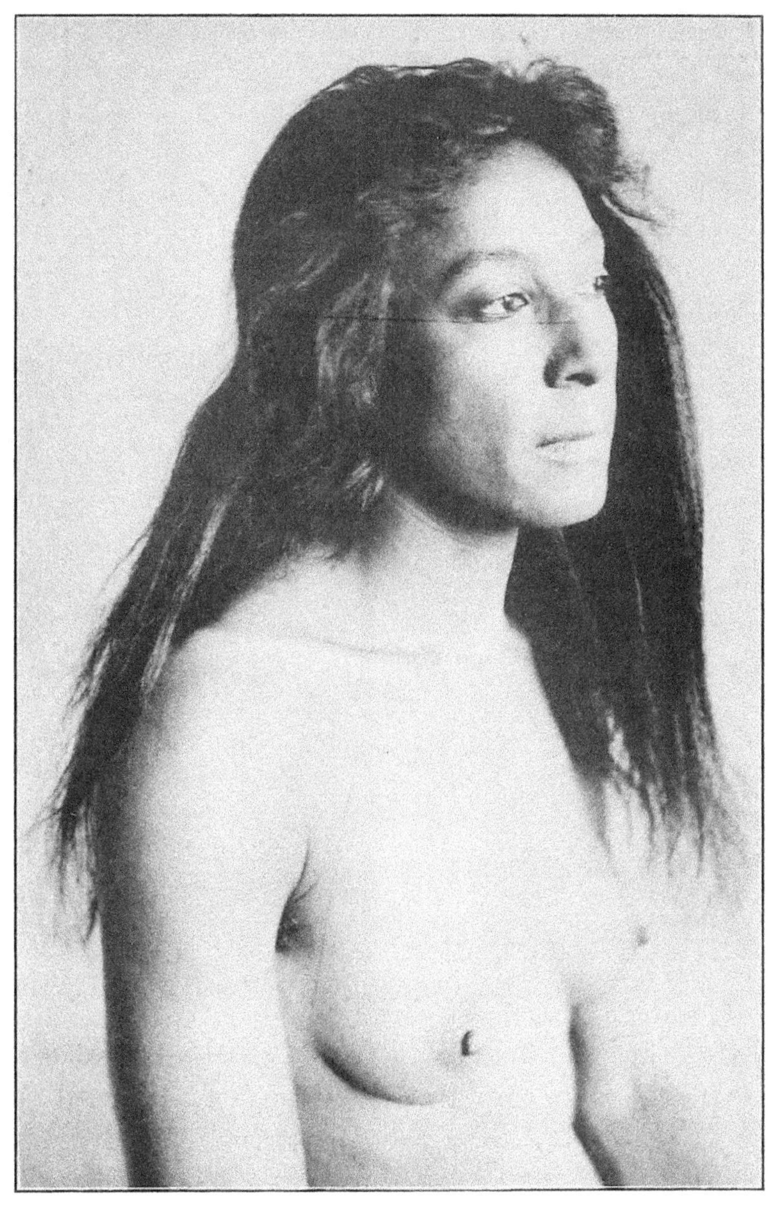

FIG 49.—SAME SUBJECT AS SHOWN IN FIGS 45 AND 46. SEMI-PROFILE.
(Photo from life by the author.)

There are those who say that the time *may* come when our relations with the Japanese may not be as cordial as they are at present;[14] that when the negroes become more restive than they are at present, owing to their continued exclusion from social place, positions of responsibility in the Government, etc., and there should arise among them leaders of ability (blacks or mulattoes) to point out to them that the only way to gain equality with the whites is by means of an insurrection,—*then,* should we at such a time have some unfortunate trouble with the Japanese, this great mass of blacks, ripe for a reign of terror, would be a very convenient element for the Japanese to use against us, and no nation on earth would know better how to handle this than Japan. It will never happen? I trust *not;* but I have a very wholesome regard for what the armies of Japan can accomplish when they undertake anything. Ask the Russians and the Germans!

This possibility, however, is well worthy of thought.

Do the people of the New England and the North Atlantic States desire *six or seven millions* of blacks to leave the South, come North in a body, and settle

---

[14] Many now believe that the feeling of cordiality is but a veneer; that the Japanese feel very strongly the part the United States took in closing the Russo-Japanese war, and even still more the exclusion of their people from California. Can one blame them? It is incomprehensible to me, in some ways, how it is that the United States will tolerate in the country over *ten millions* of a people which have been proven to be dangerous, unhygienic, non-moral, ignorant, superstitious, mendacious, and everything else that is undesirable, and at the same time close its doors to such a fine people as the Japanese! We are even so foolish—or have been for years—as to allow our country to be made the dumping-ground for the diseased and criminal class of all Europe.

over that area? Will they receive them with open arms? I think *not!* Were such a thing to happen, the same conditions would at once prevail in the North as now afflict the white population of the Southern States. Mercy knows it is bad enough in Washington at this time, without inflicting the same curse and drawbacks on the rest and now happy parts of the country.

Before closing this chapter, I will record the opinions of still others who have studied this question,—among these the negro bishop, Henry McN. Turner.

Bishop Henry McN. Turner, of the African Methodist Episcopal Church, declares that the separation of the races is the only solution of the race problem. Bishop Turner urged and still urges that opportunities should be offered to negroes to settle in Africa by a reduction of rates on steamship lines, stating that "this Nation or its aggregated people will either have to open a highway to Africa for the discontented black man, or the negro question will flinder this Government." He contends that by separation he does not mean that every one should go or must go, but that there should be an opportunity granted for the departure of "such black men and women as are self-reliant."

Mr. John Temple Graves, of Georgia, a clear thinker and very cogent writer on the negro question, has expressed his views in public in the boldest manner, both on the matter of lynching and on the ultimate separation of the two races. In one of his earlier lectures he set forth that, in his opinion, "the problem of the hour is not how to prevent lynching in the South, but the larger question: How shall we suppress the crime which always has and always will provoke lynching? The answer which the mob returns to this vital question is already known. The mob answers it with the rope, the bullet, and sometimes, God save us! with the torch. And the mob is practical; its theory is effective to a large degree. The mob is today the sternest, the strongest, and the most effective restraint that the age holds for the control of rape.

"The lyncher," he said, "does not exterminate the rapist, but he holds him in check. As a sheer, cold, patent fact, the mob stands today as the most potential bulwark between the women of the South and such a carnival of crime as would infuriate the world and precipitate the annihilation of the negro race. The masses of the negro are not afraid of death coming in a regular way. They love display, and the spectacular element of a trial and execution appeals to their imaginations.

"Expediting the processes of the law would not be adequate to eliminate lynching," said Mr. Graves. The repeal of the Amendments and the establishment of the negro's inferiority in law and society, though desirable, are not sufficient, for the negro is a thing of the senses, and with this race and with all similar races the desire of the senses must be restrained by the terror of the senses, if possible under the law.

"But this," he maintained, "like curfew edicts, separate laws for white and black, or the treatment of the crime of criminal assault as separate and outside of all other codes, are but expedients; there is no real remedy but one. No statute will permanently solve this problem. Religion does not solve it. Education complicates it. Politics complicates it.

"The truth, which lies beyond and above all these temporizing expedients," he concluded, "is that *separation* is the only solution of this great problem of the races."

My own opinion, and the opinions of others on this subject, have been set forth in a previous chapter. As such opinions, not only what the views of Mr. Graves brought out, but also to sustain what I am coming to in the next chapter—that is, the proposition of deporting the black man and his kin from the United States of America to some other country—have not been relinquished by thoughtful persons, I here introduce the words of another writer:—

To THE EDITOR OF THE NEW YORK TIMES: Your editorial of the 7th inst. fails to do full justice to John Temple Graves, who proposes to segregate and colonize the negro. *I* am a Northern man, and my viewpoint might have been like your own, had *I* remained a thousand miles removed from the South. A residence of twenty-seven years, however, in the "Black Belt," where the negroes far outnumber the whites, has given me unexceptional opportunities for studying the race question, which is also a caste problem most imperfectly understood.

Mr. Graves's proposed solution, to remove the negro to some more congenial clime, does not necessarily mean the Philippines or Liberia, nor does it mean wholesale deportation of the race in our lifetime, as most of his critics assert. Separation of the races for the highest development and happiness of both is the dominant idea of his scheme. Omitting the economic use of the negro, in the scantily supplied labor of the South, and judging from the moral side of life wholly, no thinking man could truthfully fail to agree with the school of John Temple Graves, that the separation of the races would advance the ethical conditions of the white race.

Scholarly people, like the editor of *The Times,* fail to understand this caste problem from the point of view of the "poor whites" of the South. These are laborers in full, unrestricted competition with the low-caste negroes. Every hour's work performed by a white carpenter, mason, miner, or mechanic, is paid according to the competition existing in the local labor market. The white workers of the South, desiring better homes, more varied food, and educational advantages for their children, must compete with men satisfied with cabins, filth, rags, and cornbread. The negro in the Southern States, and the Indian across the border in Mexico, can supply all his inherited cravings for half the wages of a civilized white man.

What complicates the case of the negro is that the amount of the mechanic's wages, when paid to him, tends to lower his morality. The political economists have not treated this side of the question of wages. Philanthropists declare the low-caste laboring people of English India, Mexico and the United States are all underpaid by the dominant race. They do not remember that work without wages, *i.e.,* slavery, is the first step of the barbarian toward civilization. An increasing wage equalized to his moral development is doubtless the ideal condition for furthering ethical culture in the barbarian of any race.

Liberal thinkers resident north of Mason and Dixon's line look to education and more universal schooling as the one thing needful to elevate the negro. Do they know what a school taught by negroes instills into the formative minds of the colored children? Do they realize that the friction between the races probably starts in this schoolroom? Young negroes in the South now are evidently trained to regard the white race as enemies, not as friends. There appears to be no endeavor to teach these colored children respect for the aged or for superiors, and no emulation for social position founded on morals. The money of the State spent for education should also carry an obligation to teach civic duties to all children, white and black. In case of the colored schools the appearance goes far to justify a belief that the altruistic money of the white people is spent in teaching the colored children anarchism.

Affection does now exist, and has always existed, between the cultivated whites and the uneducated blacks of the South. Between these is no competition whatever, but the caste line is recognized by both parties *as strictly as the division between Brahmans and Sudras in India.* Hence caste instinct, instead of being an evil as generally taught, is a blessing on both high and low. If the primitive doctrine of caste were to be *religiously observed,* there would cease to be any race problem. A caste instinct divides the white people of the North by minor differences into many groups; but the great gulf between the high and low caste in the South obliterates all small variations of property, profession, or calling; divides society practically into two castes, with an unchangeable division of color between them, half-breeds taking the caste of the mother.

Prosperous negro mechanics trained in slavery are always respected by their white neighbors in the South. Their children, educated in modern negro schools, I have yet to find as industrious, as useful, or as worthy as their fathers. It would be true to say of my section not a colored pupil of an industrial school, boy or girl, is now following any trade or domestic service for which he or she was supposed to be trained. The industrial schools do turn out "preachers and teachers," and thus they make the statistics they publish good by calling these "preachers and teachers" followers of the professions for which they were trained; but industrial training does not in white schools include "preaching and teaching." The negro schools of the South, however, are already beneficial in an unexpected way not intended by the Northern philanthropist. Educated (?) negroes are neither farm laborers nor domestic servants, nor do they follow mechanical trades. Hence they seek employment as porters and mail clerks on railroads all over the vast territory of the United States. While the most expensive hotels of the Northern and Eastern cities have discarded the black servants they formerly employed, as have the wealthy class of residents in those cities, the cheaper hotels and restaurants of the West are glad to obtain any service. Thus, educating the negro, permanently removing him from the cotton-fields, has benefited the white farmers by raising the price of cotton. The increased production of this crop would far exceed consumption at this time had the negro remained a cotton raiser instead of becoming a Pullman porter.

We read much of "Southern race prejudice." A prejudiced person is one who "prejudices" or expresses anticipative judgment; one not properly informed. The Southern resident alone in this country possesses opportunities for judging the black race fairly. The evidence is before him and is not present to any other. "Race prejudice" should not be charged against the English people in India, the American in the Philippine Islands, or the white man in the South. "Prejudice" in favor of the Indian, the Philippino, or the negro may exist in those who have no experience gained by personal observation. Hence, race prejudice, if it exists for or against the negro, is not chargeable to those who "post"-judge, but to those only who "pre"-judge; not to those who live South, but to those who live North. The development of manufacturing industries in the cotton States has been the greatest blessing to the impoverished whites. The taking of the women from exposed isolated rural homes to factory villages removes the constant anxiety that was part of their daily burden. Since the abolition of the caste restraint of slavery, the crimes committed by negroes against wòmen and girls of this class have principally precipitated the race troubles in the South.

The employment of white hands in the factories benefits also by lessening the competition between white and black labor. Every negro finding employment north or west of the cotton States benefits himself and the South. If this gradual exodus continues, the race problem will become national instead of local, a burden to be borne by all the citizens instead of by a few. Census statistics show as great or even a greater percentage of mulatto births in Northern States than in Southern. All history appears to prove that every slave-holding nation finally absorbed its slaves by mixing the blood of master and slave. Such a solution is only to be thought of in horror by him who reveres the morality of his ancestors, and prizes above earthly possessions the unblemished caste distinction of a thousand years of Europe's best culture. Even in the absence of ethical caste instinct, it would be opposing stirpiculture to advocate the absorption of eight millions of an inferior race by fifty millions of a superior people. What other solution except segregation can be seen by those who look into the future? The present observer counts nearly as many negroes carrying a percentage of white blood as pure African. When this crossing shall have progressed to show white-skinned, cross-bred people, with the absence of caste distinctions, who may then know the pedigree of his guests, his social acquaintances, or even his own future grandchildren?

Of several measures I already see at work, all palliative, only one radical cure has been pointed out. It is the removal of the negroes to a negro territory. Not as the Creek and Cherokee Indians of Georgia were removed by force and *en masse,* but slowly, gently, and for the benefit of the dissatisfied negroes as well as for the betterment of the whites. Public opinion may now be against this desideratum, as it originally was against the abolition of the institution of slavery. It is a move that should win the support of every altruist, and when sufficiently agitated, it or some kindred measure will protect us from the error of our fathers in bringing the African to America.

BENJAMIN W. HUNT.

EATONTON, GA., Sept. 18, 1903.

Many of our most able writers and thinkers of the present time (Nov. 19, 1914) hold identically the same views as here so ably expressed by Mr. Hunt.

Thus it goes, we see. Through the greed of gain our ancestors permitted large numbers of savages and cannibalistic blacks to be landed on the shores of a country that eventually came to be a great Republic. They were slaves and remained slaves until a fearful and prolonged war, costing myriads of lives and millions of money, freed them.

During the days of slavery, untold thousands of hybrids were produced, due to a crossing of the white and the black races; this took place principally in the South, though by no means altogether confined to that

FIG. 50.—A TYPE OF ENGLISH BEAUTY.

From "Living Races of Mankind." Courtesy of Hutchinson & Company, London. (Photo by the author.)

region. When they gained their liberty after the Civil War, much was brought to bear, from a great variety of sources and influences, that profoundly affected their history. In the forty years that followed, however, it has been amply proven that hybridization with a certain class of the white population of the United States is still actively going on; that the typical negro remains very much the same kind of being that he was on his having been brought here from Africa, and that the few who have risen to prominence in the black race in this country are not typical negroes, but have from 60 to 80 per cent. of white blood in their composition. It has further been shown that the bulk of them derive no benefit from educational measures of any kind; as for the matter of that they have never, even when crossed with the best of the white race, produced men and women in any way entitled to be recognized as thinkers, or as possessing skill in any of the sciences above the plane of mediocrity. And, as has been pointed out, this has been the case only when the individual exhibiting such prominence had a very large proportion of white blood in his composition. On the other hand, there is a very considerable amount of proof available toward establishing the fact that, in a very large proportion of cases, modern education has been downright harmful to the negro; has had the sole effect of improving his opportunities for criminal practices; of having him entertain entirely false notions of his worth and social status, and of furnishing thoroughly untrustworthy evidence of his value as a factor in modern civilization, which baseless testimony has been employed by the short-sighted, narrow-minded, and uneducated supporters of this race in the United States, in continuing their attempts to force these creatures upon a long-suffering and civilized community.

It has been shown with equal clarity that the criminality and savagery of the negro in this country has, in the case of the more criminally disposed whites, begotten crime as well as lawlessness. It is the presence of the negro among us that is responsible for lynch-law and not the tastes of our people for such brutal horrors. Among a progressive race, such as is the whites in the United States, it is the effect of their own higher and elevating civilization that, as time goes on, eliminates crime, bestiality, brutality, and all else that is ethically and morally undesirable in man's composition. But when a cultured, advancing, highly plastic and superior race of this kind introduces among it another race in large numbers, characterized by its lack of truthfulness, its sensuality, its morbid criminal characteristics, its mental density, its superstitions, and its physical repulsiveness, the influence of such an introduction is bound to be felt. The case is precisely the same as it would be to introduce into a large boarding-school, composed of refined, moral, progressive, and mentally and physically healthy boys and girls, a lot of new pupils, largely given to lying, to thieving, and to other criminal propensities. It would clearly be due to that blindness, that outcome of pseudo-philanthropy which hinders one from stating candidly what the evil effects of such an introduction would be.

Owing to his ever-present passion to ravish the women of the white race, be their social position what it may, the negro demonstrates to us every year, by scores of assaults upon our womankind,—often associated with murder and mutilation,—that, in spite of fire, hanging, and lead, in spite of any kind of penalty, he intends to gratify this heinous lust of his, be the consequences what they may. This seething mass of black bestiality, ever ready to erupt in hundreds of isolated instances and in localities of every kind, has at last had the effect of terrorizing white women throughout large sections of the country, to the detriment of the sex, individually and collectively, thus fostering a factor at once disadvantageous to the community and inimical to the progress of civilization.

The negro is too grossly and hopelessly ignorant to recognize the ruin his presence among us entails, and too sensual to inaugurate, as a race, any general movement of segregation that would relieve the people who have taken so many centuries to arrive at the state of civilization it now enjoys, and which it is so important and essential that it should preserve at all hazards.

There are plenty of uninformed people among us to say: "Oh, but give this race a chance, an opportunity for its uplifting" (uplifting is a favorite expression of such people), "and you will soon see the wonders it will effect." The answer to this is plainly that the black race is many centuries old, and yet, what has it done for civilization? Nothing!

Nowhere in recorded history has such a state of affairs as the one here presented fallen to the lot of mankind. At no historical time have two such distinct races, each numbered by its millions, the one representing the highest stage of civilization and advancement, the other practically but a day removed from savagery and cannibalism, been thrown together in the same geographical region and not separated by any political or natural barriers. This state of affairs requires some very independent thinking, and the exercise of more than usual judgment. We know from experience, however, that mixed races rarely, if ever, succeed in the world's history. The blacks have interbred with the Sicilians and other races along the shores of the Mediterranean; and although those blacks were of an infinitely better race than the stock we have in this country, it has been to the decided detriment of the whites and resulted in distinctly retarding their progress. We have no reason to hope for better results in the United States, and none to believe that they will be as good.

The great question now is: What will be the eventual outcome? Possibly, in a few places in the present volume, I may have regarded the state of affairs under consideration as a problem; while, as a matter of fact, there really is no problem. To my mind, the outcome of it all is not problematical. The mixing of a low and undesirable stock with a high and cultured one is sure to produce a mixed stock, which is not as good as either of the ones that produced it. There is but one remedy available and that is complete and thorough separation.

The placing in this country of the black race was a most supreme piece of stupidity; no one's particular fault,—in fact, a perfectly natural, though none the less glaring ethnological blunder. Having first practically exterminated the Indian occupying the South, we flood the territory with black savages and cannibals; and yet have declared that the Chinese could not land upon our soil,—a combination of idiotic and incongruous exploits which has had the most baneful influence, and which threatens to undermine the entire foundation of Anglo-Saxon civilization.

And here we are, at this late date (November, 1914), still struggling with the same problem.

We are still in the coils of the great, black snake. The daily papers still discuss the propriety of shipping as many negroes as possible out of our country. Send them here, send them there; but let us not tolerate them any longer. Africa has been proposed; Hayti has been suggested; the Philippines have been mentioned; yet nothing has been done. Still they remain, encouraging these half-breeds, who, having attained the opportunity of expressing their minds on the subject, keep advocating for the negroes "social uplifting" and permanent establishment in the United States. None of these men dare to tell the truth as Thomas did in "The American Negro." If the deportation of the negroes could be effected, I, for one, would not care a straw whether they liked it or not. I should be for sending them away all the same, and for keeping them away afterward, just as the Federal Government keeps the Chinese away. I should be in favor of shipping every negro back to the region whence they came, whether it pleased them or not. I am so loyal to anything that will sustain the purity of the best white blood in the United States; drain it of superstition of all kinds; purge it of crime and immorality, and preserve its integrity, that I would see every negro in America transported to the desert of the Soudan, rather than allow them, for any consideration whatever, to jeopardize by race intermixture the race and civilization it has taken us centuries to establish!

Today the best people, the far-seeing people, realize the career upon which the black race is now launched here in the States. Although they are eager to take up into their constitution the blood of the whites, they will remain loyal, in every single instance, to their own race, and use their advantages simply to seek further social equality with the whites. They crave political power and position; and were they sufficiently numerous, they would seize it everywhere at all hazards. It is only their inferiority in numbers which prevents them from doing so. All this, long since evident to our people in the "Black Belt," is now fast dawning on thinkers throughout the Northern States.

In closing this chapter, I desire to say a word in reference to the extension of the franchise to the negresses of the United States, in the event of this country allowing all American women to vote, through an act of Congress to that effect.

Should those women of the United States, then, who desire the ballot to be extended to the sex throughout the country, succeed in their efforts, it will, of course, be equally enjoyed by that part of our female population which is made up of several million negresses and hybrids. Have the women of the United States reckoned with *this* "problem?" I think, as a rule, not!

Mrs. "General" Rosalie Jones may think she proves the question that the ballot should be extended to the negresses of South Carolina, Georgia, and elsewhere for the reason that she and a few other females, with unusually strong pelvic limbs, were able to walk from New York City to Washington, D. C.; but such an opinion is not entertained by the author of this book.

The following bit of history will throw some light on this new method of increasing the difficulty of solving the "negro problem" in this country; it is from "The Washington Post," February 27, 1913:—

"LAUREL, MD., Feb. 26.—The suffragist 'army' which started to march from New York to Washington may not march into the Capital after all, despite the fact that the goal is so near at hand. The race problem, which has been as a cloud over the pilgrims since they crossed the Mason and Dixon line, may be the cause of the 'army' disbanding tomorrow.

" 'General' Jones, who, with her marchers, reached here late this afternoon from Baltimore, after a trying day in which they were hissed and in other ways coldly received, was told tonight that a large party of colored advocates of women's rights would join her army in Laurel tomorrow morning, to finish the march with the army.

"Not only the officers but every one of the pilgrims were aroused over the story, which was given credence by the fact that when passing through Winans, the town from which, according to reports, the recruits are to come, the marchers were met by a large party of colored women bearing a yellow banner on which was inscribed, in large letters, 'Votes for Negro Women.' The colored delegation, ignored by the regular army, marched but a short distance with it and then retired.

" 'General' Jones and a majority of her force emphatically stated that if the colored women joined the 'army,' it would be summarily disbanded, and the pilgrims would take trains immediately for New York and Washington.

"As the marchers entered Laurel this afternoon they were met by three carriage-loads of colored women, who wore 'votes for women' pins, and who followed along with the hikers into the town, cheering, and in other ways making it apparent that they were participating in the suffrage demonstration. The marchers, who had not yet recovered from their Winans experience, were dumbfounded, not only by this, but by the frigidness of their reception.

"The race problem is one which has worried 'General' Jones and the other leaders for a number of days. In Wilmington they were met by a delegation of suffrage advocates who warned them that in Maryland they would be forced to take some positive stand. This 'General' Jones has been unwilling to do, and has refused to make any statement upon the 'votes for negro women' problem until tonight.

"As she was told that the army of colored equal suffrage advocates would swell the ranks of her pilgrims tomorrow, 'General' Jones for the first time expressed herself upon the subject, and in a positive manner. 'What!' she ejaculated. The statement was repeated to her. 'An army of negro suffragists will join our army?' she exclaimed. 'Well, I guess they will—not!'

"When questioned by newspaper correspondents, 'General' Jones refused to say anything, reverting to her former policy of silence regarding this delicate

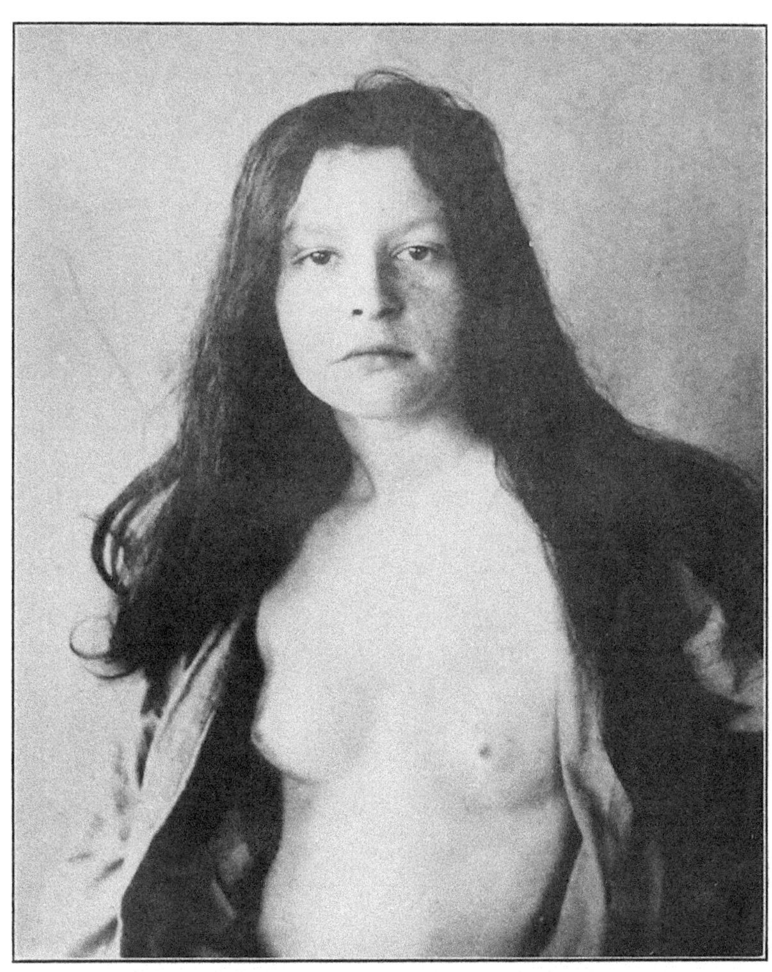

Fig. 51.—Type of the American Anglo-Saxon.

(Photo from life by the author.)

question. 'Colonel' Ida Crafts, next in command, was more positive in her statements, however. 'If the negroes attempt to march with us into Washington, then I will not,' she declared, emphatically. Others of the pilgrims stated that if the colored women tried to participate in any way in their hike they would disband.

"Few of the pilgrims will be able to gain a good night's sleep tonight, as the answer to their perplexing problem must be solved in the morning. If the colored 'pilgrims' from Winans appear with the large banner which so startled the marchers yesterday, their thirteen days' weary walk to Washington will be of no avail, and the entry planned for them into the National Capital on Friday will have to be abandoned.

"Should the recruits from the colored women's suffrage cause appear when the pilgrims are about to start tomorrow's hike to Hyattsville, each of the marchers will return to her room, don her street clothing, and take the first train for her home. The colored women who met the 'army' in three carriages at Laurel did not leave the vehicles, but proceeded at once down the road toward Winans. It was impossible to find any colored woman in Winans tonight."

This incident scarcely requires any comment from me. I have never been in favor of woman suffrage, and this experience of "General Jones" and her short-sighted "army" confirms me in my belief, that not only should all women be denied the vote in the United States, but that it will, in the event of the negro and mulatto women having it granted to them, but add another fagot to the flames of racial hatred and to the dangers of a negro insurrection in this country.

CHAPTER XI.

The Remedy.

From what has been set forth and advocated in previous chapters, the reader is doubtless fully prepared for the statement, that I am firmly of the opinion that deportation of the negro, from the United States to some other country or countries, is the one and only remedy which will avert a general race war between the blacks and whites in this country; which will prevent the horrors of miscegenation in our midst, and which will extend to the negro the opportunity for his proper development and evolution.

The soundest thinkers on this subject, having a full knowledge of all the facts in the case, agree with me in this opinion. Long ago it was the view taken by Senator John J. Ingalls, and he once wrote me to that effect. While I do not agree with him in some of his statements with respect to what would be the most useful products of civilization which the negroes of this country might take to their kindred in Africa, I do agree with the Senator in his proposition as a whole. Apart from the flowery picture of Ethiopia "stretching out her hands to God," it would seem that the taking of anything, by the negroes now with us, to their African relatives would be quite superfluous. Indeed, all they could carry they would need themselves; and surely their aforesaid relatives have long known the alphabet in thousands of instances through their European teachers in Africa. As to "the Declaration of Independence and the Bible,"—the first would be of no more use to them than a copy of the Magna Charta, while the second has always proved to be either useless or else downright harmful. However, it is now a fact in the history of this "troublesome and dangerous problem," that, over sixteen years ago (*The Chicago Tribune,* May 28, 1903), Senator John J. Ingalls was in favor of compulsory expatriation of the negroes of this country, and he said—referring to the evils I have pointed out above—that "If this condition is the inevitable consequence of the contact of the two races, separation, voluntary or compulsory, at whatever cost, is the dictate of wisdom, morality, and national safety. If reconciliation upon the basis of justice and equal rights is impossible, then migration to Africa should be the policy of the future. To that fertile continent from whence they came they would return, not as aliens and strangers, but to the manner born. To their savage kindred who still swarm in its solitudes they would bring the alphabet, the Declaration of Independence, and the Bible. Emancipated from the traditions of bondage, from the habit of obedience and imitation, from the knowledge of its vices, which is the only instruction of a strong race to a weaker, the African might develop along his axis of growth and Ethiopia stretch out her hand to God.

"The negro might not want to go. He is a native. He is a citizen. He has the right to stay. So he has the right to vote. He has the right to life, liberty, and the pursuit of happiness. He has been deprived of them all. Only the right of domicile remains. He could, perhaps, submit to the loss of this with the same resignation which accompanied his surrender of the rest. There are vague indications of cleavage. In some regions the inertia is being overcome. Communities are pervaded by aimless agitations like those which preceded the flight of the Tartar tribe across the desert. The 'exodus' of this colonization of Africa, the cost and conditions of a migration so prodigious, its effect upon the civilization of the two continents and the destiny of the two races, are subjects too vast and momentous for consideration here. —JOHN J. INGALLS."

Fortunately there are many people in this country who entertain very different opinions from those held by Mr. W. P. Garrison. Hundreds upon hundreds of negroes in this country would leave it now were only the way properly opened to them. Years after Senator Ingalls published what I have quoted from him above, and years after Mr. Garrison wrote me the letter published in the first editon of this book, the question of deporting the negroes now in the United States was as warmly advocated as ever. In support of this fact, I here reproduce the admirable address of John Temple Graves, as it appeared in the *New York Times,* September 4, 1903:—

"FOR A NEGRO REPUBLIC.

"CHICAGO, Sept. 3.—In an address on 'The Problem of the Races' before the Forty-eighth Convocation of the University of Chicago, John Temple Graves advocated, as a solution of the race problem, the establishment in the Philippines of a Negro State, where no white man should be allowed to vote. He said in part:—

" 'The experiment of political equality has had thirty-eight years of trial, backed by the power of the Federal Government, and by the sympathy of the world. It has failed. From the beginning to the hour that holds us, it has failed.

" 'The races are wider apart and more antagonistic than they were in 1865. There is less of sympathy and more of tension than the races have known since the terrible days of reconstruction made chaos in the South.

" 'Four decades after his emancipation, the negro is, in point of fact, less a freeman and infinitely less a citizen than he was in 1868. The tumult of the times about us proclaims the continued existence and the unreconciled equations of the problem that he makes, and in the common judgment of mankind, the legend "failure" is written large and lowering above the tottering fabric of his civil rights.

" 'A Chinese wall of prejudice shuts out the South on this question from the sympathy of the American people; and, although fraternal platitudes may cross it, and political affiliations may scale it, and commercial interchange may run its electric wires under and above it, and although but recently military loyalty has seemed to shatter it, this wall stands, in the sight of God and of nations, hedging in the South as a separate and peculiar people, hindered with misapprehension, held aloof in prejudice, and fretted by a criticsm which, if sometimes founded in philanthropy, is too often expressed in passion and answered in bitterness.

" 'And so long as the problem stands, the old slave States of the South, unwillingly, protestingly, despairingly, and yet inevitably, must be and will be the continuing gap in the magnificent line of our National unity.

" 'It is a problem of moral decay. It demoralizes politics. Wherever a black supremacy is threatened through a black majority, the black ballot is strangled without reserve in the black hands that hold it against the safety of the State. This is wrong. It is illegal. It is monstrous. But it is true.

" 'Never, never in a thousand years will the negro, North or South, be allowed to govern this Republic, even where his majorities are plain. We might as well fix that fact in our minds to stay. No statute can eradicate, no public opinion can remove, no armed force can overthrow the inherent, invincible, indestructible, and, if you will, the unscrupulous capacity and determination of the Anglo-Saxon to rule.

" 'In a land of light and liberty, in an age of enlightenment and law, the women of the South are prisoners to danger and to fear. While your women may walk from suburb to suburb and from township to township, without escort and without alarm, there is not a woman of the South, wife or daughter, who would be permitted or who would dare to walk at twilight unguarded through the residence streets of a populous town or to ride the outside highways at midday.

" 'The terror of the twilight deepens with the darkness, and in the rural regions every farmer leaves his home with apprehension in the morning, and thanks God when he comes from the fields at evening to find all well with the women of his home.

" 'Here, then, the issues—Unity of the Republic, material development, purity of politics, political independence, respect for the ballot, reverence for the Constitution, the safety of our homes, the sanctity of our women, the supremacy of law, the sacredness of justice, and the unity of the Church.

" 'There he stands, that helpless and unfortunate inferior. For his sake, the one difference has widened between the sections of our common country. Over his black body we have shed rivers of blood and treasure to emphasize our separate convictions of his destiny.

" 'And yet, as the crimson tide rolls away into the years, we realize that all this blood and treasure and travail was spent in vain, and that the negro, whom a million Americans died to free, is, in present bond and future promise, still a slave, whipped by circumstance, trodden under foot by iron and ineradicable prejudice; shut out forever from the opportunities which are the heritage of liberty, and, holding in his black hand the hollow parchment of his franchise as a freeman, looks through a slave's eyes at the impassable barriers which imprison him forever within the progress and achievement of a dominant and all-conquering race.

" 'Separation of the races is the way—the only way. Is the expense appalling? Is the cost prohibitive? England again offers an example. England, our mother country; England, next to ourselves, the greatest and most enlightened Government under the sun; England has just put its hand into its pocket to expend $500,000,000 in order to buy out the Irish landlords, and to heal the otherwise incurable running sore of Irish discontent.

" 'It may be that the islands of the sea were placed by Providence in our keeping to furnish an answer to the problem of the times. No reasonable or considerate plan would call for the wholesale or summary deportation of the negro. With his consent, and with Governmental aid, the movement might proceed slowly and with consideration. If only the vessels that brought foreigners to our shores from 1880 to 1885 had carried back to Africa as many negroes as they brought immigrants to us, not a single black man, woman, or child would have been left in the country in 1885!

" 'The superb inducement to the negro would be found in the freedom, the individuality, and the opportunity of an independent commonwealth, in which he would be freed from the unequal competition of a superior people, given a chance to develop a character, and to demonstrate the merits of his leaders and the capacities of the race. Let no white man vote in the negro State to harass the negro's councils, and let no negro vote in any other State than his own.

" 'The chief opposition in the South would rest upon the misapprehension which you doubtless share, that the negro is indispensable to the agriculture and labor conditions of that section. That was once true. It is no longer true.

" 'I state here, for the first time, a fact which will be as surprising to the South as it is to you. The negro no longer makes the staple or cereal crops of of the South! The cotton of Texas, of Louisiana, and of Mississippi is made chiefly by the white man and not by the negro! The negro is no longer an industrial necessity. This fact is from the census.

" 'For half a hundred years we have wrangled and fought and bled and died about this black man from Africa! Is the wrangle worth its fearful cost? Shall the great Northern section of our common country always turn its hand against the great Southern section of our country? Shall the young American of the North steel his heart against the young American of the South over an alien's cause?

" 'I appeal for Caucasian unity. I appeal for the imperial destiny of our mighty race. This is our country. We made it. We molded it. We control it, and we always will. We have done great things. We have mighty things yet to do. The negro is an accident—an unwilling, a blameless, but an unwholesome, unwelcome, helpless, unassimilable element in our civilization. He is not made for our times. He is not framed to share in the duty and the destiny which he perplexes and beclouds. Let us put him kindly and humanely out of the way. Let us give him a better chance than he has ever had in history, and let us have done with him.' "

In January, 1890, and in several other numbers of that year, *The Open Court* of Chicago published a contribution on this subject from the pen of a no less distinguished American philosopher and biologist than the late Professor E. D. Cope. It also published several rejoinders from his critics on the question. All of these contributions I have before me at the present writing, they having been kindly furnished me by Dr. Paul Carus, the editor of *The Open Court.* So valuable do I consider these articles that it would give me great pleasure to materially add to the value of this work by reproducing them here. They are rather too long, however, so I must content myself with giving only one of the replies of Professor Cope and one from one of his critics. In the issue of February 20, 1890, eighteen years ago, appeared the following two of the series to which I refer:—

"THE RETURN OF THE NEGROES TO AFRICA.

"Mr. Frederick May Holland has replied to my article on the proposed removal of the African race, in the United States, to Africa, citing various objections to such a course. These objections are well known to the present writer. He is not a Democrat in politics, and was in the days of slavery—and still is—of anti-slavery opinions. He appreciates the amiable traits of the African, and, on the ground of personal convenience, prefers him as a servant to most representatives of the white race. He does not forget his great services during the war to both the South and the North. He is aware that no citizen can be banished under the Constitution on account of race or color, nor does he lay any stress on the matter of color. Many of the Eastern representatives of the Indo-European race are black, and some of the African negroes are very light. It is a question of race and not of color.

"But all this is subordinate to two questions which are, as it seems to the present writer, of much greater importance, especially to a nation living under a republican form of government. These questions I have stated to be: first, that of negro rule, and second, that of negro mixture of race.

"When a man has a service to perform to his kind, it is essential that he shall observe the physical conditions which are necessary to the performance of it. A teacher or preacher who should so live as to be in continued ill-health could not be said to be performing his duty. A judge, attorney, or member of Congress who should eat or drink himself sick as a habit would not long retain his position.

"The people of the United States have to show mankind how order may be conserved consistently with the greatest amount of personal liberty. This we think is accomplished under our form of government. But all races are not equally capable of sustaining this relation between order and freedom. In fact, what we know as the inferior races—the Mongolian and African—have never made successful attempts to sustain republican forms of government. The negro has conspicuously failed in all but absolute governments, whatever they may be in name. It is not certain that all of the white race are capable of self-government at present. The neighboring so-called republic of Mexico is really a military despotism, although I believe that the material for a republic is there, and that at some future day that country will be in fact what it is now only in name.

"The United States have made laws excluding the Chinese from our country. We have assumed the right to do this for our own protection. On the whole, the present writer approves of these laws, although some of the reasons assigned in support of them are not good, and the maltreatment of particular Chinese is a stain on the name of our country. Many nations have, at different periods of history, removed parts of their populations outside of their borders for various reasons. It has seldom, if ever, occurred—so far as I know—that an equivalent for loss of property was granted in such cases, and as is proposed in the case of the removal of the American negroes to Africa.

"Whatever reasons may have existed, or do exist, for the removal of particular peoples, or the exclusion of particular races from any country, they exist with tenfold force in the case of the negroes of the United States. In no country, having a republican form of government, has the lowest race of mankind been found dwelling with the highest. The case is a new one, and demands some independence of thought for its treatment. So-called human rights appear to come into conflict with questions of physical fact or law. The pure idealists will sustain the former, in spite of the latter; but the wise man knows that he must bow to the latter, and acts accordingly. It seems hard to the idealist that inequalities between men exist, yet they do exist and appear to work injustice. But we cannot help it.

"I will not discuss again the mental status of the black race; it is well known except to those who will not see. The ability to weave and raise crops does not make a man just or rational, or free him from degrading vices and maddening superstitions. As to race mixture, Mr. Holland is a trifle prejudiced in his remarks. The inferior race has never been known to resist the attractions of the superior, to any great extent, so far as I am aware; least of all the negro. If Mr. Holland doubts the certainty of race-mixture, let him read history, or, better, visit all countries where races come in contact. The white race of the European coasts of the Mediterranean have not been benefited by their mixture with the African races, and these latter were and are superior to our negroes.

"The reasons why the American negroes object to being returned to Africa are self-evident. As beneficiaries of a civilized nation, they have their rights better protected than they would have under a government of their own race. It must not be forgotten that much of their orderly and 'peaceable' conduct is due to this fact. When left to themselves they are not distinguished for those qualities. They enjoy here the use of numberless inventions made by the white race. They have advantage of intellectual and ethical instructions controlled by them. These advantages are offset, to a small degree, by the outrageous treatment they too often receive from a degraded type of white men in the South, whom the Southern authorities are not sufficiently active in bringing to justice.

"I may be wrong, but I do not believe that our country ought to incur the risks incident to the existence of such a body of such a race in its midst. It is simply a question of self-preservation, far more urgent than that presented by the Chinese question. The preferences of the negroes themselves must be, in this case, disregarded. In fact, the only natural right they have in the matter is to demand to be returned to Africa, from which their ancestors were carried against their own consent. The supposition that the South is not adapted for white labor will not bear examination. The negroes can be spared, and their place will be speedily filled with whites.

"It is, however, difficult to convey to the general reader the seriousness of the difficulty as it appears to the student of species-characters in body and mind. The conclusion to be drawn from the facts is, that whatever of future progress the negro may have before him, it will take so long before he has reached the capacity to stand alone as competent for self-government, that we cannot take the risk of his presence here. Let him work out his own salvation without risking the future of the Indo-European. If he is so capable as some persons believe, it will do him no harm. If he succeeds no better in the future than he has in the past, he will not surprise some who think they know him better.—E. D. COPE.

"*PHILADELPHIA*, February, 1890."

"THE NEGRO QUESTION.

"The state of public opinion sixty years ago on the question of Negro Emigration is brought vividly to my mind by some remarks upon the subject in *The Open Court* of February 6th.

"The writer is mistaken when he says that the negro population of the country were largely opposed to emigration. The negro at the North had not at that time any distinctive influence, either in number or opinions, upon the ideas of the day, but ranged themselves in the lists of Williams Lloyd Garrison, at that time the editor of the *Liberator,* published in the city of Boston.

"Mr. Garrison, with whom I subsequently became well acquainted, was a mild-spoken gentleman in social life, a trait that formed a great contrast to his vehement, vituperative editorials as they appeared week by week in the *Liberator.*

"At that time Liberia had for Governor John Russworm, a mulatto of superior intelligence, warmly upheld by the Colonization Society, of which Mr. Gusney was president, and B. B. Thatcher, poet and lecturer, was secretary. The colored people, whatever they may have since become, were supinely indifferent to the movements made in relation to them, few attending meetings called together where their interests were at stake, and only one, Mr. Raymond (accent on last syllable), a half-breed, warmly supported by Wendell Phillips, ever pleading orally for his people.

"It was not the negro who was opposed to emigration, but such men as Garrison and George Thomson, of England. B. B. Thatcher presented the views of the Colonization Society and the growing value of the Liberian Colony, in eloquent and fervid oratory. He voiced the cultured and far-seeing ideas of statesmen and philanthropists, while the Abolitionists were looked upon as fanatics, and the negro stood between the two like the animal between the two bundles of hay.

"If we except a few members of their race, the negro has never wasted his abundant sensuality upon any questions of race improvement. Toussaint L'Ouverture was a great man, despite of race, and Count Timines, who was in this country just before the opening of the Civil War, was a man of elegant culture, educated in Paris, and holding brave hopes for the emancipation of Hayti, which was the limit of his world, and he wrote a history of it, describing the terrible war of races, which has deluged that lovely island with blood.

"The negro has never made endeavors to attain dominion or power. The negro has never made a start for liberty. Liberty has been thrust upon him,—and he receives it without dignity, uttering complaints and making statements known to be false, with constant appeals to Northern sympathy.

"It may be Utopian to think of removing six millions of people to Africa; but once let emigration turn that way, and Africa will be remunerated for the wrong we have done her. We wrenched from her a sensual, ignorant, barbarous population, and we return thither a people with civilized instincts, and it is to be hoped with aspirations that may help the dark continent to wipe out her old pagan barbarism, cruelty, and sensuality, by creating in them the hope of culture and the intimations of Empire.—ELIZABETH OAKES SMITH.

"*H*OLLYWOOD, N. C., February 12, 1890."

In the following contribution to *The Open Court* (Chicago, June 12, 1890, p. 2331), Prof. Cope closed the discussion:—

"THE RETURN OF THE NEGROES TO AFRICA.

"Criticism on my paper on this subject in *The Open Court* of January 23, 1890, having apparently ceased, I am disposed to recur to the subject for two reasons. One of these is that I wish to reply to my critics; and the other is that Mr. Henry M. Stanley is said to have taken up the subject, and to be prepared to place his knowledge of Central Africa at the disposal of the proper authorities when the project shall have been decided on.

"I am not surprised to find that the objectors to the project of transferring the negroes from this country to Africa have nothing but sentimental objections to urge against it. They call their objection ethical, and imagine that they have the support of justice in their position. Their understanding of the import of ethics and justice may differ from mine, but I suspect that their view chiefly results from ignorance of some fundamental principles of biology, and their failure to perceive the bearings of these on the problem.

"In order to present a rational objection to the plan of separating the Ethiopian from the Indo-European race by 3000 miles of water, its opponents should prove, first, that the negro and white races will not hybridize in the countries where they live together; or second, that the hybrid, if produced, possesses mental characteristics as good as those of the whites. Neither of my critics has done this, and until they do so, their objections are absolutely worthless. On the contrary, if the opposite of my position be proven, I will promptly abandon it. As to the question of injustice, we have to decide, if injustice there be, as to who shall be the sufferer. Shall we subject the higher race to deterioration; or shall we subject the lower to transportation without material loss to it? To do the former is to injure the entire human species. To do the latter is to continue the process which the abolition of slavery inaugurated, to teach the negro to stand on his own legs, a process which can no more be called injustice than the exercise of the methods of education, which the world has for us all from childhood.

"The hardships of the transportation would be trifling, and not greater than those which thousands of immigrants to this country voluntarily undergo. I have lived in various parts of the world, and I could be happy in any of them, provided my family and friends were not too far removed. Now it is not proposed to separate families and friends in this exodus, so that the picture of sufferings from this cause, drawn from one of my critics, is quite imaginary. As to the country, Stanley states that parts of the Upper Congo region are admirable as places of residence, and free from the swamps of many of our Southern States.

"Abstract objections on the one side weigh little against the facts on the other. Objections against compulsory education and against compulsory vaccination are of the same character, and are generally admitted to be valueless as against the important benefits accruing to mankind from the enforcement of these provisions.

"I repeat what appear to me to be the facts of the case. The characteristics of the negro mind are of such a nature as to unfit him for citizenship in this country. He is thoroughly superstitious, and absolutely under the control of supernaturalism, in some generally degrading form, and the teacher of it. He is lacking in rationality and in morality. Without going further, these traits alone should exclude him from citizenship. Secondly, these peculiarities depend on an organic constitution which it will require ages to remove. Corresponding qualities in the lower strata of the white race are modified or removed in a comparatively short time on account of superior natural mental endowment. Thirdly, if he remains in this country he will mix with the whites until, in a half-century or less, there will not be a person of pure negro blood in it. It follows from this that there will be, in accordance with the usual rate of increase, an immense population of mulattoes, where there should be an equal number of whites. The deterioration thus resulting would tell disastrously on our intellectual, moral, and consequently on our political prosperity.

"In view of these facts, it appears to me that the surplus in the treasury could not be better spent, and the navy of the country be better employed, than in the transportation of these people to Africa, where they can work out their own destiny, whatever that may be. The necessity seems to me to be great and urgent, and nothing but an ignorance of the facts of the case can prevent its being felt to be such by every white citizen of this republic.

"It is not denied by me that the negro has various merits, and that in particular instances men of that race have risen to deserved prominence. But the general result is not altered by these exceptions. Senator Morgan's bill, or something like it, should be passed promptly, and its provisions carried into effect before the burden becomes greater, and the material conditions beyond our control."

These last words are prophetic in the extreme. Cope has now been dead a number of years; it looks very much as though "the burden" had most decidedly become "greater, and the material conditions beyond our control." The negroes themselves are not nearly so much averse to leaving this country as many would have us believe; indeed, a very large proportion of them are heartily in favor of some kind of emigration scheme. In support of this I here publish some of their views on the subject, set forth in the newspapers of this country for the past twenty years or more. Thousands of them at this date, Nov. 21, 1914, are ready to emigrate now. The issue of *The Evening Star,* of Washington, D. C., of October 23, 1893, printed an article on this subject:—

"To South America.

"Topeka, Kan., Oct. 20, 1893.—In 1885, fifty prominent negroes of Kansas, Missouri, Arkansas, Kentucky and other States met in Topeka and organized the 'Central and South American Immigration Association and Equal Rights League of the Western Continent,' the object being to organize the colored people of the United States into colonies and send them to South or Central America, there to found a new empire, build new homes, and in time solve the race problem in this country by simply allowing the Anglo-Saxon to have full and unlimited sway.

"When this scheme was first advanced it was talked about all over the country and discussed pro and con in the newspapers, several prominent statesmen, notably John J. Ingalls, taking a hand. But finally interest waned and effort ceased, until recently, when the association developed an entirely new plan, and announced that active efforts would soon be made toward the deportation of negroes to South America by the various States, and that influential negroes would be sent into the lecture field to explain fully the plan of operation.

"Col. John M. Brown, the negro county clerk of Shawnee County, Kan., is president of the association, and S. W. Wine, of Kansas City, secretary. Brown is one of the ablest colored men in the West, and has been a prominent candidate for State auditor. In political campaigns he renders valuable service on the stump for the Republicans, and is recognized by the opposition as a forceful and convincing speaker. He came to Kansas twelve years ago at the head of an exodus from Mississippi, where he held a county office. He lived in the 'black belt,' and the overwhelming negro majority made it possible for him to secure a political position. He is thoroughly conversant with the negro problem in the South, and after twelve years of study and investigation he believes his plan the only one that will ever bring peace and happiness to his race. It will, he says, solve the vexing problem in the South, and at the same time deport these people to a country where there are no social distinctions, but where with the Latin races they would become cemented and a part of the whole.

"When Col. Brown first launched his colonization scheme on the public, he was met with strong opposition from leading colored men all over the country; they did not believe it practical, and declared that a wholesale emigration of negroes would tend to fasten upon them a greater servitude than that complained of on the cotton and sugar plantations of the South. Then the negroes were unacquainted with the social conditions existing in the South American countries; but since Col. Brown and his co-workers have, through printed matter and from the lecture platform, removed the prejudice which first existed, a wonderful change has taken place, and he is constantly receiving letters inquiring about the movement. Several years ago he laid his plans in detail before ex-Senator John J. Ingalls. That gentleman scouted the idea of colonizing the negroes in South America, and advanced the opinion that his plan of sending them back to Africa, their natural home, was the only feasible one by which the race question would ever be eliminated from society and politics in this country. Col. Brown, however, caused Ingalls to weaken on his proposition when he showed him the disadvantages of his African scheme. He pointed out the fact that it would cost at least a hundred dollars a head to transport the negroes to that country, and that the great vessels necessary in the shipment of them across the ocean would, of necessity, have to come back empty, for the reason that this country receives nothing from Africa in the way of staple products. On the other hand, to land them on the eastern shore of South America, would not cost over fifteen dollars a head, and on the return trips sugar, coffee, and other South American products could be transported at a nominal cost.

"Recently this association has formulated a new plan. Each State of the Union will be requested to organize a society for the purpose of pushing the scheme. Each State will be required to raise a fund sufficient to send from twenty-five to a hundred families to South America as an experiment, and to provide for their wants for several years, in case they are unable to secure homes and make their own way. When these societies are formed among the negroes of the various States, during the coming winter, a board of directors will be chosen by each State association. Later, all these boards will come together and select a national board to go to Brazil, Bolivia, Argentine Republic and other South American countries, and arrange with the government offering the best advantages for either the purchase or lease of lands for the American colonies. Each State board will have charge of the deportation from that State, and in order that the plan may be favorably received by the Afro-Americans, and finally accepted by them as the best and surest way to solve the race problem, only industrious, intelligent and thrifty negroes will be taken in the first shipment. If they have sufficient money to make the trip, they will be expected to pay their passage; if they have not the necessary means, the society of the State from which they go will pay the expenses. None of the indolent and shiftless classes will be allowed in the first instalment. The success or failure of the movement depends upon the class of people who first go to the new country, and the leaders will see to it that good report comes back to stimulate others.

"It is proposed to make every State society a stock company and solicit from Afro-Americans sums of from ten to fifty dollars, which will go into a common fund for advancing the movement. One of the plans on foot is to build several large vessels to ply between New Orleans and points on the eastern coasts of South America to be paid for out of this fund. If a head of a family wishes to aid the enterprise, and at some future time desires to cast his lot with his brethren in the new Eldorado, his subscription will be received, placed to his credit, and when he is ready to go the amount will be applied on the passage of himself and family to his new home. These vessels, Col. Brown thinks, would be a profitable investment for the association, because they would bring in a good revenue for carrying to the United States on their return trips the products of South America, which this country must have. Thus, while the deportation of the negroes from the United States to the new Southern home was going on, the association would reap a rich harvest in bringing back to this market the products of South American countries.

"Col. Brown says negroes can be transported from points between New Orleans and St. Louis for about fifteen dollars a head. He believes that after the first settlement is made, and the plan is proven a success, as he confidently believes it will be, the association will not be able to take all who will want to go. He says there is ten times more vacant land in Brazil alone than all the negroes in the United States could properly cultivate. He has received letters from that government recently, saying that all the negroes who will may come and be assured of protection, homes, and a competency. He also has letters from the Argentine Republic and Bolivia, offering very flattering inducements. He is favorable to Brazil, and if the present troubles do not disturb his plans he will undoubtedly favor negotiations with that government. The climatic conditions are favorable, and there is plenty of land at very low prices. Speaking of the social question as it relates to that country, he said: 'There the color line is obliterated and we would stand upon the same footing with the natives. Here we can never hope to enjoy that privilege.'

"He believes that the first deportation of negroes

for the new Eldorado would create great excitement among their brethren in the South, and that thousands would want to join the procession. On this line he said: 'Let a boat-load of negroes, bound for the new country, leave St. Louis, singing their old plantation songs as they float down the Mississippi, and it would be almost impossible to hold the multitudes that cultivate and pick the cotton from the plantations along the banks. They would want to join the throng, because they would see beneath the lowering clouds that have shut out the light of freedom and independence, a silver lining, and they would feel that a brighter era was dawning. They would realize that there was in store for them in their new home something better than a life of drudgery and ceaseless toil, from which they are barely able to live. And this is not all; for the first time in the history of this country the old ex-slave drivers and plantation magnates of the South would feel the sands slipping from under them. The cheap labor from which they have been able to amass fortunes would depart for a Southern clime in another country, and their plantations would grow up in weeds. The Winchester rifle and shot-gun, potent factors in Southern elections, would rust in their racks, and the race problem would be settled, and settled forever in this country. The public domain is exhausted and the restless young men crowding West would turn to the deserted fields of the new South, where plantations would be divided and subdivided, until the Yankee had a voice in the politics of that section. All we ask is that Senator Ingalls, and other statesmen who believe themselves burdened with the responsibility of settling the race problem, will allow us to carve out our own destiny. We believe the South American emigration plan will solve the negro problem in this country, and, if it does, these statesmen who have been so solicitous about our welfare ought to be satisfied.' "

Some years ago *The World*, of New York City, printed the following as a news item bearing upon this question (November 29, 1903):—

"NEGROES CALL FOR *HELP* TO EMIGRATE.

"BIRMINGHAM, ALA., Nov. 25.—If the cause we represent were less deserving of consideration at the hands of the people of America, we would hesitate to make this appeal on the eve of that day when we Americans are more than at any other time in the year appealed to to meet the demands made upon us by deserving humanity. We believe, however, that of all the obligations the American people owe to humanity, the debt we owe the people that were once our slaves is possibly the greatest.

"It is true that the purses of the philanthropic people of this country have been and are always wide open, when the real needs of the colored people are made apparent. Churches, schools, colleges, and many other institutions of much importance to the race are prominent landmarks throughout the Southland, speaking eloquently of the generosity of the Anglo-Saxon toward these people, and more eloquent still are the intelligent, educated men and women of the race, who have been qualified by those means to lead their people out of the darkness thrown around them by long years of servitude. But with all this there has sprung up possibly a greater menace to the progress of these people.

"The colored people believe that they have been discriminated against, ostracized, disfranchised, and otherwise oppressed to such an extent that emigration to Africa appears to be the only means that will afford them relief. This society will have, by February or probably sooner, a colony of from three to five hundred sturdy pioneers, men, women, and children, ready to embark on a chartered steamer at Savannah, Ga., for their new homes in Africa.

"Many of these people, in fact nearly all of them, are financially unable to undertake this venture without the moral support and some financial aid from their Anglo-Saxon friends. It is true that Liberia, the place where they are going, offers them every natural advantage and opportunity for making a living, and to establish themselves comfortably in a home of their own; but as a matter of fact, with little means they would have a hard time for the first few months after landing there; therefore this appeal is made to the generous and philanthropic people of America, to contribute at least a mite to assist these people for a short while after landing in Liberia.

"They will need, first: provisions, medicine, and the immediate necessities of life. Then houses, household necessities, farm implements, seeds, and things of that description will be needed to enable them to get an early and successful start. If only a few of their friends will contribute these things in kind, or the money with which to buy them, many souls will be made glad and a worthy cause aided very materially. Will not each one who reads this contribute a dime, a dollar, or several dollars? You will be happier for doing so.

"Persons wishing to aid these colonists can receive further information by addressing the Liberian Colonization Society, Birmingham, Ala., or donations can be sent direct to it. This appeal comes directly and indirectly from fully four million souls who are crying out for relief from what they believe to be unjust oppression, and many hearts will be glad and prayers go up to an all-wise God for every favor contributed. —LEE COWART, President."

The following is the most sensible and feasible proposition they ever attempted. It was proposed in October, 1893 (*The Evening Star,* Washington, D. C., Oct. 30, 1893), and had the scheme been methodically carried out and accomplished, the so-called "negro problem" would, in so far as this country is concerned, have been settled a number of years ago. Here is the plan:—

"A BILLION FOR COLONIZATION.

"A delegation of colored lawyers from the South is in this city to carry into effect a resolution of the recent Afro-American Convention, held in Chattanooga, Tenn. The delegation is composed of S. L. Hutchins, R. C. O. Benjamin, J. G. Burge, John E. Patton, M. C. Parker, and Samuel R. Lowery. They are here to present to Congress a memorial asking for $1,000,000,000 to be appropriated by Congress to colonize the colored race in some other country.

"The memorial will be presented to Congress by Representative Murray, the colored member from the Seventh South Carolina District, but Mr. Murray is not in sympathy with the colonization scheme; he believes that the colored race will make better progress by remaining with the white race, emulating it, and receiving the inspiration of a higher civilization."

Such utterly chimerical plans as the following—although proposed by negroes—are noticed here only to show how ignorant these people are of the actual conditions existing in regard to them. Of course it is nonsense to talk about setting two States aside for their exclusive occupancy; for to ship them from one part of the country to another is no solution at all. Besides, it is at once more than dangerous and harmful, and can but be a scheme to spread the existing trouble. *The New York Times* (Tuesday, Nov. 10, 1903) published the following:—

"TWO STATES FOR NEGROES.

"WASHINGTON, Nov. 9.—The first paper read at the opening meeting today of the National Sociological Society, in session in this city to consider "The Race Problem in the United States," came as a shock to many members of the society present. The author of the paper was Bishop Lucien Halsey, of the African Methodist Zion Church, who proposed to have the National Government set aside one or more States of the Union for the segregation of the negroes.

"A warm discussion followed the reading of the paper, but no resolutions on the matter were introduced.

"A permanent organization was made with ex-Representative White, of North Carolina, as Chairman, and a number of Vice Presidents.

"At the afternoon session an address of welcome was made by Commissioner MacFarland, and responded to by the Rev. I. L. Thomas, of Baltimore."

A few months earlier (August 17, 1903) the following, which in reality meant nothing more than the natural spread of the race and danger to the country, appeared:—

"NEGRO EMIGRATION SCHEME.

"TACOMA, WASHINGTON, Aug. 16.—The Rev. J. F. Davidson, pastor of the Mount Olivet Colored Baptist Church, arrived from New Orleans yesterday with a party of twenty-five colored men, whom he will colonize in Tacoma or in the vicinity. Mr. Davidson hopes to be able to purchase a large tract of land, upon which he will establish a colored community somewhat coöperative in character. At present a certain part of the wages of the colored men will be set aside every month as a nucleus for a fund for buying this land.

"Mr. Davidson expects thousands of colored people will come North from time to time. He himself is one of the Western agents of a colored organization, with headquarters in Boston, the object of which is, if possible, to depopulate the South of negroes by inducing emigration on a monumental scale to favorable regions of the Northwest.

"Mr. Davidson is enthusiastic over the prospects of those of his race who are transplanted to the Pacific Northwest, declaring that under favorable conditions they will become intelligent members of society, and prove themselves capable of developing into important factors in civilization in this country. One result of this immense immigration of negroes will be to relieve the labor shortage along the entire coast."

I publish these opinions of negroes, newspapers, and others, given twenty or more years ago, in order to show how long this state of unrest among the blacks has existed. Such opinions, too, are interesting and important from an historical standpoint. They point out the facts and conditions which are just as true today (Nov., 1914) as the day they were uttered or published. They also are of advantage to bring out the characters of the countries to which negroes may be deported; where they will be received and where they will not; the matter of cost of transportation, and associated questions. Some of the negroes who have given the foregoing opinions are still living, and in the light of development of recent conditions affecting the colored race in this country, they are more than ever convinced that deportation is the only solution of this problem. Opinions of those of the present day will be given further on in this chapter.

Only a little more than a year ago, the following opinion was rendered by a very well known Congressman of one of the Southern States. It was published in *The Evening Star,* of Washington, D. C., in its issue of October 16, 1913, having been extracted from a long letter written by Representative Frank Clark, of Florida, to the governor of that State, in regard to a threatened colonization of a tract of land in Florida by the Japanese. In the course of his remarks Mr. Clark said:—

"I was astonished when I learned that there was a real serious movement on foot to colonize Japanese in the State of Florida. The people of Florida are burdened now with the solution of a race problem that will tax the ingenuity, ability and patriotism of generations to come to solve. I regard it as the most perplexing question which has ever challenged the attention of any people upon the earth.

"Here are two races of people living upon the same soil, under the same government; one recognized as the most superior and advanced race in the world, the other as inferior. It is utterly impossible for these two races to inhabit the same territory upon terms of absolute equality, either social or political.

"The white people of Florida, and of the United States, in my humble judgment, will never consent to assimilate with the negro; and, stupendous as the task may seem, the only solution of this question which will preserve the integrity of the white race, and at the same time be fair to the negro, is deportation of the negro, and settlement in a land of his own, under a government he shall control."

A contributor to *The New York Times,* September 30, 1906, expresses an opinion in which he attempts to point out that on account of its expense and magnitude, the question of deportation of the negroes is not feasible. He also endeavors to show that they cannot, as laborers, be spared from the South. In fact, in his contribution, he practically raises the points usually raised by those desiring to retain the blacks in this country, and expresses himself precisely as such an objector would express himself at the present time. I shall endeavor to answer all such objections at the close of this chapter:

"From the *Charleston News and Courier:*—'Separation of the races is the only radical solution of the negro problem in this country. There is nothing new about it. It was the Almighty who established the bounds of the habitation of the races. The negroes were brought here by compulsion; they should be induced to leave here by persuasion.'

"Certainly this would be a 'radical' solution of what is termed the negro problem. We are not surprised that it should occur to Southern men under the immediate influence of the events at Atlanta last week. Putting aside for the moment the question whether the solution is the only one, it is worth while to consider how it can be applied. The Charleston writer mentions an estimate made fifteen years since of $32,000,000 a year for ten years, $320,000,000 in all. We do not know if that estimate included compensation to the property owners among the deported race; if it did, it was obviously defective. The total expense would probably be many times the amount mentioned.

"At the last census, the negroes, including all those of negro descent, were reported to be 8,840,789, and the whites to be 66,990,802 in the whole country; that is, the negroes were about one-ninth of the population. But if we take the fourteen States south of the old Mason and Dixon's line, the negroes were reported to be 8,067,824, and the whites to be 17,436,-495; that is to say, in these States there were in 1900 forty-six negroes to each hundred whites, and the negroes were, roughly, one-third of the population. There are four States, however, in which the negroes are less than one-fourth of the population—Texas, where they are 26 per cent. of the whites; Maryland, where they are 22 per cent. of the whites; Kentucky, where they are 15 per cent. of the whites, and Missouri, where they are but 5 per cent. of the whites. This leaves ten of the Southern States in which the proportion of the negroes is much higher, and in eight of these ten the proportions are as follows: For every 100 whites there are in South Carolina 150 negroes; in Mississippi 145; in Louisiana 90; in Georgia 88; in Alabama 82; in Florida 75; in Virginia 55, and in North Carolina 50. If we put aside the population of Missouri, Texas, and Kentucky, we find that the total white population in the remaining Southern States was, in 1900, 10,202,674, and the negro population was 7,001,162. The negroes were 70 per cent. of the whites, and somewhat more than two-fifths of the entire population.

"Now here—if we are to take seriously the advice of *The News and Courier*—is the real 'problem' of the negroes: How is the South to get rid of two-fifths of its population, including the greater part—practically the whole—of its agricultural laboring class? In the first place, where are they to go? What reason is there to think that the Republic of Liberia, named by the *News and Courier,* could provide homes and living for them? Next, how are they to be 'induced' to go 'by persuasion?' How much would be required to compensate them for their present holdings, how much to pay the cost of their deportation, how much to ensure the reasonably attractive employment or settlement in Africa, and who is to furnish all this enormous sum? These are perfectly practical questions. They must be answered, and it is 'up to' the proposers of the plan to answer them.

"But they are by no means all that must be answered. There is another list relating to all the industries now dependent on negro labor in the South. They may be summed up in the simple question: What is to replace negro labor? Grant, to start with, that negro labor in the South is not what it should be, is not nearly what the South needs; but there it is, the only labor available for the time being. There is a great mass of it. The body of the eight millions of negroes in the South support themselves in some way. They contribute the greater share to the $454,000,000 worth of cotton, the $56,000,000 worth of wheat, the $28,000,000 worth of corn, the $18,000,000 worth of oats—$556,000,000 worth of farm products in all—raised South. Assume that it is possible to 'induce' them to go to Africa, who are to take their places, who are to do their work? Quite apart from the almost incalculable cost of their deportation, which the South must bear if the expense is to be incurred, where is the South to find the arms to replace their arms? It will be an enormous task; it will take a long time; it will involve immense sacrifices. Without pronouncing judgment on the 'solution,' we venture to ask whether those who advocate it have considered these elements of the 'problem,' and what is their opinion regarding them."

I am not certain as to whether M. F. Walker, the author of "Our Home Colony," is a man or woman, negro or Anglo-Saxon; the reader must judge of this from the following part of a paragraph that I find in the *Preface* to that very instructive little pamphlet; it reads as follows: "Our own personal experience, in no way, has been allowed to bias our judgment. No one could entertain higher regard for the American white man and his magnificent civilization than the writer; and it is the appreciation of this fact, along with the infancy of Negro freedom, that forces the conclusion upon our mind that it is contrary to everything in the nature of man, and almost criminal to attempt to harmonize these two diverse peoples while living under the same government."[1]

On page 34 of this little treatise, the author very truly remarks: "The people of this Republic should understand the great danger that confronts them by a delay in putting into practicable operation some plan to relieve this country of the congested Negro population of the Southern States. There is to our mind no other rational plan but Emigration for the Negro. Every principle of the science of social development is opposed to the unnatural relation existing in this country between seventy millions of the white and ten millions of the black race. This condition would never have occurred had the members of the white race pursued the courses dictated by natural laws. The association of the races in this country originated in a *crime,* and is *unnatural.*"

The author then proceeds to give the true reason why it will never be possible for the negro to rise in the United States; to properly develop, or ever become the social or intellectual equal of the dominant race,—and *it is* impossible.

"The Negro has often been credited with possessing a strong patriotism; yet the treatment given him at the hands of his white fellow-citizens is designed ultimately to make of him an enemy to the government, and a menace to peace and order. . . . It

[1] Since the above paragraph was written I have received a very interesting letter from M. F. Walker, dated December 17, 1914. He is the Manager of the Cadiz Opera House, Cadiz, Ohio. In his letter he states: "As to my identity will say I am what you would call a mulatto, born and raised in this State, but have traveled much of our country." R. W. S.

is impossible for the American Negro to feel the same warmth of patriotism for the United States that swells the bosom of an Anglo-Saxon, or that makes it pleasant for an Englishman or Frenchman to die for his country. These people are filled with a national pride arising from the achievements of their fathers and the sacred, inherited trust of maintaining them inviolate to their posterity."

Then follows paragraph after paragraph giving the real status of the negro in the United States, and the utter hopelessness of his situation. "If the white man refuses to take the Negro as a citizen of this Republic on perfect social, industrial, and political equality, then the fate of the black man is sealed. He must either leave the United States, be practically reduced to slavery or be exterminated. It will be impossible for the Negro to have industrial or political equality with the white man without social equality; and this, as we have said, he can never get."

In fact, as this writer thoroughly believes and is eminently correct in believing, every negro in this country who entertains the opinion that either he or she, or any of his or her descendants, will ever attain to social equality in the United States, is simply following a will-o'-the-wisp. By social equality I mean an equality characterized by a freedom so great that the two races intermarry without restraint or stigma attached to the union; by the negro entering, without surprise to any one, into all of our social gatherings, both of home and those of State and Federal function; in short enjoys, without comment or protest from any one, all that this civilization has brought us in private and public life. It is not that the white race in

America desires in any way to be unfair to the negroes in the country; but we have gone as far as we ever shall go along the social equality line. And I will say to the entire negro multitude in this country: We will never go one single peg further. It is always the fate of a numerically and mentally subordinate race, when occupying the same country with a higher race, to be held in strict subordination by the latter, and it is no more than natural that it should be so.

Walker very truly points out that "The Negro is attached to this country more by the hope of equality with the white man than by dread of Africa. . . . Thousands of Negroes in the South are ready and willing to leave the United States if cheap means were provided for them to do so. The recent effort, which is meeting with considerable success, to divert part of the great stream of European immigrants to the Southern States will only force the Negro to the North, and make more acute the already troublesome problem. When the 'black belt' moves north of 'Mason and Dixon's line,' the Northern white man may see more clearly the necessity of moving it across the Atlantic Ocean, where of right it belongs." (This is what Mrs. Annie Riley Hale contends, and is set forth in her letter published on a previous page.)

It is not necessary for me to point out what would happen were a fine class of European immigrants from various nations to pour into the South and drive the negroes out. White would be substituted for black; cleanliness and progressiveness for filth and idleness; clean marriages and homes for negro concubinage and squatters' hovels; social, industrial, and political equality for alien subordination and protested rights of complete citizenship. Where is the boasted mental acuteness of the negro in America if he fails to see this written all over his future career, so long as he remains in the United States?

If you ever attempt to gain what you, as a race, so yearn to possess—complete social equality—by force of arms, there will be, in this country, no history of Haitian independence for you, nor could forty such men as Toussaint lead you to it. It would mean extermination in very short order—but *not* of the Anglo-Saxons. You deserve a far better fate than that, and it is the plain duty of this country to assist you in every possible way, financially and otherwise, to secure you room in the world where you can properly advance and develop. Are you any nearer social equality in Washington today than you were in 1866? Essentially you are *not,* and you *never* will be.

Your own "ministers of the gospel" are hoodwinking you as a race, and in doing so they are traitors to your best interests and welfare. They should forcefully teach you that this is a *white man's* country; that its rulers and its people—apart from a certain percentage who think otherwise—think of their God as *white;* of his Son, the saviour of their souls, as *white,*—and he had twelve *white apostles.* Walker remarks in his pamphlet "Our Home Colony," from which I have been quoting: "Many good-meaning men of both races urge upon the Negro to trust his cause to God and all will come out well. There can be no question about this if there was any proof that God would give it immediate consideration." Now you ten millions of blacks and mulattoes in the United States might implore the powers that be for social equality with the whites in this country until the crack of doom, and it would have no more effect than did another celebrated prayer (October 4, 1914), in the way of bringing peace to war-distracted Europe.

"The gods help those who help themselves," is what your churches should teach you, and teach you every day, Sunday not excepted. What does American civilization mean to you if you are not part of it, *can not* enter into it, had nothing to do with its origin, and can have nothing to do with its real progress and future, beyond being considered a "problem" and a "black peril?"

Men like Booker T. Washington and W. E. D. DuBois are traitors to their race in this country, and are the worst enemies the negroes in the United States have today. There are thousands of the best white families in this country at this writing who would not sit at the same table with either of these men—and why? Simply for the reason that they are members of the subordinate race.

It will make no difference how *wealthy* any particular negro may become: he will never be able to *buy* his way into the inner circles of the American white aristocracy; it would be the accomplishment of a feat quite as unthinkable as a full-blooded negro becoming President of the United States.

Walker fully appreciates the fact that the *only remedy* which will save these two races in the United States, and admit of the subordinate one evolving as best it can, is their *complete segregation* and the *deportation* of the blacks in this country. Most forcefully does the author of "Our Home Colony" present this remedy as the only effective step to prevent the rottenness of morals now pervading the country where negroes reside. As a part of the discussion to which the present chapter is devoted, I will quote quite fully what is set forth on that point. On pages 42-47 he says:—

"The Negroes generally expect the day to come when, through the effect of education and the accumulation of wealth, they will enjoy full social equality with the white people of the United States. Some are so ignorant of the nature of the marriage relation that they argue it is only a step from concubinage between white men and black women to the Divine institution. These persons do not seem to know that concubinage has its motives in the animal desires, and that the marriage relation never should be entered from considerations based on the passions or impulse. There is absolutely no analogy between concubinage and marriage. The motives that lead to the marriage relation are drawn from considerations that do not enter the mind of the illicit lover. We wish to make it clear that persons living in a state of concubinage are not only not approaching the marriage relation, but the very motives under which they act precludes even its proper consideration. As we have before said, the temptations to an immoral life are the most deplorable features in the present conditions of the Negro race. The Negro will never get social equality with the white race, hence there is no escape from a condition that will ultimately deprive him of all moral sense. There is no use in trying to go contrary to the known laws of human nature.

"We wish every thoughtful white father and mother in the United States, and every Negro interested in the welfare of his race, could fully appreciate the wide prevalence of concubinage between white men and Negro women all over the land, but especially in the Southern States. This crime needs earnest consideration because its continuance and spread will ultimately sap all that is good from the American home. This form of vice as it exists between the races is nothing less than a grade of prostitution, and of the most dangerous sort.

"The concubinal white man is a lecherous being, and the Negro concubine a human without the least trace of moral sense. Offsprings from such unions swarm the Southern States. What is to prevent this progeny from being worse than animal? Such creatures are more dangerous to society than wild beasts; for these last can easily be hunted and shot, while the former go on procreating their lecherous kind without hinderance.

"This species of vice is the most common and persistent of the many that always attends the bringing together of alien races. Women of the subordinate race are unable to resist the temptations to an immoral life. The struggle for existence and a disposition to ape after the ideals of the dominant race are too much for her feeble intellect and will. Mankind shall have to become perfect before alien races can inhabit the same country and remain free from this cancerous form of vice. If the danger to social institutions which concubinage surely holds was well and rightly understood, there is no doubt but that a sentiment would soon be aroused that would endeavor to cure the conditions under which it invariably thrives.

"It seems to us, and the view is supported by all

human experience, that the Negro race in the United States can never have its women develop that high and pure morality which is the bulwark and pride of every civilized people.

"How long would the Indian maiden last if she were to leave the Reservation? What is the moral tone of the mongoloid women who infest New York City and San Francisco? Can they ever be saved? Far more hopeless is the condition of the Negro woman! For fear some of our readers may think our view of this phase of the Negro Problem is overdrawn, we shall quote a few observations made by notable white men. The Montgomery Advertiser reported this statement by Dr. J. A. Rice, pastor of the Court Street Methodist Church, of Montgomery, Alabama: 'I hesitate before I make another statement which is all too true. I hesitate, because I fear that in saying it I shall be charged with sensationalism. But even at the risk of such a charge I will say, for it must be said, that there are in the city of Montgomery four hundred Negro women supported by white men.' The same Dr. Rice also stated that in addition there were thirty-two Negro dives operated for white patronage, and the statement was quoted in the Montgomery *Advertiser*. The New Orleans *Times-Democrat* of February 15, 1906, used the following language to describe the prevailing crime: 'It is a public scandal that there should be no law of this kind (against miscegenation) on the statute book of Louisiana, and that it should be left to mobs to break up the miscegenatious couples. The failure to pass a law of this kind is attributed to white degenerates, men who denounce social equality yet practice it, men who are more dangerous to their own race than the most inflammatory Negro orator and social equality preacher, and who have succeeded by some sort of legislative trickery in pigeon-holing or killing the bills intended to protect Louisiana from a possible danger. Such men should be exposed before the people of the State in their true colors.'

"In January, 1907, District Attorney J. H. Currie, in his address to a jury in Judge Cochran's court at Meridian, Mississippi, used these strong words: 'The accursed shadow of miscegenation hangs over the South today like a pall of hell. We talk much of the Negro question and all of its possible ramifications and consequences, but, gentlemen, the trouble is not far afield. Our own people, our white men with their black concubines, are destroying the integrity of the Negro race, raising up a menace to the white race, lowering the standard of both races, and preparing the way for riot, mob, criminal assaults, and finally a death struggle for racial supremacy. The trouble is at our own door. We have tolerated the crime long enough, and if our country is not run by policy rather than by law, then it is time to rise up and denounce this sin of the Earth.'

"Ray Stannard Baker, in the 'American Magazine' for April, 1908, says: 'Negro women, and especially the more comely and intelligent of them, are surrounded by temptations difficult indeed to meet. It has been and is a struggle in Negro communities, especially village communities, to get a moral standard established which will make such relationships with white men unpopular. In some places today, the Negro concubines of white men are received in Negro churches and among the Negroes generally, and honored rather than ostracized. They are often among the most intelligent of the Negro women; they often have the best homes, and the most money to contribute to their churches. They are proud of their light-colored children.'

"From these statements there can be no doubt as to the wide extent of this degrading evil, and the alarm already aroused in the minds of some thinking men. What is needed is a cure. What shall it be? All ask this question, but few give the answer that ultimately must be given if the homes and firesides of this Republic are to represent all that is best in honor, morality, and religion.

"The sort of education that is possible for the American Negro woman cannot be relied upon to keep her from becoming the white man's concubine. Experience shows that hundreds of educated Negro girls are living the life of kept women in every Southern State; and the number is increasing notwithstanding the spread of schools. The whole trouble is that the conditions under which the Negro must live are opposed to the development of true moral character. Teach the Negro girl art, music, and literature; but without *morals* she will become a concubine at the first opportunity!

"If there were no other reasons for separating the two races, consideration of the moral conditions of the Negro, and the hopeless task of improving it under existing circumstances, ought to convince the most reluctant mind that no other remedy will cure the present evils or save the Republic from more terrible calamities. Against the desire and duty to act for the general welfare of both races, the money cost or the magnitude of the undertaking ought not to prevail.

"There can be given no sound reason against race separation. All experience, and every deduction from the known laws and principles of human nature and human conduct are against the attempt to harmonize two alien races under the same government. When the races are so differentiated in mental and physical characteristics as the Negro and Anglo-Saxon, the government that undertakes the experiment rests at all times on a volcano.

"The subordinate race grows more and more restless under discriminating laws and customs as the people learn to recognize their social, industrial and political ostracism. Nothing can prevent this unrest except giving to the subordinate race full and equal rights in every particular.

"There is absolutely no probability for any such event to occur. The longer the discontent continues the stronger it will grow. Other circumstances will contribute to arouse the resentment of the dominant people against the subordinate because of their obnoxious pretensions. From bad to worse the situation must ever tend.

"Every true friend of humanity must hope that some means may be found to avert the dangers that can already be seen gathering over this grand Republic.

"Our fear is that the remedy will not be seen until the evils have accumulated to such proportions, and the passions of the people so fired that calm and dispassionate reason will be impossible.

"The American people have met with honor and

courage every difficulty which has seemed to threaten the welfare and existence of their government,"—and it is high time that the people of the United States should say frankly to the negroes we have living among us: It was our forefathers who were responsible for the crime of cruelly and forcibly removing you from your own land, and retaining you as slaves in this country. But you must remember that America passed through all the horrors and expense of a long war, one of the results of which was to give unto your race its freedom from slavery. Since that war, many well-meaning white citizens of the United States have endeavored to place your race on a plane of equality in all respects with their own; but, notwithstanding the tremendous efforts made along such lines, they have, in the main, been abortive, and your race can never properly develop as it now exists in the United States. We have the greatest possible sympathy for you in your dilemma, and we stand ready to aid you in every way in our power. Our atonement for the crime committed by our ancestors can, however, take but one form: to assist you to migrate to some other land where you can build a civilization of your own, where your people can be made happy, prosperous and powerful, and attain a position in the world which they never can attain under Anglo-Saxon rule in America.

The matter of the deportation of the negro from the United States can be effected with far less difficulty and expense than most people think. In one way it is a stupendous task to achieve, and in another a very simple one to bring about, provided this country makes up its mind that it is the best thing to be done for *both races* and must be done at all hazards. One thing simplifies the problem very much: A very large number of negroes in this country are ready to enter into any good plan for their deportation at the present time. Four-fifths of our own race are strongly in favor of the movement, especially those who appreciate the horrors of allowing the negro to remain in this country.

On this point, then, it but requires the exercise of every possible means *to show all the people at all times* the pressing necessity for the removal in question. This can be accomplished in many ways: from churches, in speeches, in newspapers, magazines, and other prints; in motion pictures, and in the schools.

As the negro vote has long been but a *matter of barter,* the privilege, as set forth in constitutional amendments, should next be repealed. The negroes would lose absolutely nothing by this, for they would, in any event, carry their vote with them to their own land, wherever that may eventually be.

The next step would be the enactment of a Federal law to the effect that all negroes and descendants of negroes, within the boundaries of the United States of America, shall leave this country for all time within ten years after the passage of said law; this to be rigidly enforced by the entire power of the United States Government.

It is not at all necessary that all of these millions of negroes and their half-blood relatives go to the same country, or leave at the same time. By the enforcing of such a law no hardship whatever would be entailed by a single member of the race subjected to it. It could be carried out in the most *orderly, friendly,* and *helpful* manner, and from the very nature of it, it would be so carried out.

Within the ten years allowed by the law, ample time would be given for the transfer of all real estate or other holdings that the negroes and mulattoes have in this country. They would only have to part with such of their estates as could not be conveniently taken with them. The transfer of real estate would, in ten years, give no trouble, for it would, in half that time, be taken up by the real estate speculators, by the incoming white immigrants, and in small part, perhaps,—where it would prove advantageous,—by the State or Federal Governments. Moreover, if any negro or half-blood could not, without sacrifice, dispose of his or her holdings *in ten years,* such a one could arrange to leave it and dispose of it subsequently through agents in this country. It is fortunate that the negroes have amassed such great wealth in the United States since 1865, for it will very materially facilitate their migration, and powerfully aid in making the start for their empire in some other land.

Then, too, when financial stringency became evident at any point during the deportation, this country could well afford to ease it by the expenditure of any reasonable appropriation for the purpose, commensurate with the object to be accomplished: the saving of the debasement of our race; the atonement for a national crime, and the horrors of a racial war in the future. Fifteen millions or more a year for ten consecutive years, would mean nothing to the United States, were the "problem" solved in that way, without any harshness or jar. Think of it for a moment; it cost this country ten millions to keep General Funston and his army in Vera Cruz for only a few months; surely the accomplishments in either case are hardly comparable. United States undoubtedly would have to furnish transportation and keep for a large number of the negroes who are entirely without means. These latter would have to be organized and led by the dominant men and minds of their own race.

It is by no means necessary that all the negroes should go to the same country, as most people seem unable to get out of their heads. Three millions of them could easily be distributed over South America, *where they would be welcome.* Half a million could find their way into Mexico and the West Indies, aside from Haiti, which latter country could easily accommodate three millions more. They could be transported to those countries just as easily as the Kaiser has transported his armies to and fro, from the trenches in Flanders to the firing-line in Poland, during the present war, and with far less expense and discomfort, especially in the matters of loss of life and national accomplishment.

United States could well afford to assign an island in the Philippines to them to accommodate a million or two, and there they could establish, under this country's protection, a government all their own, where no white man could vote or have a word to say. It could be made a strong ally of the United States in the East, and a starting-point where the African race, under the most favorable conditions, could build an empire of its own.

In these days, the transporting of that many negroes to the Philippines *in ten years* would mean but little, in so far as any difficulty attached to it in the matter of its accomplishment. Naturally, many negroes in this country look to Africa as the land to which they would much prefer to go. It is a magnificent country in all respects, and Walker says in "Our Home Colony," in regard to this and the whole project of negro deportation, that "We believe that the Negro race can find superior advantages and better opportunities on the shores of old Africa, among people of their own race, for developing the innate powers of mind and body than anywhere else upon the face of the earth, and the reasons of this belief we shall try to give in the following pages.

"In 1822 a Colony of free Negroes from the United States was settled upon the west coast of Africa, mainly through the efforts of the American Colonization Society. There was no difficulty in procuring sufficient land for these people who desired to emigrate; nor was there at that time any disposition among free Negroes to oppose the opportunity of returning to their native land.

"In 1827 free Negroes of Baltimore, Md., and Washington, D. C., memorialized Congress to provide financial aid to transport all who might desire to go to Liberia, as the country provided for them in Africa was named.

"In 1847 the independence of Liberia was declared, and in 1848 it was recognized by England and most of the continental countries. The United States did likewise a few years later, in 1861.

"This Colony since 1847 has exercised full sovereignty over a territory embracing nearly 35,000 square miles; as large as Connecticut, New Jersey, Massachusetts, Maryland, and Delaware combined, and one and one-half larger than the State of West Virginia. It is no longer an experiment, but a fact. Liberia stands today a recognized Sovereign State among the family of Nations. The Liberians are today exercising all the functions of a free and independent government. If they have not shown the advance some would like to see, it can be easily shown they are far in advance of their Negro brethren left behind in the United States. The few thousand American Negroes who have returned to Africa and builded for themselves and posterity a national edifice recognized and respected by all nations, are deserving of praise and honor from every Negro in the world. These people have demonstrated to mankind that the Negro is capable of organizing and maintaining a civilized government in the very midst of intellectual and moral darkness.

"In the early days of African Colonization, Negroes were transported to Liberia for the small sum of twenty dollars a head, and vessels made but one or two voyages per year. With the improved ocean steamer of today and the increased facilities for handling traffic, there is every reason to believe that this sum of twenty dollars for passage could be materially lessened if the scheme of deportation was undertaken on a large scale. It is objected to any scheme of Colonization that it would not appreciably reduce even the natural increase of the race, and hence would have no effect on the congested Negro population of the Southern States. This objection is urged more strongly by white men than by negro enemies of Emigration.

"A few figures from statistics will show the absurdity of this objection, and prove conclusively that in a few years the fear of Negro domination even in the States most densely populated by the black race would have no terror for the most timid. If $85,000,-000 had been expended during the period from 1820 up to the present time, not more than 1,500,000, and probably not 500,000 Negroes would be in the United States today. The census of the United States for 1820 shows 233,530 free negroes and 1,538,128 slaves, a total of 1,771,658. Now, a fair allowance for natural increase would be 3 per cent. of the total per year, making in round numbers 53,000.

"The American Colonization Society was able, as has been stated, to transport Negroes to Liberia for twenty dollars per head, and at this rate could have carried the 53,000 increase to Africa each year for $1,060,000. If just that much had been done for eighty-five years, we see the outlay would be less than $90,000,000, and the original stock of 1,771,658 lessened by reason of the loss each year of the most prolific of the race.

"This plan of deporting the Negroes willing to return to Africa was ably advocated by many true friends of the race, and most notably by those who were advocates of gradual emancipation. The same plan applied to conditions as they exist today, would show equally favorable results. By the census of 1900 the population was 8,849,789, an increase during the decade from 1890 to 1900 of 1,352,001, or 12.2 per cent. Now to transport this increase of 1,352,001 at twenty dollars would cost $27,040,020. If this task were undertaken by the General Government the sum would be less by one-half. Who will deny that the great and powerful Government of the United States could not afford to expend even $100,000,000 per year to accomplish an object so fraught with beneficial results to two races, alien and incongruous?"

As the departure of the negroes took on shape, it would naturally be of the most gradual character at first. Indeed, the first year or two of the ten years could be profitably spent in this country in making the arrangements to leave; the mapping out of the tracts in the countries to be occupied as their future homes, the correspondence entailed, the comfortable transfer of holdings, and finally all the arrangements this country would have to put on foot for transportation and other matters. However, once under way, the stream of migrants would rapidly increase in numbers, and this would be accelerated by the knowledge of the operation of the law, and the probability of another law being enacted, to the effect that under no circumstances could they return to the United States for any purpose, any more than certain other races can that are now debarred from enjoying certain privileges in California.

As time passed the departure of the negroes from the United States would be greatly quickened through the knowledge of the fact that those who were on the ground first to establish themselves would reap the greatest advantages in the matter of securing the best land locations and positions in the new government.

As I have said in a former chapter, as the negroes left, the whites now coming to this country daily *by the thousands* from Europe, would take their places almost without attracting any particular attention as it gradually happened.

Furthermore, it is fair to presume that the present terrible race war, now converting only too large a part of Europe into a veritable slaughter-pen (February 22, 1915), will come to a close as suddenly as it commenced; and when this much hoped-for day arrives, not only will shiploads of the white races of many of the continental peoples come to the United States seeking homes and employment, but these, upon the whole desirable contributions to our population, would not only include the day laborers, the tradespeople, and the artisans, but also a fair proportion representing the various professions, and the votaries of art, science, and the *belles-lettres.*

With the blacks and their hybrids out of it, the *relief* to this country would be felt with ever-increasing benefit, and what a "problem" we would have solved!

GLOSSARY.

[Compiled by the author especially for the present work.]

A

Abolitionist: *abolition,* to abolish; hence one who favors the doing away with anything; one who stands for the abolition of slavery.

aborigines: the original inhabitants of any country or place; first applied to the people of Latium, the Roman ancestors.

abstract: conceived apart from matter and from special cases (as a number in arithmetic, where it stands without designating anything).

aery: the site of the nest of an eagle, including the nest itself.

alien: a resident of one country living in another and not possessing citizen-rights in the adopted country. Very different in character or nature. Hostile.

allegories: parables; fiction written to illustrate truths; symbolic representations in literature.

alpha and omega: first and last letters of the Greek alphabet,—hence the beginning and end of anything.

altruistic; altruism: action or acts prompted by benevolence or by any of the worthy emotions; being regardful of the welfare and feelings of others. *Altruist,* one who practises altruistic methods. These words are the opposite of *egotism, egoist,* and *egoistic.*

ambiguity: uncertainty or doubtfulness.

amblystoma: one of the tailed batrachians; they are related to the newts, etc. (see aquatic batrachians).

ameliorating: making better or improving; meliorating.

amplification: the act of enlarging or extending; amplifying.

analogue: anything that possesses something in agreement or in correspondence with something else. In zoölogy usually applied to structure, functions or relations. There are also *analogous* terms or words; *analogy,* agreement. That which agrees or corresponds is *analogous.*

aneurism: an enlargement or dilatation in the course of an artery caused by pressure of the blood on a localized and weakened area.

Anglo-Saxon: a person of that race; applied generally to the pure strain, white, English-speaking people.

animalism: generally applied to those human beings in whose organizations a desire for the sensual exceeds that for the intellectual. A mere animal. Dominated by strong animal passions.

ankylosed or anchylosed: immovably joined together, as when two bones become firmly united, as the bones of the skull for example.

anterior lobes: divisions of the brain; the pair of fore-parts of the cerebrum. Either half of the cerebrum is divided into three lobes: the anterior, middle, and posterior.

Anthropidæ: the family in zoölogy containing man, generally considered as a single genus and species (*Homo sapiens*).

anthropofauna: collectively speaking, the various races of men found in any particular country or district, or of the entire world (Shufeldt).

Anthropoidæ: a family in zoölogy to contain the higher apes or simians.

anthropoid apes: the man-like apes, as the gorilla, chimpanzee, orang, and gibbon. The *Simiidæ*. They are all man-like in a great many particulars, both mentally and physically.

anthropologically: in an anthropological manner or way.

anthropology: the science of man or mankind collectively.

antithesis: contrast or something in opposition, as *antithetic* opinions or propositions; *antithetical,* pertaining to antithesis.

aortic segment: the *aortic valves* at the origin of the aorta, in the heart; the three semi-lunar valves.

aponeurosis: a thin, broad, flat tendon, glistening white in color, connecting thin, flat muscles, as the *aponeurosis frontalis,* riding over the top of the skull in man, it being the *aponeurotic* part of the *occipito-frontalis* muscle.

a priori: in the first case or instance; from the former; from cause to effect.

aquatic batrachians: those members of the order *Batrachia* which, in their early stages, breathe by gills and live in the water; especially refers to toads and frogs. It also includes the newts, tritons, salamanders, etc.

Archencephalia: a group containing man alone; conterminous with *Bimana,* etc.

atavism: to revert or the reversion to a preceding type through heredity, as when black children are born to white and mulatto crossings. *Atavistic,* pertaining to atavism.

auto-erotism: the gratification of the sexual desires through self-practices.

B

basal and bulbar ganglia: a ganglion is an enlargement in the course of a nerve; the basal ganglia are found at the base of the brain (cerebrum).

bestiality: beastliness; unworthy of a refined and intellectual man's nature; having the qualities of a beast, whether a human beast or otherwise.

Bimana: an order of the *Mammalia* including man, the only *bimanous* animal, strictly speaking, in the world's fauna. Not now in use, as, zoölogically, the higher apes would have to be included in it.

bimanous: having two hands. See *Bimana.*

biologist: one learned in biology, the science of life and the forms of life of all kinds in the world of nature.

brachycephalic; brachycephalous: heads or skulls whose diameter from side to side is not much less than it is from back to front; opposed to *dolichocephalic* (which see).

brain-pan: the cranium or that portion of the skull in which the brain is found.

C

calcaneum: the large bone of the foot forming the heel (*os calcis*).

canine: one of the dog-tribe(*Canidæ*) or a *canid,* a carnivorous mammal of the canine family, sometimes referred to as the *Canina.* The dog-tooth or *canine*-tooth, which in shape is *caniniform. Canis* is the Latin word for dog.

cannibalism; cannibal: those people who feed upon human flesh; also any other animal that eats of its own kind. A human flesh-eater of the human species; a human man-eater as found among some of the black races. An anthropophagite.

cardio-vascular-renal disease: a disease in which the heart, blood-vessels, and kidneys are involved.

carnal gratification: satisfying, to a greater or less degree, the sexual instinct or appetite (which see).

carnivorous: to feed upon flesh; to subsist upon an animal diet, as in the case of the *carnivores* of the order *Carnivora* or what pertains to that *carnivoral* group of the Mammalia.

Caucasian: a member of the highest type of mankind; the best of the white races of the world.

caudal appendage: the tail in animals possessing one.

cerebrum: the brain or larger brain mass of the encephalon.

certitude: beyond all doubt; certainty.

chastity: purity in sexual matters; chaste; absence of all depravity and obscenity; guiltless of sexual intercourse from one cause or another.

Chellean type: a type from the Chellean deposits, formed in one of the earliest paleolithic periods,—that is, in France (Chelles), a short distance from Paris, on the right bank of the river Marne. The type of the flint instruments of the Chellean age of Europe.

chimpanzee: one of the man-like monkeys (*Troglodytes niger*); the anthropoid ape of that name; a species most nearly related to the gorilla, and in its form and organization very closely related to man (*Homo sapiens*).

Christianity: the religion said to be founded by Jesus Christ; also applied to the body of people who believe in what it is reported that Christ set forth as a guidance in morals and conduct.

chyluria: a disease characterized by the presence of milky urine. The color is due to emulsionized fat in great quantities, and it will frequently coagulate on standing. There are other symptoms.

cicatrices; cicatrix: scars, welts, or other marks formed on the body as the results of cuts or other wounds.

coalesce: unite, come or join together; to combine. To form one body.

co-efficient: acting in coöperation to the same end or purpose.

cohabit: to live together; to dwell together as man and wife; or where unmarried men and women live with each other as husbands and wives. Generally used as a term for sexual intercourse, which it does not always imply.

coition: sexual congress; carnal union between the sexes of any animal. The act of performing *coitus*. Copulation. A coming together, a meeting.

concensus: a collective opinion; a state of general agreement.

concomitantly: that which exists or occurs together.

concrete: (in logic) particular; individual (opposed to abstract), a class-name or proper name.

concubinage; concubinate: sexual intercourse among people in the absence of legal marriage. *Concubine,* a wife holding an inferior position in the family or household, also applied to the male sex; a paramour; a mistress. *Concubinal* practices, as having *concubinary* relations, or one who lives as a *concubinarian.*

condoned: that which has been forgiven or pardoned; *condone,* to overlook a fault.

conterminous: contiguous; possessing the same limit; to border upon, or in contact at any boundary; equal extension. Also, with the same meaning, *conterminate.*

convolutions: objects or things that are *turned* or are winding, as the convolutions seen on the outer surface of the brain; the gyres of the cerebrum.

cortex: that which covers some anatomical structure in the manner of bark or fruit-rind, as the *cortex* of the cerebrum or brain.

cranial bones: those bones of the skull which encase the brain; brain-box; bones entering into the brain-cavity in animals.

cranial sutures: boundary lines where the margins of the cranial bones come together or articulate.

criteria: the plural of *criterion,* a test of truth or falsehood; also standards of criticism or judgment for anything being considered. Occasionally used in the sense of a law or a principle; rule of guidance.

D

decimate: to destroy a great number of anything, generally people.

degeneracy: the tendency to pass from bad to worse or to deteriorate. A race or nation is in a state of degeneracy when well started on a downward course.

degenerate: (when used as an intransitive verb) impaired; to lose and assume the place of a lower type. As an adjective: the state of having been reduced to a lower type; a worse state or degraded condition. We may also use the word as a noun, meaning one who has passed from a normal type to a lower or debased one.

demography: vital and social statistics as applied to mankind. The *demographer* in his *demographic* researches contributes to the science of anthropology.

deportation: the removing from one place or country to another and generally a more distant one.

diametrically: directly or to an extreme degree, as opinions which may be diametrically opposite.

diastemata: in animals with true teeth, a *diastema* is an interval between any two consecutive ones, as the diastema between a canine and a premolar tooth. Such *diastemata* are also found between the canines and the lateral incisors.

digits: fingers of hands and toes of feet.

dissemination: the act of spreading abroad for any special purpose; the extension of influence; sending an opinion broadcast.

dogmatic: relating to *dogma* or principles propounded upon authority. Dogma usually refers to religious doctrines as opposed to proven and demonstrated facts, usually those of science.

dogmatically: pertaining to dogma,—dogma meaning an authoritative religious doctrine, or principles based on authority rather than on experience or demonstration.

doliochocephalic: heads or skulls in which the antero-posterior diameter is markedly longer than the one passing from side to side; opposed to brachycephalic (which see).

ductless glands: those glandular organs of the body that are without ducts; there are four of them, namely, the spleen, the adrenals, thymus and thyroid.

duress: hardness; sternness; durance; restriction of personal liberty, under pressure.

E

edentate: toothless; where the front teeth are absent as in the *Edentata.*

El Dorado: a country which Orellana claimed to have discovered somewhere on the Amazon River (1540-41), which was rich beyond all imagination in jewels and gold.

elephantiasis: skin diseases of several kinds bear that name; leprosy (which see).

emasculation: castration; to deprive a man or any other male vertebrate of the testes or a single testicle should only one be present—hence to deprive of vigor or render effeminate.

emesis: act of vomiting; evacuation of the stomach by the mouth.

emolument: remuneration in connection with the salary of any office.

emotionalism: subject to *emotion,* or possessing a tendency to emotional excitement as an *emotionalist* is.

empirical: that which is derived through experimentation or experience; also charlatanical; quackish. Empirical in medical practice. That which is derived through insufficient observation or experience.

eoliths: objects from the *eolithic* age,—that is, the early part of the palæolithic period.

epidermis: cuticle or scarf-skin; the outer layer of the skin or the non-vascular cuticle. The integument.

epitomized: that which is shortened or abridged; to make an *epitome* is for the *epitomist* to prepare an abstract of a subject.

erotic: amorous; dealing with love; prompted by amorous desires.

esthetics: pertaining to beauty; the love of the beautiful; refinement and taste in the arts.

ethics; ethical: the science of right and wrong conduct of life; the doctrine that has to deal with man's moral obligations as they refer to himself or to those with whom he comes in contact.

Ethiopian: an inhabitant of Ethiopia; when used in an extended sense means an African in general.

ethnic: that which pertains to or is peculiar to a race of men.

ethnological: relating to *ethnology*, or the science of the various tribes and races of human beings, including their history, customs, civilizations, etc.

ethnologist: a student of the science of *ethnology*, or that science which takes into consideration the study of the races of men in the world,—their history, characters, customs, and institutions. There is a vast *ethnologic* or *ethnological* literature extant.

euphemisms: mild or agreeable words or expressions for disagreeable ones which might give offense; a *euphemism* is a word thus used.

expatriation: to banish or to remove a person or a people from the country where they have been living.

extenuation: the act of making less blamable; to mitigate the degree of a fault.

extirpation: the act of rooting out; total destruction or removal, as a surgeon would *extirpate* a diseased appendix in appendicitis. Errors may also be *extirpated,* that is, if they be *extirpable* at the hands of the would-be *extirpator.*

F

facial angle: an angle formed by a straight line in a plane tangent to the face of the skull in man (and other vertebrates), with a line in the plane of the base of the skull. It has been taken differently by various *craniometrists,* as the facial angle of Camper, of Cloquet, of Jacquart, and of Geoffrey Saint Hilaire. The facial angle may be nearly 90 degrees in certain skulls, and its average is much greater in the skulls of the superiorly intellectual among the white races of mankind than it is among the lower races of men, as the negroes and their allies.

fallacies: errors; deceptions; falsehoods; delusions; delusive reasoning.

fasciculus: a bundle (in anatomy), as a bundle of nerves such as go to form the spinal cord. A bundle of muscular fibers composing a part of a muscle. There are many such *fasciculi* in the anatomy of any of the higher animals.

fetishism: a form of religious belief where the worshippers set up a *fetish* as their god. Many of the negroes of the west coast of Africa regard their *fetishes* with great awe, and these are usually small charm-objects or talismans. All *fetishistic* practices are highly imbued with superstition.

filariasis; filarial infection: refer to the disease caused by the infection of the parasitic nematode worms of the family *Filariidæ*. *Filariate,* to infect with *filaria,*—that is, thread-worms.

fissure: a cleft or narrow, elongate groove, as the *fissures* separating the convolutions of the brain.

fœtus; fetus: the young of viviparous animals in the uterus or womb up to the time of birth. Occasionally applied to the young of oviparous animals in the egg.

folk-psychology: science of the phenomena of the mind in various races or peoples.

fortuitous: casual; that which takes place or occurs by chance. Lucky.

fraternization: the act of combining as in a brotherhood; associating with common interests; *fraternize,* where people with similar aims, tastes, sympathies, etc., unite in a brotherhood or *fraternity.*

fratricidal: a person who kills his brother is a *fratricide,* and anything pertaining to such a murder is of a *fratricidal* import.

G

genesis: creation; procreation; production; formation; act of begetting; mode of generation-processes of natural propagation.

germ cells: a germ with the structural value of a single cell, as an ovum when first impregnated.

germinal sexual elements: the ova in a female and spermatozoa of the testes in the male.

glandular secretions: secretions from certain glands in animals, as the urine by the kidneys, milk in the female, etc.

gluteal: pertaining to the *gluteus muscles,* or to the buttocks in man, referring to the natal region.

gonococcus: a cell of the micrococcus found in the discharges coming from a gonorrhea,—one of the venereal diseases.

gorilla: the largest known anthropoid ape (*Troglodytes gorilla*). It is found in certain parts of Africa, and in its anatomy it closely resembles man.

H

hallux: in man, the great toe; the innermost of the five digits of the hind foot in the vertebrata. *Pollex* is the thumb in the hand of man and in some of the higher mammals.

helix: the prominent, curved and thickened posterior margin of the outer ear in the Primates,—that is, in men and in most monkeys and apes.

hemaglobinuria fever: a fever associated with the disease or condition of that name. *Globin,* the proteid substance which, combined with *hematin,* forms the larger part of the red blood-corpuscles.

heredity: the possession of mental or physical qualities through transmission of descent. The influence of parents upon their children. Characters in offspring derived from parental stock. (See atavism.)

heterogenous: mixed; incongruous; very unlike; different in kind or character.

hippocampus minor: a structure which is a part of the brain, but not peculiar to man; it consists of a longitudinal eminence found in the lateral ventricle, or rather the floor of the posterior horn of it.

Hominidæ: the zoölogical family containing all the species and subspecies of men. There is but one genus, that is the genus *Homo,* Mankind.

homogeneous: essentially alike; the same kind or nature,—generally refers to parts of one whole.

Homo sapiens: the zoölogical name for man, of which there are a number of subspecies or geographical races.

homo-sexuality: having sexual desire for one of the same sex. There is a class of sexual perverts described as *homosexualists.*

Hottentot: a member of one of the South African races of people. They are a small, stupid, ungainly stock, with dark yellowish-brown skins and often apish faces. Many of their women are steatopygous (which see).

humerus: the long bone of the upper arm. It articulates with the scapula at the shoulder-joint and with the two bones of the forearm at the elbow.

hybridization: cross-breeding; *hybrid* is a half-breed or half-blood. *Hybridize,* to produce hybrids; *hybridist,* one who *hybridizes.*

hypotheses: an assumed proposition or one taken for granted; a supposition. Propositions held to be probably true for the reason that according to known laws they have been proven to be true.

I

idealist: one who advocates the doctrines of *idealism* and believes that the psychical reigns in all that is real in nature: in other words the real, or the doctrine of the *realist,* is but of the nature of thought. *Idealistic* doctrines are of many kinds and have been held by many men of eminence.

ideation: the acts or processes through which *ideas* are formed. *Ideational,* pertaining to the formation of ideas or to the faculty of *ideation.*

idiosyncrasies: mental or physical peculiarities of persons; certain antipathies or susceptibilities inherent in people.

incidence: an incident; a casual happening; also in physics the ray of light or heat which, impinging on a surface, is refracted at a certain angle,—the "angle of incidence."

incitement: anything that moves to action; the act of inciting or instigating; to *incite* is to spur or to stimulate.

inculcation: forcible teaching; particularly where it assumes the form of repeated admonitions.

Indo-European: a member of any race speaking the Indo-European languages (the Aryan). The races are all white, and hence the word is sometimes employed to designate the white races of the world as a whole. Strictly speaking, an Indo-European is an Aryan.

ineradicable: that which cannot be eradicated or rooted out.

in extenso: in full; at füll length, as an unabridged manuscript is given *in extenso.*

inherent: intrinsic; existing as an attribute; innately characteristic.

inhibit: to check or repress; to forbid; to restrict or hinder by some obstruction. Prohibit. *Inhibition,* the act of *inhibiting.*

insectivorous: plants and animals which subsist upon insects are said to be *insectivorous* and belong, in so far as animals are concerned, to the *Insectivora,*—a very complex group.

inter se: Latin expression meaning among themselves.

in utero: within the *uterus* or the womb of woman and other mammals. A child or fœtus is *in utero* up to the time it passes into the vagina during a normal birth.

invidious: obvious; envious; to discriminate offensively.

J

jurisprudence: science of law and legal practice. The laws of any nation or community.

juxtaposition: placed near to or close together. *Juxtapose,* to place two objects side by side.

L

lascivious: lewd; filled with lust; wanton; that which excites lustful desires or emotions.

lechery: lewdness; unbridled indulgence in sensuality or the carnal appetite (see these definitions under their headings).

leprosy: a name applied to various diseases; strictly speaking it is the *lepra cutanea* or elephantiasis Græcorum.

lethargy: stupor; inactivity; a prolonged condition of inactivity; extreme dulness; sluggish. A dull *lethargic* state is a torpid one, or one of *lethargicalness.* Some climates seem to have a *lethargogenic* effect upon those who live in them; the effect is to *lethargize* or stupify the people.

lewd: in its usual meaning or as commonly used, lascivious, lustful, libidinous; while strictly it means ignorant and untaught or unlearned; worthless, of no use; rude and uncultivated.

libidinous: filled with eager lust; an intense desire for sexual indulgence.

licentiousness: sexual immorality; the state of being loose or dissolute in morals. Wanton.

lues: a pestilence or a plague. (*Lues venerea,* syphilis or any of the venereal diseases.)

lust ceremonies: certain dances and customs of savage tribes, associated with lustful acts. In ancient times they were also practised in cities of Italy and Greece.

lycanthropy: human beings that are supposed to possess the power to transform themselves or other persons, either for the time being or forever into wolves or other ferocious animals.

M

malar bones: cheek bones (jugal bones).

malevolent: malicious; one inspired by evil intent or having an evil disposition. Hostile.

Mammalia: in classification, the highest class of vertebrated animals, or those which suckle their young; includes all *mammiferous* animals.

mandril: one of the baboons; the hog-ape; the great, ferocious blue-faced species often seen in zoölogical gardens. They inhabit the coast of west Africa.

manumitted: to have been released from slavery; such *manumission* or emancipation was given the negro slaves by President Lincoln. *Manumit,* to free from bondage.

manus: the hand in those animals possessing one. Also applied to the bones of the fingers and wrist in the skeleton. The *manus* of the pectoral limb in birds, etc.

marmoset: common name for a group of little apes or small monkeys. The squirrel-monkeys of South America.

maxim: a rule based upon a proposition; apt expressions employed as rules for conduct, etc. Such guides may be true or false, and are generally pseudoethical rules for conduct.

mendacity: a lie; habitual lying, being *mendacious.*

mendicity: the condition of a *mendicant* or a beggar; beggarliness, the state of a *mendicant,* or one given to *mendication.*

menstruating: a discharge of the menses in the female. *Menstrua,* menses or catamenial discharges. *Menstrual,* to occur once a month; *menstruant,* a woman who *menstruates; menstrous,* having the monthly flux of the female.

Mesvinian: a type of palæolithic weapons or stone implements of an earlier form than those known as the Chellean type (which see). Prehistoric weapons of the earlier eolithic types have been long known and abundantly described.

metaphysics: philosophy in its wider sense; philosophy as applied to any of the sciences. The mental sciences in general.

miscegenation: a mixture of races through indiscriminate crossing; a term commonly applied to the sexual union of the whites and negroes.

mitral ring: the circumference of the auriculo-ventricular orifice of the left side of the heart in man and in other mammals, to which is attached the *mitral valve* or segments.

monad: a single-celled organism or animal of the extreme simple type. Its meaning in metaphysics is quite complex and does not require definition here.

Mongolian: a *Mongol,* or an individual of the *Mongol* race of *Mongolia,* situated in northern China and southern Siberia.

monogamic marriage: that form of human marriage in which but one wife at a time is legally permitted.

morphological: pertaining to the science of *morphology* or that science which treats of organic forms of life, including plants, their external forms and internal structures.

motor control: having power over one's movements.

mucous membrane: one of the most extensive membranes of the body; lines the entire alimentary canal and its annexes, including the air and urogenital passages.

mulatto: a man or woman having parents one of whom is white and the other a negro. The father or mother may be either black or white in any case.

myology: the science which treats of the muscles in man and other animals. *Myological,* referring to the muscles.

mythology: the science of myths.

N

nasal apertures: the nostrils; openings that lead into the cavity of the nose.

nasal bones: two small bones of the face forming the outer wall of the nose; they vary greatly in size and form.

natural environment: the normal surroundings of any animal in nature and those surroundings into which its habits may normally lead it.

nefarious: wicked; abominable; vile.

negligible: that which may be disregarded.

negroid: resembling a negro or being akin to one of that race.

negrophiles: persons who possess a great love for members of the negro race.

nephritis: inflammation of the kidneys, of which there are a number of forms.

newt: (see salamander).

nidus: Latin word for nest.

nolens volens: willing or unwilling.

O

odoriferous glands: those glands in animals the secretions of which possess an odor of a greater or less strength, as for example the sweat-glands.

omnivorous: indiscriminate feeding; all-devouring; an animal classed with the *Omnivora,* as the pigs and hippopotamuses.

organically: the adverb of the adjective and noun *organic* which has numerous meanings, as instrumentally, in an *organic* manner; by or through *organization. Organic,* operating as an instrument or *organ* to accomplish anything. Having reference to or pertaining to the organs of animals and plants. Making up a whole with a regular or systematic arrangement.

organic evolution: animal evolution or the evolution of organic life in nature; usually as distinguished from the evolution of plants.

orientation: the act of taking one's proper bearings mentally.

orthognathous: those human skulls in which the jaw is straight and thus give a vertical profile and a wide facial angle. The opposite of prognathous.

ostracism: expulsion; social separation; banishment of all kinds, with a general reference to society. *Ostracize,* to banish from society.

P

palæolithic: pertaining to the "stone age," characterized by the existence in it of *palæoliths* or unpolished stone implements made by prehistoric man.

palæontologically: in a *palæontological* sense,—the science of *palæontology,* having to do with the former life on this planet, as shown by the fossil remains of animals, plants, etc., in the geological strata and periods.

palliation: the act of *palliating;* concealing or rendering less offensive the circumstances of misdemeanors or crimes; mitigation in general; alleviation.

pellagra: a disease of southern Europe, which has quite recently developed in the United States; after running a few years it is frequently fatal.

pelvis: the bony basin supporting the backbone and with which the lower-limb bones articulate. It varies greatly in form in different persons and in the two sexes.

perfidious: basely treacherous or lacking in faith. Having the character of a traitor.

persona grata: person who is welcome or acceptable; one in favor.

phylogeny: tribal history. That department of biological science that undertakes to define the ancestral histories of plants and animals from the development of the individual, and the characters observed during the processes of such development. Opposed to *ontogeny,* which refers to the development of individual organisms. *Phylogeny* and *phylogenesis* mean the same thing.

physiologically: in a *physiological* sense, or from a *physiological* viewpoint. *Physiology* is the science of the functions of the organs of animals and plants or of living things in general.

Pithecanthropus erectus: name given to the remains of an extinct animal found by Dubois in Java. These remains indicate that they belong to a form nearer man than any of the anthropoid apes now existing. It was doubtless a bominiform mammal forming a veritable missing link between man and the higher apes.

plantar surface: the under surface of the foot, as opposed to the upper or dorsal surface.

plantigrade: said of those mammals which normally walk with the heels on the ground, as the racoons and bears which belong to the *Plantigrada.*

plasticity: *plastic,* capable of being molded or given form to, hence that property of matter whereby it may be given form through being fashioned or molded.

pliocene age: in geology, that division of the Tertiary which is the most recent.

polydactylism: possessed of fingers or toes exceeding the normal number of five on either hand or foot.

polygamy: that form of human marriage where two or more wives are permitted at a time.

posterity: descendants, when taken collectively; the breed or race that descends from an ancestor or progenitor.

potentialities: *potential* has many meanings, as mighty and powerful, potent; that which may become possible or effective as opposed to the actual,—hence *potentialities,* those states or qualities which possess inherent capability or development into the real or actual state; possibility.

precociousness: the state of being prematurely developed mentally; forward. *Precocity.*

preëxistent: that which previously existed.

prehensile: taking hold of; grasping or seizing; formed for *prehension,* as the tail of certain monkeys, opossums and porcupines.

prescription: direction; also the written directions for a patient in the use of medicine or in treatment. In law, holding possession sufficiently long so as to secure title to one or more persons to rights against others; to acquire possession through prescription.

Primates: the highest order of the *Mammalia,* including man, all forms of apes and monkeys, and the lemurs.

primeval: belonging to the first or early ages. Also first in other things, as primeval forests, etc.

pristine: primitive; original; belonging to an early period.

proclivity: proneness; tendency; inclination. *Proclive,* to incline.

procreative instinct: the desire to have children; the desire to cross with the female with the hope of having children.

prognathism: being *prognathic* or possessing protrusive jaws (same as prognathous).

promiscuous: confused; mixed together regardless of order or arrangement; common, indiscriminate, as promiscuous sexual congress among people or races.

prostitute: a harlot; a woman who resorts to indiscriminate sexual intercourse; base; infamous; to devote to anything base.

Protozoa: that group of the subkingdom of the *Animalia* which comprise the cell-animals or the primordial forms of life.

psoas parvus: a small muscle attached to the brim of the pelvis, in front of the *psoas magnus* muscle, and which arises from the sides of the bodies of the first lumbar and last dorsal vertebræ. According to M. Theile, it is found in about one in twenty among the whites.

psychologically: in a *psychological* sense or from a *psychological* viewpoint. *Psychology* is the science of the mind or mental functions and their phenomena, and those who devote themselves to it are the *psychologists.*

psychopathia sexualis: diseases of the sexual system which depend upon the mental ones, or where the mental functions are involved. The diseases of sexual perverts.

puberty: the time in the lives of boys and girls when they become able to reproduce their kind, or to give or bear children respectively.

puerile: trivial; boyish; childish, lacking in intellectual strength.

putridity: rottenness; corruption of any kind. In its correct use only applies to *putrid* matter.

Q

Quadrumana: an order of the *Mammalia* in which are grouped all the apes, monkeys, marmosets, and their near allies. *Quadrumanous,* four-handed, as the animals just named.

quadrupeds: four-footed animals.

R

religiosity: religious sentimentality; being extremely susceptible to religious sentiments and influences; superstition associated with awe, wonder, and extreme religious reverence.

religious emotionalism: excitement, where the exciting cause is religion; or the fear prompted by religion or superstition.

retina: the expanded end of the optic nerve at the back of the eyeball. It receives the optical impressions imaged upon it through the focussing of the crystalline lens.

retrogradation: a going backward; the state of degeneration.

S

salamander: one of the tailed batrachians (see aquatic batrachians). Also includes tritons and newts.

sclerotic: the white enveloping tunic or membrane of the eye in the Anglo-Saxon, and in numerous other races. The *sclerotica.* It is very frequently deeply tinged with yellow in negroes.

segregation: the act of separating.

semi-metamorphosed: incomplete transformation.

sensuality: the unbridled gratification of the sexual or carnal instincts and promptings; immoderate indulgence in carnality or worldly pleasures. Through example, certain characters may be *sensualized* or rendered *sensual,* the *sensualization* taking place in greater or less lengths of time in different individuals.

sensuous: pertaining to the senses, as *sensuous* pleasures; keenly awake to pleasurable sensations through the senses.

sex centers: those structures in animals and plants which pertain to the sexual system, and the excitation of which gives rise to sexual desire.

sexual appetite: the normal desire for copulation,—though it is frequently appeased through other expedients.

sexuality: having sex or the state of being sexed; sex in the abstract; the distinction between the two sexes.

sexual madness: a loss of control over the normal sexual impulse or desire.

Simiidæ; Simians: the *simians* are the higher or anthropoid apes; they are grouped in the family *Simiidæ,* which, next to man, is the highest family of the order *Primates.* They form the suborder *Anthropoidea.* Many of the lower forms of Africans possess *simian* characters in their anatomical organizations, as well as in other respects.

skatological rites: *skatology* is the science of fossil feces or excrement. A study of such fossils (coprolites) often contribute to our knowledge of the animals themselves. The rites referred to are of the order of certain forms of witchcraft, but more particularly those religious rites where fecal matter, excrements, and urine play a part. In some savage rites, *scatophagy* is practised,—that is, the eating of the dung and excrement, etc.

sociological: that which pertains to human society. *Sociologic* customs are those exacted on the part of society.

spine: spinal column or the series of vertebræ forming the backbone.

steatopygous: having monstrous fat buttocks, as the *steatopygous* Hottentot women. *Steatopygy,* the state of having big, fat buttocks, the condition being termed *steatopyga.*

stirpiculture: the breeding of special kinds or stocks by careful selection.

Strepyea: a type of palæolithic weapons of an earlier form than those of the "Chellean" type (which see).

sublimation; sublimated: in addition to its meaning in chemistry, it means the act of refining or purifying. Highest point of anything so refined. To rid of baser qualities.

substratum (moral); the underlying moral support of a person or a race of people.

sulci: the plural of *sulcus,* a name for the furrows, grooves, or fissures found between any two convolutions (gyri) of the brain; upwards of 50 of them have received names by which they are distinguished, as the *carotid sulcus,* the *frontal sulci,* etc.

superstitious: addicted to or believing *superstitions,* generally of a religious nature. *Superstition,* fear of the unknown or mysterious. All religions are based more or less upon *superstition.*

supracondyloid foramen: *foramina* are holes or other kinds of openings that occur normally in different bones of the skeletons of all mammals, which have passing through them nerves, arteries, etc.; for example, the optic nerve of the eye passes through the *optic foramen* at the base of the orbit to the eyeball; the *supracondyloid foramen* or *supracondylar foramen* (also known as the *epitrochlear foramen*) is a foramen that pierces the inner lower end of the *humerus* (which is the single long bone of the upper arm). It transmits a nerve and a vessel,—that is, the brachial artery and median nerve. It is of rare occurrence to find it in man.

supraorbital ridges: elevations occurring on most human skulls just above the orbits,—one on either side.

syphilis: a serious venereal disease of an infectious character that may be communicated from person to person through sexual intercourse, or by contact with *syphilitic* discharges left anywhere, or by heredity. *Syphilization* of the system may be brought about by repeated attacks or by inoculations, and one is then said to be *syphilized.* Negroes seldom suffer from *syphiliphobia* or the fear of having contracted syphilis, as do many Anglo-Saxons; the former never commit suicide upon that account, while the latter frequently do.

syphilologist: one versed or learned in syphilitic or venereal diseases. *Syphilology,* the science which treats of *syphilis.*

T

testicles: male organs of generation found in the scrotum, and which secrete the spermatozoa or sexual germ cells in the male sex.

tibia: the larger and inner of the two bones of the leg, between the knee and ankle.

tribal orgies: ceremonies among savage races characterized by great excesses, lewd dances and general debauchery.

triton: (see salamander).

U

uncinariasis: a disease caused by the presence in the intestines of the hookworm (*uncinaria*). Hookworm disease.

uterine filiation: "What is still more general than the clan, is the institution of the maternal family or *uterine filiation,* but this familial type is not invariably deduced from a previous familial clan. . . . As a matter of fact, in humanity, as well as in animality, the uterine family establishes itself spontaneously, whenever the male abandons the female and her progeny. . . . In every ethnic group living in promiscuity, for example, *uterine filiation* shows itself, and it will be the same under a polyandric régime, unless fictitious paternity is established. . . . The uterine family is far from being rare in negro Africa." (Letourneau.)

Utopia: an imaginary place where everything was perfect in every respect, as its government, laws, etc. (Sir Thomas Moore's "Utopia," 1516.) The name of the island—one of ideal perfection—is responsible for the coining of many words referring to such imaginary places founded upon chimerical perfectness. *Utopist* is an optimist entertaining *Utopian* ideas, and frequently believes in his *utopianism.*

V

variability (laws of): those laws which have been formulated by biologists setting forth the ability animals and plants possess to vary or change their forms, function, structures, colors, sizes, and so on,—to lose or gain in character and thus depart from parent or ancestral types and forms, which plasticity or modifiability is due in large part to the conditions of environment, habit, food, etc. These laws are often very complex, and there is a large literature on the subject.

veneer: to cover with a thin layer of anything; superficial ornament; meretricious disguise; bad or indifferent qualities disguised by superficial and more worthy ones.

vestigeal: pertaining to a vestige; in biology, the remains of atrophied organs or other structures; rudimentary, as the vestigeal remains of the intrinsic muscles of the external ear in man.

vocative: compellative; the act of naming, addressing or calling by name, as the *vocative* case in grammar.

W

wisdom teeth: the last molar tooth on either side of the mandible, or lower jaw. It usually erupts at the age of twenty to twenty-five; it has also been called the "wit-tooth" (*dens sapientiæ*), as one is supposed to have arrived at the age of discretion when these teeth appear.

C.

I.

J.

K.

L.

M.

www.ingramcontent.com/pod-product-compliance
Lightning Source LLC
LaVergne TN
LVHW052335100826
845147LV00020B/1066

* 9 7 8 1 6 3 9 2 3 7 7 6 0 *